TOTALITARIANISM AT THE CROSSROADS

TOTALITARIANISM AT THE CROSSROADS

edited and with an introduction by
Ellen Frankel Paul

Transaction Books
New Brunswick (USA) and London (UK)

Published by the Social Philosophy and Policy Center and by Transaction Publishers 1990

Library of Congress Cataloging-in-Publication Data

Totalitarianism at the crossroads / edited and with an introduction by Ellen Frankel Paul.
p. cm. -- (Studies in social philosophy and policy)
Includes bibliographical references.
ISBN 0-88738-351-3 (Transaction Books). -- ISBN 0-88738-850-7 (Transaction Books: pbk.)
1. Communist state. 2. Totalitarianism. 3. Democracy. 4. Government, Resistance to. I. Paul, Ellen Frankel. II. Series: Studies in social philosophy & policy.
JC474.T72 1990
321.9'2--dc20 --dc20 90-30066
CIP

Cover Design: Kent Lytle

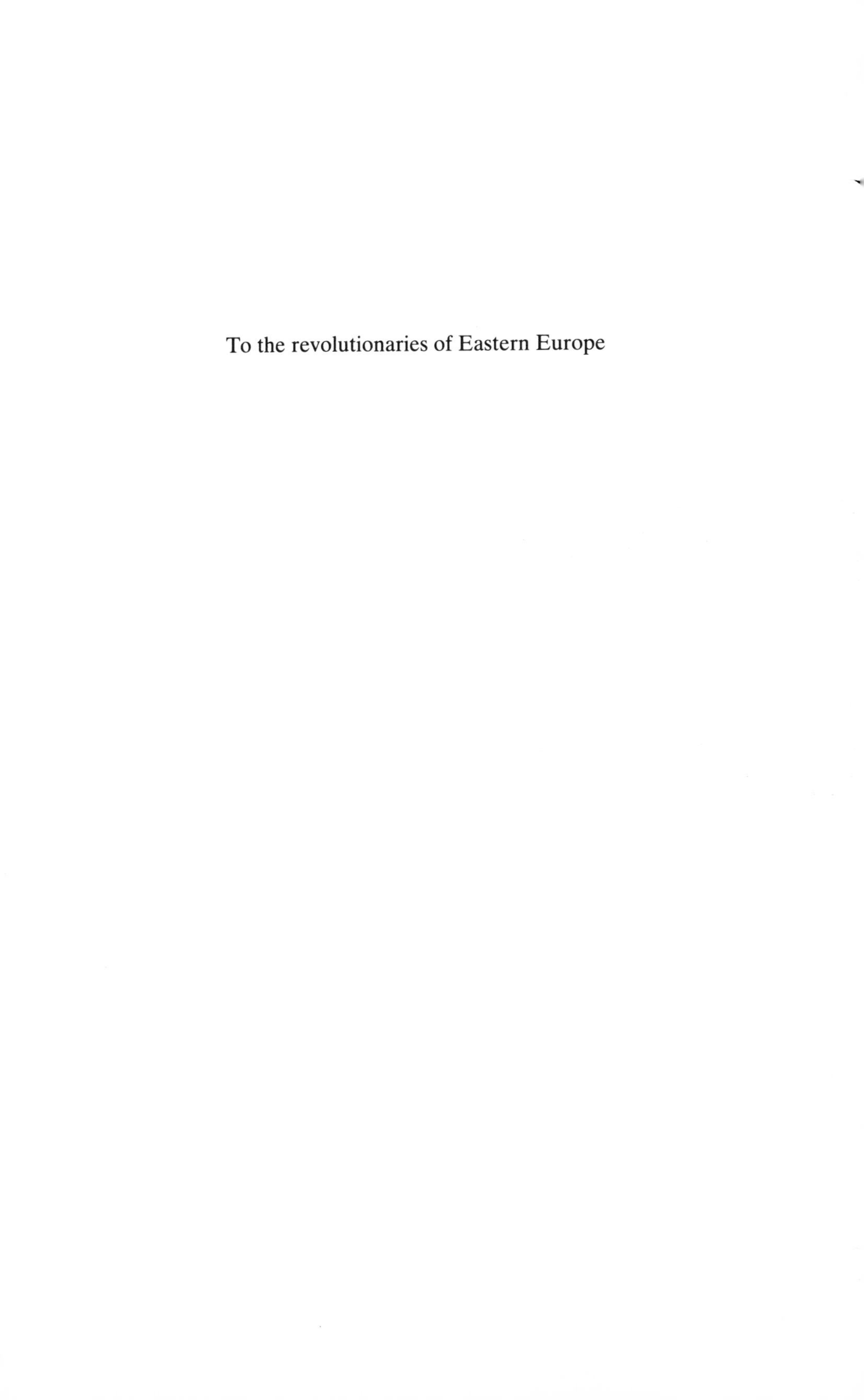

To the revolutionaries of Eastern Europe

TABLE OF CONTENTS

Introduction

Not long ago we were at a crossroads—where was the world going; toward further confrontation, the aggravation of ideological hostility, the whipping up of military threats, or toward cooperation, mutual understanding and the search for agreement? The choice has more or less taken place. And now the challenge is to quietly and thoroughly move toward a new, peaceful period.

Mikhail S. Gorbachev,
November 14, 1989

The twentieth century's remaining totalitarian experiments—all of Marxist genesis—are in deep crisis. Marxist totalitarianism, wherever it seized power, demonstrated a fundamental antipathy toward liberty, attempting to eradicate every vestige of political, economic, religious, and civil liberty that formerly existed among its subjects. With the apparent unwillingness of the Soviet Union to preserve socialism in its satellites with tanks, the antipathy of the colonized towards the imposed, ideological state has erupted with remarkable zeal and apparent spontaneity in one Eastern European satrapy after another. For the first time, nations are seemingly overcoming totalitarianism from within.

Change in Eastern Europe is proceeding at a dizzying pace. What seemed impossible yesterday is tomorrow's old news. Nearly a decade separated Solidarity's formation in the Gdansk shipyards from the ascension of the first non-Communist prime minister since the Communists secured power. The Hungarian Communists' removal of the old guard, transformation into a socialist party promising free elections, and failure in a plebiscite to dictate the conditions of the first election took only a year. Surprisingly, the hard-line regimes of East Germany and Czechoslovakia crumbled with even greater alacrity. A scant two months after East Germans encamped in Western embassies in great numbers and availed themselves of the opportunity to escape to the

West through the opening in the Hungarian border, the Berlin Wall—the preeminent symbol of the imprisonment of mind, spirit, and flesh under Communism—could not withstand the hunger of the people for freedom and democracy. Czechoslovakia's old-guard leadership did not have the luxury of years or even months of resistance to change; it was swept away in a whirlwind of events in a matter of days.

The prospects for liberty and peace in much of the world will depend on the success of these first tentative steps toward de-totalitarianization. The purpose of this volume, *Totalitarianism at the Crossroads,* is to explore the nature of totalitarianism and plumb its essential aspects, to speculate about the prospects for success of totalitarianism's subjects in liberating themselves from its deadening and often deadly embrace, and to discuss the uncharted path back from the ideological state to a "normal" existence, from central planning to markets, and from thought control to a liberation of the human mind.

Totalitarianism in Disarray

Perestroika and *glastnost,* the one betokening economic restructuring and the other openness or truth-telling, are slogans of the Communist Party of the Soviet Union that have captured the imagination of journalists, politicians, and their audiences throughout the world. Despite this worldwide euphoria, *perestroika* is in retreat in the USSR. Mikhail Gorbachev, its chief architect, now frequently denounces the few successful cooperatives (private enterprises) that have sprung up at his invitation. Enterprises caught between the edicts of central planners, price controls, and the new insistence on profitability have resorted to simultaneously raising workers' wages and discontinuing inexpensive product lines, thus exacerbating the chronic shortages of consumer goods. Long lines, endemic to the system, are now longer and the payoff more meager; rationing abounds; staples disappear from the shops never to reappear, even in the major cities.

Glasnost, however, has been more successful, if we measure it by the revelations it has engendered, the revolutionary icons it has undercut, and the mental liberation it has fomented. But its "success" must look like something of a double-edged sword to the men who sit in the Politburo. Gorbachev insists that his reforms have the salvaging of socialism as their objective, to redeem its promise of a better life for the Soviet people. Yet what *glasnost* has revealed to these same people is the millions of slaughtered peasants in the name of the collectivization of agriculture, the added millions who perished in the Great Purge of the 1930s, and the impoverishment of the Soviet worker compared to his counterparts in the developed world. Social ills formerly assigned solely to the capitalist West are now revealed under *glasnost* to have even more dire manifestations in the East. Soviet readers are treated to a daily feast of poverty, ecological decimation, alcoholism, food shortages, horrific medical care, and a deepening housing crisis.

Glasnost's revelations have undercut the very foundations of the Communist Party's claim to rule. In the Soviet press, one writer calls the October Revolution a coup, another defiles the chief icon, Lenin, as the instigator of concentration camps and the perpetrator of policies that cost millions of lives, and another declares Lenin's co-conspirators no better. In this turbulent atmosphere, it is not surprising that each day brings news of demonstrations, demands for the end of one-party rule, or even more radical calls for independence by one non-Russian republic after another. From Lithuania to Turkestan, Estonia to Georgia, subject peoples are taking the first opportunity since their subjugation to demand an accounting of the historical crimes of the Communist regime and their own manumission.

The erosion of belief in Communism, even the outright detestation of Communism by the peoples of the Soviet republics, ought to be apparent to the Soviet rulers by now. But if they have failed to note this root cause of their troubles in their homeland, it is impossible to evade in the nations captured and held by Soviet tanks. It is an historical truism that once empires cease to expand they crumble; in Afghanistan, the Soviet empire retreated. This undoubtedly gave impetus to the political earthquakes that shook Eastern Europe throughout 1989. If the Soviets retreated in one arena, could they not be vanquished elsewhere?

In such unlikely places as East Germany and Czechoslovakia, tiny coteries of dissidents—suddenly augmented by fractious mobs of mostly young people—took to the streets, risking assault from the riot police. Communist totalitarianism was revealed as a hollow vessel, despised by its progeny and unable to maintain itself in its usual form, once it became clear that tanks from the East would not roll as they had in 1956 and 1968. The "New Man" of Marxism-Leninism, forged in the crucible of an education of indoctrination, censorship, and loyalty to the party, now marched in the streets demanding liberty, free elections, and even a return to private property and capitalism. The notion that the "ideological state" must be replaced by a "normal" state and with it a "normal life" is echoed throughout Eastern Europe. Apparently Marxism-Leninism, at least as judged by those forced to live by its dictates, does not constitute a "normal" life. The revolution to expunge the past—to rid society of its history, laws, customs, and religions—has proven a colossal failure. Human nature proved resistant to human design, and evolution more "normal" than revolution.

Yet the victory celebrations may be premature; the putrescent beast may still have a few convulsions left in it before it finally succumbs, as the carnage in Tiananmen Square demonstrates. There is, however, one difference between the Chinese and the Soviet predicaments, and this difference may prove decisive: those who called out the troops to shoot the students in China were of the revolutionary generation, while the leaders of the Soviet Union are three generations removed. Perhaps it takes a certain fanaticism that Gorbachev's generation of *apparatchiks* (i.e., Party officials) lacks in order to call out the troops to decimate its own people. Perhaps they do not have the stomach for the mass slaughter, arrests, and deportations that clinging to power may require. Perhaps it is simply too soon to tell, although the gassing and clubbing of peaceful demonstrators in Tbilisi, Georgia by elite Spetsnaz troops under Politburo control suggests that even careerist Leninists can turn murderous.

Amidst the general euphoria in the West over the seeming collapse of Communism, several disturbing notes have gone generally unremarked. As in previous periods of relaxation between the two blocs—of détente—the foreign arm of the KGB is more active than ever, stealing military and technological secrets and suborning foreigners to its service. Events in Eastern Europe seem too pat, maybe even too good, to be true. One day after the breaching of the Berlin Wall, Bulgaria announced the ousting of its supreme leader, Todor I. Zhivkov, and his replacement by a new Communist chief, one embracing reform who said that the people must decide whether the party will maintain its "leading role in society." Where were the dissidents, the huge crowds in the street demanding change? They appeared only afterwards. Instead, it was a case of pure "revolution from above." Bulgaria prompts the skeptic to wonder whether Moscow might not have a grand design lurking behind the apparent chaos, especially when it seems to be egging the chaos on. Do Gorbachev—Andropov's disciple—and his KGB cronies who are now elevated to the Politburo have a grand deception in mind, something that would make the Trust of the 1920s (see John Gray's contribution to this volume) look like a Sunday school picnic? Is Gorbachev willing to offer a Finlandized Eastern Europe in exchange for the breakup of NATO and the disarmament of the West?

Let us hope that the skeptics are, for once, dead wrong, and that what we are witnessing is really the death knell of the Marxist-Leninist totalitarian project. Millions have been sacrificed to realize its utopian dream; new generations ought not lead twisted lives on the altar of its power, now bereft of promise.

The Essays

Vladimir Bukovsky's "Totalitarianism in Crisis: Is there a Smooth Transition to Democracy?" documents the tremendously destructive impact of Communist totalitarianism in undermining human health and moral character, in decimating the physical environment, in destroying voluntary economic relationships and replacing them with a highly inefficient and technologically backward command economy, and in eradicating legal norms and substituting for them party ukase. Ironically, Bukovsky points out, Marx's dire predictions for the future of capitalism came to pass not for the system that he condemned, but rather in a system whose ruling party embraced Marxian collectivism. The crisis that we are now witnessing is nothing less than the "end of socialism," Bukovsky argues, brought about by the exhaustion of all sources of wealth, both physical and human. Although it was apparent by the 1950s that virtually all of the predictions of "scientific socialism" were erroneous and belief in the ideology had ebbed, the Soviet system nevertheless persisted. What finally brought the colossus to crisis was the enormous drain of resources to support its far-flung empire and the competition from resurgent, prosperous democracies whose economic might and inventiveness the inherently wasteful socialist economy could not match. This system of "social engineering by the means of terror" leaves in its wake a "biological exhaustion, a fatigue of human material." Remarkably, the human spirit has somehow survived almost a century of darkness to arise and demand liberty and national independence, and it may yet withstand the final crisis of totalitarianism.

In "Perestroika and Ideology," Adam Ulam contends that *perestroika* is the result and acknowledgement of a deep ideological crisis. In the past, belief in Marxism-Leninism had been used to justify and mitigate the travails of Soviet society. It enabled the regime to claim that the sufferings of the forced collectivization of 1928–33, of the terror of the 1930s, and the general repressive character of the Soviet state were a necessary price for erecting a more just society in the USSR, and (eventually) a peaceful and stable Communist world order. These beliefs began to crumble in 1956, with the official revelations about the crimes and abuses of the Stalin era. The Sino-Soviet dispute and other fissiparous developments of the international Communist movement demonstrated the unsoundness of the international aspect of Marxist-

Leninist doctrine. Now, in the Gorbachev era, adherence to the canon of Marxism-Leninism has been in fact, even if not explicitly, abandoned by the rulers of the leading Communist state. *Perestroika* has demonstrated the obsolescence of much of Marxism, as well as of its Leninist offshoot. It remains to be seen, Ulam writes, whether and in what form the Soviet regime can survive its current ideological disarray.

In Andrzej Walicki's " 'The Captive Mind' Revisited: Intellectuals and Communist Totalitarianism in Poland," the author engages in a lively reexamination of Czeslaw Milosz's thesis that the uniqueness of totalitarianism consists in attempting to coerce people from within, through controlling their thoughts and feelings. Milosz's classic, *The Captive Mind,* offered a penetrating analysis of the genuine temptations of the totalitarian "New Faith," and a fascinating description of the techniques that the captives employed in an attempt to salvage their separate identities while paying obeisance to the obligatory new faith. The testimonies of other Polish intellectuals who had experienced the heavy pressure of Stalinist ideology, as well as the Russian dissidents' analyses of "dual consciousness," show the remarkable accuracy of Milosz's descriptions. The gradual de-ideologization of the Communist regimes, which took place after Stalin, gave birth to attempts to redefine totalitarianism through deemphasizing its "ideocratic" aspect. Walicki finds all of these attempts unconvincing. He claims that the end of ruthless "ideological mobilization" entails a gradual dismantling of totalitarianism. This is what happened to the Soviet Union and, on a much greater scale, to Poland. Thus, while the classical model of totalitarianism is still useful as a heuristic device, it is necessary to develop a theory of de-totalitarianization.

In "Totalitarianism, Reform and Civil Society," John Gray argues that the totalitarian project is principally one of suppressing civil society, with its distinctive institutions of private property and contractual freedom under the rule of law. In the paradigm Soviet case, this project succeeded in suppressing commodity production and replacing it with the institutions of socialist central planning. Six important episodes in Soviet history are examined in order to show the primacy of Marxist-Leninist ideology and of the institutions of totalitarian bureaucracy in the Soviet state. Totalitarianism is theorized in general terms as a condition of economic chaos contained in a political "state of nature" created by a lawless state. On Gray's analysis, totalitarianism can be reformed by peaceful means and a stable post-totalitarian order achieved only where important institutions of civil society have survived intact. Where civil society has been altogether destroyed, its peaceful recreation is likely to prove difficult or impossible.

Zbigniew Rau's "Four Stages of One Path Out of Socialism" offers a conceptualization of the transition from the totalitarian system to parliamentary democracy and the market economy in the Soviet Union and the Eastern European countries. He analyzes this process in terms of a rebirth of civil society: that is, of the emergence and steady growth of independent social groups and movements and their impact upon the totalitarian system. The essay focuses on four stages in the process. The first is the emergence of dissident groups which challenge the system by the creation of alternative concepts and institutions of public life. The second brings about the establishment of "revindication movements" which organize and mobilize the population outside the system. The third is characterized by the launching of independent political parties within these movements which eventually formulate their own political programs in order to compete with the ruling Communist parties in free elections. The fourth and last stage is a takeover by independent political parties and the formation of a non-Communist government.

Roger Scruton, in his essay "Totalitarianism and the Rule of Law," examines the question of whether or not totalitarianism is compatible with the rule of law. If it is not, what possibilities exist for totalitarian societies to change in a legal direction? To answer these questions, Scruton argues, we need to define 'totalitarianism' and 'the rule of law'. The first, he suggests, is defined by a *project:* the total control of society by the ruling party. The second is characterized by the existence of a legal order and the subjection of all power, including the ruling party, to that order. He explores what these conditions involve and shows that, from a study of Communist law and its practice, the totalitarian project and the rule of law are fundamentally incompatible. Finally, he considers the changes that are necessary for a legal order to reemerge from the grave of communism.

Ellen Frankel Paul
December 8, 1989

Totalitarianism in Crisis: Is There a Smooth Transition to Democracy?

Vladimir Bukovsky

In order to define what totalitarianism is, one is usually forced to write a lengthy theoretical treatise or an equally lengthy description of the governmental structures and social institutions typical of a totalitarian state. This is a difficult and thankless task, for apart from being incomprehensible to a non-specialist, such scholarly definition fails to convey the very essence of the subject: its utter inhumanity; its danger for mankind; and the degree of horror and desperation experienced by those unfortunate nations which are entrapped by it. In a way, it also obscures the subject, because we inadvertently tend to compare a totalitarian system with a free democratic one. In doing so, we only compound the confusion. The difference is so enormous that such comparison leads to simplifications, distortions, and ultimately to a notion of "moral equivalence," best expressed in the phrase: "They might be cannibals, but we are not vegetarians either."

A much better way of defining totalitarianism is by comparing it with an ordinary dictatorship; although the difference is still enormous, our minds are more prepared to grasp it. Thus, trade union activity is forbidden under some dictatorships, and this certainly is a violation of the right to organize independent public associations. Totalitarian regimes, however, are still worse in this respect precisely because they have almost 100 percent unionized labor, while their trade unions are just an extension of the ruling party's apparatus, created to grasp the work force even tighter and to prevent any genuine trade-union activity. This is certainly much worse for someone trying to defend the rights of employees, as he will be forced to struggle not just against the employer—which is difficult in itself—but against a huge organization of professional manipulators with unlimited power. But, if we try to compare free trade unions in a democratic country with totalitarian "trade unions," the differences will be obscured by endless structural and procedural details, incomprehensible to a non-specialist. All we would get after such a comparison is a false impression that the systems are essentially similar except for some technicalities and that, unlike a dictatorship, totalitarianism does permit trade union activity.

The same would be true if we were to compare any totalitarian governmental or social structure and its "counterpart" in a democratic society. In this sense, a totalitarian state will be better defined as a dictatorship which made an additional step away from democracy: instead of simply closing down democratic institutions, it replaced them with look-alike pseudo-institutions designed to prevent any independent public activity. However, the system thus created is immeasurably worse than the most vicious dictatorship one can imagine. Unlike the latter, a totalitarian state controls all spheres of human activity. It forces people to live not only in slavery, but in an atmosphere of constant lies. Above all, it mutilates and corrupts society to such an extent that the way back to democracy becomes practically impossible.

Indeed, while we do not know of a single example of a totalitarian state transforming itself into a democracy (except as a result of a foreign occupation), there have been quite a number of dictatorships even in the last ten to fifteen years which have done so. Furthermore, in most cases the process of transformation was remarkably smooth, quick, and painless, often triggered simply by the death of a dictator (Spain, Portugal), or by a coup (Paraguay), by a failure to suppress the opposition (the Philippines), by international pressure (Chile, South Korea), or even by a dictatorship itself which did not want to maintain its rule any longer (Turkey, Argentina). Needless to say, none of these scenarios could have happened in a totalitarian state. Supreme leaders died (sometimes quite often) or were deposed, but the system continued practically unchanged, and it never hesitated to crush any opposition with the utmost cruelty. As for international pressure, totalitarian regimes—unlike ordinary dictatorships—always enjoy considerable public support in, and special treatment by, the democratic countries. Whatever the reason, one can rely on a democratic society to persuade itself not to put pressure on its totalitarian neighbor.

But most revealing is the ease with which democracy establishes itself in a former dictatorship. One can see how little the fabric of the society was affected by the years, sometimes decades, of dictatorial rule.

Clearly, as Plato said, every democracy carries a germ of dictatorship, and every dictatorship a germ of democracy. Both belong to the same civilization.

Not so with a totalitarian regime. Such an Orwellian society is usually built on the basis of some all-embracing theory, or a religion, embodied in its every structure and institution. Even when no one believes in this theory any longer, the system continues to exist until it exhausts "the original sources of all wealth—the soil and the labourer."[1]

I. Political Dimension

The events of the last decade leave little doubt that we are witnessing the end of socialism, its final stage—a worldwide crisis of the totalitarian system created according to the recipe of "scientific socialism." The idea itself was in trouble for a long time, and like another utopian dream of humanity—perpetual motion—it was at odds with science even at the beginning of this century. Further developments in the natural sciences, particularly in genetics and neurophysiology, ruled out any possibility of such miracles as the creation of a perfect New Man by perfecting social conditions, so much so that Stalin had to proclaim them "bourgeois pseudo-sciences." And contrary to Marxist theory, "collective labor" proved to be far less productive than individually rewarded labor. By the 1950s, virtually all the predictions of "scientific socialism" were obviously incorrect, and the much-expected "world crisis of capitalism" was nowhere in evidence.

But the system still persisted and even continued to expand its influence. If nothing else, the sheer inertia of this giant, its ideological rigidity, the absence of any feedback mechanism in its structure (except for the automatic suppression of dissent), as well as the self-interest of the ruling elite, still kept it going. Propaganda replaced achievements, coercion replaced belief, fear and apathy replaced revolutionary fervor, while subversion, manipulation, or military expansion were employed to promote "inevitable" socialist revolutions abroad. Internally, it was too powerful and ruthless to be successfully challenged by the people; externally, ideological sympathy and the specter of nuclear holocaust paralyzed the will of Western democracies, and no intentional challenge was ever presented.

There were, however, two factors limiting its life: finite internal resources and the ever-growing burden of external competition. No matter how peaceful their intentions might be, the mere existence of prosperous democracies and their more than modest efforts to maintain credible defenses in the postwar period were a constant challenge to the totalitarian system's striving for superiority. Besides, the cost of expansion in the Third World grew in proportion to its success, as it created more and more unproductive states unable to survive without external subsidies. All these expenses, combined with an inherently wasteful socialist economy at home, finally exhausted the resources of the totalitarian world. The system simply could not exist any longer in its traditional form, let alone carry on its "historic mission of liberating humanity from the chains of capitalism."

It should also be noted that the current crisis of totalitarianism coincides with a remarkable revival of the Western economy, which made the expected "crisis of capitalism" even less likely. On the contrary, this revival was to a large extent brought about by a "conservative revolution"—that is, by a reversal of socialist trends in Western countries, including the introduction of stricter monetary policy, reduction of income taxes, privatization of previously nationalized industries, and other measures reducing governmental control over economic life. The spectacular success of this reversal in some countries made it impossible for others not to follow. Even in France, Australia, and New Zealand, where socialist parties came to power for one or another local reason, they had to abandon their socialist principles and introduce similar policies of dismantling socialism in order to withstand the pressure of international competition.

Not surprisingly, totalitarian regimes—where socialism is not just a passing trend but a basic principle built into every structure—were the biggest losers. Suddenly, the gap between them and the rest of the developed countries widened dramatically: while the world entered into a post-industrial stage of development, they were still struggling to complete industrialization; while the free world's economy was rapidly expanding, theirs was shrinking, and there were no more resources, human or natural, to make a new heroic leap forward. In short, the choice was limited: either these regimes would readjust to the new reality, or they would cease to exist. No wonder most of them have promptly started reforms, restructuring, and readjustments.

Still, it is not quite clear how well their rulers understand the nature of the crisis or how far they are prepared to go. Some of these regimes, as we know, started on the path of reform earlier, and have gone much further. Hungary, Yugoslavia, and Poland abandoned collectivized agriculture in the 1950s, while China undertook such reforms only after the death of Mao, and the Soviet Union is only now contemplating them. Yet, even in the Eastern European countries, with the exception of

Hungary, the real depth of the crisis is not quite appreciated by the ruling parties, which still insist on staying in power or on confining any reform within a "framework of socialism." Popular discontent in East Germany toppled an intransigent, hard-line regime and forced reform upon new party leaders bent on salvaging what they could of the party's power. As for China and the Soviet Union, both still hope to get away with a minimal, within-the-system readjustment, and China, after the crackdown in Tiananmen Square, seems intent on retrenchment. The model of reform embraced by the Chinese and the Soviets ignores the lessons of Eastern Europe; that model has been tried and failed, thus driving those regimes to more fundamental reforms, each at its own pace.

Ironically, even the opposition forces in countries like Poland, where they are strong enough to matter, have accepted the "framework of socialism" as a limitation and have therefore deprived themselves of the only realistic alternative platform. Whether it is a tactical concession or a genuine belief in a "different socialism," the results are going to be the same. An opposition which fails to offer a way out of the crisis and to try to win power from a bankrupt and unpopular government is bound to lose public support. Such an opposition is more of a prop for the ruling party than a hope for the people.

Thus, in Poland today both sides seem to be pleased with themselves and with their part of the bargain. The Communists, who are clearly unable to govern any longer, believe they have found an ideal way of retaining their ultimate power without constantly relying on military force by becoming a kind of senior partner of a company, with at least 65 percent of the stock remaining in their hands; whereas the opposition believes it will gradually reduce the Communist's power to a mere formality and "dissolve" socialism, all without a confrontation with the government and, therefore, without bloodshed.

Preoccupied with each other, neither side even bothered to find out: what would be the people's attitude to their deal? Will they respond by enthusiastically increasing productivity and modernizing the economy at the expense of their immediate well-being? And, while the entire world applauded the spirit of "moderation" in Warsaw, no one bothered to ask: is this new deal a solution, or is it just a way to prolong the agony?

No sooner was the "round table agreement" signed than it became clear that the people rejected it. As a result, we have witnessed a situation without precedent in human history: a victorious opposition had to persuade a reluctant population to vote for a clearly defeated government in order to avoid victory. Can we imagine anything like that in the Philippines in the Marcos-Aquino contest, or in Chile in the recent referendum? Would the world have applauded such behavior on the part of the opposition there?

And the worst is still to come: the Polish people will reveal their disdain for the deal struck between the government and the opposition, and further economic deterioration will bring a wave of strikes and riots. Will the Solidarity government try to "calm" the workers, hand in hand with the police, or will they join the strikers and therefore cease to be a government? In short, by signing the "round table agreement," Solidarity has gotten itself into a no-win situation; in due time it will be either completely discredited or in the very same confrontation with the Communists that it had tried to avoid in the first place.

Try as I may to be more optimistic in my forecast, this depressing scenario seems very likely. Dismantling socialism is not an easy task. It took Margaret Thatcher ten years to perform this task in Britain, where socialism has never been even remotely as omnipresent and well-rooted as it is in any Eastern European country. Even in Britain it was a quite painful process, initially causing a decline in the people's well-being, and the task is still far from completion. The scale of human suffering that this process must bring in a purely socialist country will be mind-boggling. A more gradual transition will simply make it unbearable for the population. Besides, as the Hungarian experience has already indicated, the more gradual the reforms are, the less they are successful. Therefore, a gradual transition is bound to produce minimal economic results accompanied by considerable popular unrest. This is particularly true for the Soviet Union, where the situation is significantly worse than in Eastern Europe; there is simply no time left for experimentation.

If the British people chose to endure a period of hardship in a fair and democratic election, and consequently endured it with relative equanimity, a hardship imposed by a hated Communist regime is not likely to be accepted as an unpleasant medicine, even with the opposition's blessing. The party, which robbed and abused the people for decades (and finally caused the crisis), cannot count on any public trust. In particular, one cannot expect the entrepreneurial element of society—a prime target of Communist abuses throughout, yet an absolutely essential element for economic recovery—to start laying golden eggs into a Communist nest. Certainly, the Soviet population still remembers the fate of those who believed the government in the 1920s and followed its slogan to "enrich" themselves as private farmers and tradesmen. Millions of them ended up in Siberia in the 1930s after the New Economic Policy (N.E.P.) was terminated. After such experiences, often replicated in Eastern Europe, even a slight uncertainty—let alone Communist control of the Army and police—is bound to discourage private initiative. In short, one is forced to conclude, as Hungarian Communist Party leader Imre Pozcgay did recently, that the Communist system cannot be reformed and must be liquidated.[2]

This conclusion, however, is unacceptable even in Warsaw, to say nothing of Moscow or Beijing. The ruling party, as we have seen in China this spring, is still prepared to murder for the sake of socialism (or for the sake of staying in power, which is the same thing). And with good reason, because this "new class" (to borrow Milovan Djilas's expression) committed crimes against humanity every day of its existence and they are bound to be held responsible as soon as power is not in their hands. There is hardly a family in the Communist countries which was not affected by repressions at one period or another, and the amount of hatred accumulated in any totalitarian society could only be measured in megatons. The ruling class has no choice but to cling to power and, in doing so, will commit more and more crimes.

But this, in turn, is the reason why the opposition in any Communist country is so reluctant to advocate a confrontation with the authorities, let alone a revolution. Unlike a dictatorship, where the ruling elite guilty of the regime's crimes is tiny, a totalitarian regime creates a whole class of rulers. In the Soviet Union, Gorbachev himself has said that this bureaucratic class numbers 18 million strong; it has a proportionally huge repressive apparatus. One can expel Ferdinand Marcos and his henchmen to Hawaii, or imprison a few officers in Argentina, but where can 18 million people go? Bearing in mind that they will be fighting for their lives, what can be the result of a revolution in a totalitarian country but a senseless bloodbath?

Thus, a peaceful transition from totalitarianism to democracy seems extremely unlikely. Since it remodels the whole society according to its ideology, a totalitarian regime replaces all social institutions and governmental structures with its own pseudo-institutions. In doing so, it creates a whole class of professional organizers, supervisors, and rulers incapable of any other function in society. Not only their vested interests are at stake, but their very lives, because a totalitarian regime always involves a large proportion of the population in its crimes. In the Communist countries, as in Dostoevsky's *The Possessed*, a complex technique of social engineering ("class struggle") is employed to tie the ruling class up in a blood circle. Unable to rule by more sophisticated methods than "command and control," they become an obstacle in the way of progress; yet, they are too strong to be forcibly removed from power. They are a state within the state, an occupation force, which cannot be finished off by a coup and cannot be forced to withdraw—they have no place to withdraw to. Since foreign occupation is out of the question in the nuclear age, only a civil war or a total collapse of the economy (or, most likely, both at the same time) can terminate a totalitarian regime. A strong and well-organized opposition could minimize the violence, but totalitarian regimes are usually too powerful to tolerate it.

Having said this, I should acknowledge the differences among the existing totalitarian regimes, as these might be quite important in the final stages of their crises. Thus, Hungary has a much better chance for a more peaceful transition to democracy, for at least three reasons. First, it was a relatively liberal regime for the last thirty years; therefore, its ruling elite—not being involved in outright repressions—could step down with a minimal risk of a mob trial, should they decide to do so. Second, by the time the crisis hit the Communist world, Hungary was far ahead of other Communist states in reforming its economy and dismantling socialism. Third, the Hungarian ruling elite seems to be aware of the real depth of the current crisis and accepts the possibility of relinquishing power.

Eastern Europe, in general, might have a slightly better chance of recovery than the Soviet Union. This is likely not just because some of these countries began their economic reforms before the Soviets, but mostly because they became socialist much later and never went as far, particularly in agriculture. Also, the "megaton-count" of hatred might be somewhat lower in Eastern Europe; after all, socialism was brought there by the "Russians." However, those who expect an overnight collapse of the Communist regimes upon the termination of the "Brezhnev Doctrine" are going to be quite disappointed. It is enough to look at Afghanistan after the Soviet withdrawal to see the importance of the national "new class" in any totalitarian country. The difference between a traditional empire and a Communist one is as enormous as the difference between a dictatorship and totalitarianism, or between a foreign occupation and a self-occupation. In the final analysis, it does not matter how socialism entered a country, or who brought it; far more important is the fact that it took root there. Even with the recent changes in view, the transition is far from over.

Needless to say, the worst scenario could be expected in the Soviet Union, the cradle of socialism, where at least three generations were born and grew up under totalitarian rule. The nationalities problem will only aggravate the crisis. It is far behind its neighbors in economic reforms and far ahead in repressions. But let us make no mistake: even if all the Communists miraculously disappear in every socialist country, this alone will not resolve the crisis. For, unlike a dictatorship, totalitarianism leaves behind a mutilated, deformed society, a ruined economy, exhausted resources, and general degradation.

II. Economic Dimension

Even the most absurd dictatorship, obsessed with its own power, would not try to dictate to a producer how to produce or to a tradesman how to trade, but every bolt and nut produced under socialism was produced because the central government made a decision to produce it: how to do it, when, where, of what quality and quantity, to whom it should be sold, and at what price. Moreover, we were told, universal happiness is only possible if the production of every bolt and nut is controlled in this manner. There will be wars and crimes, poverty and slavery—all because of the uncontrolled bolts and nuts. Surely we don't want that to happen, do we?

In order to understand a socialist economy, one should first study Kafka and only then Karl Marx. Otherwise, one would never grasp the connection between a production process and a process of turning a man into an insect.

> The mode of production of material life conditions the social, political, and intellectual life process in general. It is not the consciousness of men that determines their being, but, on the contrary, their social being that determines their consciousness.[3]
> Modern industry, by assigning as it does, an important part in the socially organized process of production, outside the domestic sphere, to women, to young persons, and to children of both sexes, creates a new economic foundation for a higher form of the family and of the relations between the sexes. . . . Moreover, it is obvious that the fact of the collective working group being composed of individuals of both sexes and all ages, must necessarily, under suitable conditions, become a source of humane development.[4]

Marx argued, therefore, that the development of "capitalism" will inevitably lead to a "proletarian revolution" and to the emergence of "socialism."

> One capitalist always kills many. Hand in hand with this centralization, or this expropriation of many capitalists by few, develop, on an ever extending scale, the cooperative form of the labor process, the conscious technical application of science, the methodical cultivation of soil, the transformation of the instruments of labor into instruments of labor only usable in common, the economising of all means of production by their use as the means of production of combined,

> socialized labor, the entanglement of all peoples in the net of world market, and with this the international character of the capitalistic regime. Along with the constantly diminishing number of the magnates of capital, who usurp and monopolise all advantages of this process of transformation, grows the mass of misery, oppression, slavery, degradation, exploitation; but with this too grows the revolt of the working class, a class always increasing in number, and disciplined, united, organised by the very mechanism of the process of capitalist production itself. The monopoly of capital becomes a fetter upon the mode of production, which has sprung up and flourished along with, and under, it. Centralisation of the means of production and socialisation of labor at last reach a point where they become incompatible with their capitalist integument. This integument is burst asunder. The knell of capitalist private property sounds. The expropriators are expropriated.[5]

It is not difficult to notice that all his economic constructions, all three volumes of *Das Kapital*, were created as a "scientific" justification for his youthful dreams of the proletarian revolution. He simply invented a model of economic development that would logically lead to an inevitable revolution. Thus, he completely rejected the most essential part of the market economy—the market itself, with its mechanism of price formation—and instead invented a mysterious "value" of a product, measured by an "average socially necessary labor-time" spent on its production:

> Socially necessary labor-time is the labor-time required to produce any use-value under the conditions of production normal for a given society and with the average degree of skill and intensity of labor prevalent in that society.[6]

All that is really valuable in human labor, all the treasury of human inventiveness and initiative, is thus excluded from Marx's formula, and the only way left for the wretched "capitalist" to get a profit ("surplus value") for his pains is to rob the worker by underpaying him. If that were the case, then Marx would indeed be right. The economy would be doomed to develop extensively, progressively consuming more and more resources with less and less profit, while the number of proletarians would grow proportionally and their living standard would decline to the level of absolute poverty. Meanwhile, the only way to survive the competition would be through a further monopolization and centralization, and the only way to increase productivity would be through a further division of labor, large-scale industry, and machinery, until an absolute majority of the population turned proletarians, working at one huge assembly line. Needless to say, such a society could not possibly exist for very long, with its economy working full-blast just for self-reproduction at the expense of producing consumer goods, with its resources depleted and its average rate of profit falling, with huge masses of hungry, overworked people ever ready to revolt.

However, a hundred years after Marx died, the "capitalist" world's development still does not follow his predictions. In fact, the free world's economy developed in exactly the opposite direction. Ironically, his predictions did materialize with frightening accuracy in the socialist countries, precisely because those countries followed his prescriptions to the letter. It is a bizarre twist on a self-fulfilling prophecy, ironic and tragic at the same time.

It is not difficult to see how and why it could happen that, while building a "socialist paradise," followers of Marx have actually constructed exactly the model of depraved capitalism invented by their teacher. According to Marx, all necessary conditions and features of socialism, including the "socialist consciousness" of the proletarians, will be prepared by capitalism itself. Victorious proletarians would only have to perform the simple task of canceling private ownership of the "means of production"—or, to use his expression, the task of "expropriating expropriators."

> What we have to deal with here is a communist society, not as it has developed on its own foundations, but, on the contrary, just as it emerges from capitalist society; which is thus in every respect, economically, morally, and intellectually, still stamped with the birthmarks of the old society from whose womb it comes.[7]

While political structures will be taken care of by the "dictatorship of the proletarians," there is not much to be altered in the economy except that the distribution must be made fairer. Until the next stage comes, a leading slogan of socialism must be: "From each according to his ability, to each according to his labor!"

Thus, there will be no "surplus value" expropriated by the capitalist; the worker will be paid the whole value of his labor, calculated on the basis of the "socially necessary labor-time." Besides, since collective labor is a more progressive (and more productive) form, a system of collective reward through social benefits will be introduced which excludes any inequality. It is ironic, but not surprising, that when the Soviets attempted to follow Marx's prescriptions, the resulting socialist economy developed extensively, consuming ever more resources with declining effect. Who would bother to work for a collective reward?

Why kill oneself working extra hard if the value of your product is calculated according to an "average socially necessary labor-time . . . under the conditions of production normal for a given society and with an average degree of skill and intensity of labor prevalent in that society"?

It goes without saying that the new socialist society could not tolerate any market—the notorious hotbed of profiteering, inequality, and corruption. Instead, after nationalizing all enterprises, big and small, the centralized Soviet state-created planning organ (Gosplan) regulated all production and distribution in the spirit of Marx's absolute justice. Monopolization, as we remember, was bad for capitalism, but it certainly must be good for socialism, helping to socialize labor.

Indeed, every socialist state, being the only employer of the whole nation, proudly built giants of industry, gigantic factories, dams, and canals, instead of building many smaller enterprises capable of competing with each other. And why shouldn't they? After all, Marx predicted that the whole world would inevitably follow the socialist pattern. So, the sooner the better. Besides, it is much cheaper to build one gigantic plant than a dozen smaller units, and it is easier to manage them from the center if a central government must plan every nut and bolt.

Finally, these gigantic constructions of the "biggest in the world" plants and factories, the famous "construction sites of socialism," were tangible proof of the advantages of the socialist system over the capitalist one. Collective labor of the victorious proletarians must constantly march from triumph to triumph, demonstrating its unlimited power by turning rivers backward and converting deserts into blossoming gardens.

And so it happened that the "capitalists" were moving away from the Marxist model prescribed for them by demonopolizing industries, encouraging small enterprises, modernizing machinery, and intensifying productivity through individual incentive, while the world of socialism was rapidly moving toward the crisis (of capitalism) predicted by the master.

Let us assess the Soviet and United States economies by comparing Marx's most important indicators. Marx predicted that capitalism would lead to: (a) the growth of the proletarian class as more and more people are compelled to lose their independence and work for the big capitalists; (b) the increasing poverty of the proletarians as capitalism progresses, gradually being driven towards mere subsistence; (c) monopolization, centralization, a falling rate of profit, and increased production of producer goods as competition forces capitalists to mechanize or succumb; and (d) modes of production that will become fetters upon productive forces.

A. Extent of the Proletariat

One cannot even find such a creature in the United States as a "proletarian," but if we use the original Marxist definition of one as an industrial and agricultural worker (including workers in forestry, fishery, mining industry, construction, manufacturing industry, transportation, and communications), their number in 1986 was 39,943,000 out of a total population of 238,740,000, or 16.24 percent. One should not count them all as "proletarians," because this number includes everyone employed in those industries, including management, office employees, and even the capitalists themselves.

The Soviet Union at the time of the revolution had a tiny proportion of its population employed as laborers—that is, as proletarians. By 1986 61.7 percent were workers, 12.1 percent collective farmers, and 26.2 percent "intellectuals" out of the total population of 278,800,000 people.

Even if we do not count collective farmers as "proletarians," the ratio is still 1:3.79. If we include the collective farmers, who in reality are nothing else but proletarians, the ratio is 1:4.5.

Thus, industrial development in a socialist country brought about numerical growth in the proletariat; it cannot continue without the availability of even more proletarians. This is precisely the predicament that Marx anticipated for capitalist systems. The United States has 4.5 times fewer proletarians than the Soviet Union, plus about 7 million unemployed people, while the Soviet Union has a shortage of labor which seriously obstructs their industrial growth.

B. "Pauperization of the proletarians"

In 1986 the minimum wage in the United States stood at $3.35 an hour. With an 8-hour, 5-day week, this amounted to $589.60 per month. The minimal wage in the Soviet Union is 70 rubles a month. Even if we equate rubles and dollars, the ratio will be 8.4:1. The official rate of exchange will still give us a big difference of 5:1, although no one would accept that the purchasing power of 60 rubles in the Soviet Union is equal to the purchasing power of $100 in the United States. The black market rate will give us a ratio of 58:1!

But since we do not know how many of the "proletarians" earn a minimal payment, we should turn to an average wage. Soviet statistics only give us the overall average earning in the country—201 rubles a month in 1987, a figure which must include all the categories from a collective farmer to a general. On the other hand, U.S. statistics do not give us a national average, but do provide the average earning of an industrial worker in 1985—$19,300 a year. Still, a comparison gives us a ratio of 1:4.8 in the official rate of exchange (1:56 with a black market rate), or 1:8 if we equate the currencies.[8]

As we can see, the ratio is consistent for both minimal and average earnings. No matter how we figure it, the disparity is still huge—at least five times lower in the Soviet Union.

This, however, only gives us a vague idea of the poverty in the Soviet Union. Recently, a Soviet newspaper published some statistics on poverty, according to which 35 percent of the Soviet population lives below the poverty level, earning less than 100 rubles a month per capita.[9] "There are still many families with an income of less than 50 rubles a month per capita, and even less," claims the paper.

According to the Soviet Deputy Minister of Finances, Victor Semenov, Soviet people pay only 8.6 percent direct income tax, but more than 60 percent as indirect tax. The latter is hidden either in the retail prices or in the wholesale prices as a tax from the profits of the enterprises. One wonders: is this not a "surplus value"?

But the real picture of Soviet poverty cannot be accurately reflected by just the family earnings. Constant shortages and deficits, appalling lack of housing (as a result of which several families have to live in the same apartment sharing all facilities), an inflationary rate currently estimated at 12 percent per year (and no automatic indexation), squalor and alcoholism (which also does not improve the family budget), a constant need to pay black market prices and bribes for basic services, and much more must be taken into account if we want to get a true picture. Surely, this is exactly what Marx meant by "pauperization of the proletarians."

C. "Historical tendency of capitalist accumulation"

I already mentioned that the monopoly of production did not become a feature of "capitalism," but rather became the very essence of the socialist economy. But what about the other features of "capitalist accumulation"?

The free market economy does not differentiate between the "means of production" and consumer goods; both are just goods on the market which anyone can buy. Their production is as profitable as that of any consumer good. How, indeed, can one distinguish them in our time?

What is a computer? a car? a sewing machine? a washing machine? Are they "means of production" or consumer goods?

In the Soviet economy, however, these are entirely separate "groups" of industry: "group A" (production of the means of production) and "group B" (consumer-goods production). This is as it should be in a true Marxist state, because all means of production must be in the "public hands." Also—as it should be according to the Marxist model of capitalist accumulation—the share of group A has steadily grown, while the share of group B has declined. The ratio of groups A and B was: in 1928, 39.5 percent to 60.5 percent; in 1940, 61 percent to 39 percent; in 1960, 72.5 percent to 27.5 percent; in 1980, 73.8 percent to 26.2 percent; in 1985, 74.8 percent to 25.2 percent; and in 1986, 75.3 percent to 24.7 percent.

Moreover, as a Soviet economist recently disclosed, practically all growth indicated in the Soviet statistics falls into the group A category and therefore does not affect the standard of living. National income growth is therefore a statistical fiction. The economy is working practically for self-reproduction, and even that is barely maintained.[10]

Nevertheless, new industrial constructions are started in great number, although there are no resources to complete them. This mad expansion aggravates the already existing shortages. The first thing that becomes apparent is a shortage of labor. All who could be turned into proletarians have already reached that point. Still, the author discloses, at least one quarter of the jobs in the manufacturing industry are not filled.

Then it was the turn of energy resources. I calculate that there were more energy resources used in the last fourteen years than during the whole previous history of the country. And yet there is a shortage of energy so acute that sometimes planes cannot fly and flights are canceled. Sometimes trucks cannot deliver goods, although oil production reached an all-time record of 600 million tons a year.

At the same time, the Soviet Union produces more steel than the United States, more electric energy, and more tractors—and it is still not enough. Even shoes are produced in huge numbers (800 million pairs a year), but no one wants them because of their poor quality. And each year 800 million pairs of shoes are stubbornly produced as planned, the workers receive their payment and their bonuses, the GNP and national income figures include them, but no one buys them.

Meanwhile, as Marx predicted *for capitalism*, the average profit is falling. Another Soviet economist calculated this decline at 3 percent annually, which is equivalent to a loss of 40 billion rubles.[11] The leading Communist Party magazine, *Kommunist*, sums it up:

> Further movement along this course in the situation when the possibility of involvement of labor, raw materials, and natural resources into production is reduced could only lead to an increased number of unfilled jobs, to an excessive growth of expenditure for development and transportation of mineral resources, and for protection of the environment. This way of development has no prospects now: more and more investment would yield less and less results. In the present conditions, this would be a dead end.[12]

Of course, a dead end. The very same dead end that Marx called "sapping the original sources of all wealth—the soil and the laborer."

D. Development of the productive forces

As we know, the market economy did not turn out to be an obstacle to the further development of "productive forces," new technology, or new ideas of management. On the contrary, it could not survive without encouraging their development. The "capitalist" self-regulating economy is prospering and does not show any signs of a crisis.

Not so in the Soviet Union. The prominent Soviet economist Tatyana Zaslavskaya writes:

> In the last 12–15 years one can notice a tendency of a marked decrease in the growth rate of the national income. If in the 8th Five-year Plan its annual growth was 7.5%, and in the 9th Five-year Plan 5.8%, then, in the 10th it fell to 3.8%, while in the first few years of the 11th it is about 2.5% (at the population growth average of 0.8% a year). This does not provide either for the necessary increase in the people's standard of living, or for an intensive modernization of production.[13]

Further on, she defines the reason for the crisis as "the lagging of the system of production relations, and hence of the mechanism of state management of the economy which is its reflection, behind the level of the productive forces."[14]

Such an explanation could never have been applied to a socialist economy before.* According to Marx, this is what should happen under capitalism. According to Zaslavskaya, however, it will lead to "either a period of acute socio-economic and political cataclysms within the given

*According to dogma, there could not be a contradiction between the system of production relations and the level of productive forces under socialism because socialism is the most progressive system of production relations. Such a contradiction could only happen under capitalism or feudalism. As I mention later, that such a contradiction is now attributed to socialism is an indicator of growing revolution.

formation, which modify and readjust production relations to the new mode of production, or there comes an epoch of a general crisis of the given social formation and of its downfall caused by a social revolution."[15]

"Radical reorganization of economic management essentially affects the interests of many social groups, to some of which it promises improvements, but to others a deterioration in their positions." And where did this "social group" (or what, less politely, would be termed "class enemy") come from after seventy years of socialism in the state of workers and peasants? Apparently, it was always there posing as an "advance-guard of the proletarians."

"Neither in the times of Ivan the Terrible, nor in any country at present, which did not experience nationalization of private property, could bureaucracy control the main stock of the means of production," writes Andrei Nuikin, another Soviet economist. "One assumes it is not without some serious scientific foundations that people start talking about the creation in the 1920s of a 'class of bureaucratic supervisors.' For property relations, first and foremost, ownership of the means of production defines the division of the society into classes."[16]

* * * * *

Thus, after making a comparison of the Soviet and United States economies and socioeconomic tendencies, according to criteria provided by Marx, I am forced to conclude that the socialist countries which followed Marxist teachings have actually created the very same model of depraved and doomed "capitalism" that was invented by Marx. It is in the socialist countries that a real division into classes has occurred: classes of the exploiters and of the exploited, of proprietors and proletarians. It is in the socialist countries that the monopolistic economy evolved, leading to the insane race for economic self-reproduction at the expense of the people's consumption and the plunder of natural resources.

Finally, it is the socialist system which turns out to be incapable of further developing productive forces and appears to be an obstacle in the way of progress. There, and not in the countries with a free market economy, can the crisis predicted by Marx be seen. And if in our time, one hundred years after Marx died, one still can see the fading apparition of the Great Proletarian Revolution somewhere, it is in the world of socialism that spreads from Havana to Hanoi and from Belgrade to Beijing.

Scared as they are by the prospect of an approaching Doomsday,

Communist leaders are ready to admit their past crimes and mistakes, ready to "reform" and apologize, as if their apologies can change anything now. They are even prepared to sacrifice their precious ideology and to bend it in any way required. But where is a solution? How can "capitalist" competition be introduced into the workings of a gigantic factory, the biggest in the world and the only one in the country? What can be done with all these gigantic dams, canals, and artificial lakes which destroyed ecosystems and yet failed to produce enough electricity? How can a market economy be introduced in a country where neither a market nor an economy existed for sixty years? And where is the time to gradually dismantle socialism, when every day brings them closer to the abyss? Even if all Communists miraculously disappear, the crisis will remain.

There is no one to be blamed: neither Stalin, nor Brezhnev, nor even Lenin. They did not invent "expropriation of expropriators" nor a "class struggle." No one, except perhaps Karl Marx for a slight mistake; people, after all, did not turn out to be just like insects and did not respond to social conditioning. Man did not prefer equality to freedom. But who could have known that in advance?

III. Human and Natural Dimensions

What else will the Communists leave behind, apart from a deformed society, a ruined economy, and depleted resources? A scarred earth, stinking swamps, and a degenerate populace, in which the very class of a hardworking person has been exterminated. For, unlike a dictatorship, a totalitarian regime is not simply engaged in terror for the sake of retaining power (although it does so as well) but is also engaged in a form of social engineering by means of terror. All social strata, psychological types, or, sometimes, the whole nation are subjects of this policy, not because they pose any threat to the rulers, but because a totalitarian regime strives to change the very fabric of the society. It is a kind of "unnatural selection," a survival of the unfittest, which leaves a long-lasting effect. Many skills and trades are lost forever, and fear seems to reside as deep as genes. One should not forget that at least three generations in the Soviet Union were born and grew up under the present regime, watching the slow destruction of their country, culture, and fellow countrymen (two generations in most other Communist countries). Unlike the case of Hungary or China, there are no peasants in Russia, only collective farmers, and the generation which still remembers how to work the land is dying out. This is one reason why reforms could revive agriculture in China, but it may be too late for Russia.

No one can tell exactly how many people were killed by the Soviet regime since the October Revolution: thirty, fifty, or perhaps even sixty million, but the number is certainly large enough to qualify as genocide. One should also recall that a huge proportion of the population went through labor camps, where forced labor is the rule and, therefore, any work for them is forever a punishment. In a sense, though, working conditions anywhere under Communism are not much different from forced labor, with a similar effect on the people's working habits.

Besides, one of the main goals of the Soviet regime in handling the population always has been to convince them that they are in a no-win situation; that there is no escape from their misery, either physically or emotionally; and that there is no way to improve their condition or to escape abroad. Any initiative has always been severely discouraged. This pattern is known as "learned helplessness" in experimental psychology; it leads to the inability of the subject to discover how to escape, even when escape is available. And this is apart from the fact that, for three generations, people were obliged to listen to and repeat obvious lies of the official propaganda. This constant conflict between reality and propaganda is alone sufficient to produce a profound psychological trauma, to say nothing of the ever-present fear, suspicion, and misery.

In short, the current condition of the Soviet people (and, to a degree, the condition of any nation under totalitarian rule) is not just apathy and resignation, but a biological exhaustion, a fatigue of human material. Its signs are high infant mortality, low birth rate (below the replacement rate in some republics and close to zero among the Russians), life expectancy of about sixty, and an exceptionally high percentage of children born physically and mentally handicapped (about 6-7 percent by the end of the 1970s, and projected to be 15 percent by the end of the 1990s). The latter is partly due to massive environmental pollution, but it is mainly a product of alcoholism. A document smuggled out of the Soviet Union in 1985 indicates that in 1983 there were 40 million "medically certified alcoholics"; that figure is projected to grow to 80 million by the year 2000.

Even nature seems to be exhausted by 73 years of Communist rule. Unlike the West, where public opinion could prevent the worst excesses of industrial pollution, there were no forces in the Soviet Union (or any other Communist country) to stand in the way of the state. The very idea that nature should be "protected from man" was totally alien to the revolutionary philosophy. "We cannot wait for favors from nature. Our task is to take them from her." This was the slogan of socialism—which, after all, believes that, given the appropriate conditions, one can make an apple out of a pear and a minister out of a cook. Sixty years later, this philosophy resulted in a major environmental catastrophe.

By the end of the 1970s, air pollution had reached a "threatening level" in more than 1,000 cities, a level of "immediate danger for health" in over 100 cities, and 10 times higher than the "immediate danger" level in about 10 cities. Total damage caused by air and water pollution at the end of the 1970s was calculated by official Soviet estimates to be 20 billion rubles; by 1990, it may reach 120 billion. Soviet rivers carry about 20 times more pollutants to the Baltic Sea than the Rhine delivers to the North Sea. Since land reclamation is too expensive, only about 8–12 percent of the land destroyed by quarries and other methods of mineral resource exploitation is reclaimed annually. Thus, about 77,200 square miles of territory were destroyed at the end of the 1970s, with an additional 400 square miles being destroyed each year.

Even more land is destroyed by huge artificial lakes and seas created in the process of constructing hydroelectric power stations. The area submerged by these lakes equals 46,320 square miles, while the subsequent soil erosion has made a staggering 243,180 square miles of once excellent pastures, water meadows, and fields unusable (with biological productivity being reduced by 80 to 90 percent). Not only did these projects destroy huge areas of arable land and pastures, but they also destroyed rivers, turning them into stinking swamps, with the destruction of the balance of water. Finally, they failed to produce the required amount of energy when the level of water dropped. Evaporation, agricultural irrigation, and the rapid expansion of industry aggravated the problem even further. Natural lakes and seas—Aral, Azov, the Caspian Sea—may simply disappear by the next century. The ecology of the Black Sea is already damaged and will have to sustain further assults. A shortage of water will affect development plans in both industry and agriculture.

Another problem is the barbaric extermination of forests. Soviet official sources admit that the stretches of forest cut annually for timber are as big as those destroyed by fire—namely, about 100,000 square miles. As a result, additional areas turn into swamps or become affected by erosion.

The total loss of land is equal to the territories of England, France, Italy, West Germany, Switzerland, Luxembourg, Belgium, and Holland combined.[17] An estimated 100 to 200 years will be needed to restore it.

* * * * *

In conclusion, one can only try to be more optimistic. If human nature could withstand such a devastating blow, such protracted destruction, misery, suffering, and still not give in, still stand for Liberty and Dignity, Honesty and Truth, one simply wants to believe that it will withstand the final crisis. It may take a generation, or even two, it may exact a high price, but it must triumph. For if the human spirit survived almost a century of darkness, like that candle in the wind, it must be indestructible.

It could have been worse, and a dead silence might have been the only response when the great retreat of totalitarianism finally began. And yet, from the Baltic Sea to the Caucasian mountains, and from the Danube to Siberia, former captive nations are rising up to demand their national independence. In Russia itself, recent "elections," restricted and manipulated as they were, showed a clear vote of no confidence in the Communist Party. In the wake of inflation, a wave of strikes is gathering momentum. According to recent reports, even policemen in Leningrad are about to go on strike. In short, the people have spoken: they want democracy. Not a "socialist" one, not "democratization," just plain old-fashioned democracy for all. And no force can stop them now.

The scars will be deep and lasting. Unfortunate is the country where simple honesty is perceived at best as a heroic deed, at worst as a mental disorder, for its fields will not yield bread. Woe be to a nation which has lost its sense of dignity, for it begets crippled children. But if only one among them differs, they will not perish.

This is why no good definition of totalitarianism will ever be found, for it is worse than a nuclear holocaust.

NOTES

1. Karl Marx, *Capital*, vol. 1 (Moscow, 1974), pp. 474–75.
2. An interview with Radio Free Europe on May 29, 1989.
3. Karl Marx, "A Contribution to the Critique of Political Economy," Marx & Engels, *Selected Works*, vol. 1 (Moscow, 1973), p. 504.
4. *Capital,* p. 454.
5. *ibid.,* pp. 714–15.
6. *Capital*, vol. 1 (Penguin Books, 1976), p. 129.
7. "Critique of the Gotha Programme," Marx & Engels, *Selected Works*, vol. 2 (Moscow, 1962), p. 33.
8. All the figures above are from: *The Statesman's Year-Book: Statistical and Historical Annual of the State of the World for the Year 1988–1989,* Macmillan Reference Books.
9. *Trud*, June 26, 1988.

10. V. Selyunin, "Tempy Rosta na Vesakh Potreblenia," *Socialisticheskaya Industria*, January 5, 1988.
11. V. Tomashkevich, *Socialisticheskaya Industria*, August 30, 1988. The annual fall of 3 percent occurs in what is called "fondootdacha" (a profit on capital investment) which is equal to a loss of product equal to the sum of 40 billion rubles. "Fondy" in the jargon of socialist economics is anything including equipment—i.e., "capital" in Marxist terminology. Thus, Soviet economists calculated that there are "dead fondy" in the country (unused equipment, capacities, etc.) equal to a sum of 400 billion rubles, and the process of "mortification of fondy" grows at 3 percent annually.
12. Kommunist, 11 (1985), p. 62.
13. Novosibirsky Document, Samizdat Archive #5042, p. 3.
14. *ibid.,* p. 4.
15. *ibid.,* p. 4.
16. Novy Mir, #1, 1989.
17. Boris Komarov, *The Destruction of Nature in the Soviet Union* (White Plains: Sharpe, 1980); all the environmental statistics above are from the same source.

Perestroika and Ideology

Adam B. Ulam

I. What Went Wrong

Communism, almost everybody (including its partisans) would agree, is going through difficult times. In the Soviet Union, the regime has been trying to shed its repressive and over-bureaucratized integument, but it is still far from clear what new structure could take the place of the old, and whether any new arrangement would contain the social and ethnic turbulence released by *glasnost.* In China, Mao's successors are trying to recoup their repressive control over society while persisting in a very un-Marxist restructuring of the country's economy. It has often been noted that much of the Marxian idiom about capitalism could much more appropriately be applied to Communist society.[1] And, indeed, what do we see in the USSR and China but the most palpable manifestation as yet of the "inherent contradictions" vis-à-vis the state?

To characterize the present situation in the USSR as a crisis of the system would not only be platitudinous, but almost redundant. Crisis has been a permanent feature of Soviet history. The Revolution and the Civil War were immediately succeeded by a struggle for power, then by a disastrous war waged by the regime against the peasant majority of the nation, then by massive terror that struck at all elements of society. It is as if Communism by its very nature abhors normalcy and tranquility and requires of its subjects no only obedience (as has been customary with other authoritarian systems) but also constant and feverish anxiety. In the Soviet official vocabulary, that anxiety has usually been translated to "vigilance." Normal human passions and concerns had to be subordinated to constant watchfulness: against foreign and domestic enemies; counterrevolutionaries—whether of the right or left; "enemies of the people"—to be found not only among the opponents of the regime, as common sense would suggest, but quite often within its highest political and military circles as well as among ordinary persons completely loyal to the established order.

The war, and especially its pre-Stalingrad victory phase, represented the ultimate crisis situation. And following the passing of real danger to the country and the regime, one might have expected that those largely contrived crises with their phantasmagorical atmosphere would no longer recur as the Soviet Union—now a superpower and having passed its most severe test—would turn its energies to the task of rebuilding. But Stalin's despotism could not dispense with a demonology: how could the Soviet Union feel secure when threatened abroad by the American imperialists and at home by those who craved the ways of the West and its freedoms—e.g., the "cosmopolites" denigrating Russia's past and Soviet achievements?[2] The alliance with the democracies and the victory itself were thus taken to be portents of domestic danger. There is much to suggest that had Stalin not died, he would have sought to deal with that danger in a manner reminiscent of 1937–39.

But the despot's death, while freeing the country from those largely contrived crises and their surrealistic atmosphere, had opened the period of what might be called the organic crisis of the regime and the society. After thirty years, Stalinism had become virtually synonymous with Communism as practiced in the Soviet Union and its dependent states. Stalin's successors were at first rightly concerned whether the system could survive the man who had been both its maker and its embodiment. As Khrushchev recalled:

> We were scared, really scared. We were afraid the thaw might unleash a flood which we wouldn't be able to control and which could drown us. How could it drown us? It could have overflowed the Soviet riverbed and formed a tidal wave which would have washed all the barriers and retaining walls of our society. *From the viewpoint of the leadership* this would have been an unfavorable development. We wanted to guide the progress of the thaw so that it would stimulate only those creative forces that would contribute to the strengthening of socialism.[3]

These words epitomize the dilemma faced by the regime from March 5, 1953 to the onset of *perestroika:* how to keep "the barriers and retaining walls" of the totalitarian system without diminishing its power. At the time, their fears proved superfluous. Among the legacy of those thirty years was also the social inertia and fear which precluded the possibility of revolt. From "the viewpoint of the leadership," this passivity of society was a welcome surprise: it made any basic reforms unnecessary. All one had to do was to eliminate the possibility of the rise of another Stalin and remove another feature that had made life hazardous, not only for the people at large but also the leaders themselves: the intermittent use of mass terror. Other basic features of Stalinism could and did remain—absolute control of society by the Party; the essentially conspiratorial rule of the Party by a small self-perpetuating elite; and the utter helplessness of the individual citizen, whether a manual worker or a great artist or scientist vis-à-vis the state.

None of those essential features was the target of Khrushchev when he delivered his famous speech at the 20th Party Congress. It is not surprising that the regime has remained unwilling for so long to make the document public, though the contents of the speech become rapidly and widely known. For the speech was not merely, as intended by the First Secretary, an indictment of Stalin as a person. It was a revelation not only of the criminal acts of one man, but the first official (if unwitting) acknowledgment of the absurdity of the system which both allowed that man to achieve supreme power and continued essentially unchanged after his death. The speech was bound to spur not only a feeling of revulsion against the "cult of personality" (and how feeble a euphemism it was for what it purported to describe), but also a wave of critical thinking about history and politics. Decades of official mystification and myth-building had well-nigh eroded the people's ability to appraise their political environment realistically. Now the blow at the "cult of personality" was also to be felt by the cult of the Party. Did the latter go astray only in 1934, as the First Secretary wanted his listeners to believe, or did the trouble start before—perhaps even in Lenin's time? It was the secret speech which both prepared the ground for dissent and hastened its appearance.

Krushchev sought to cleanse, rather than to reform, the Soviet system. His restlessness, so evident in his pyrotechnics on the international and domestic scenes, was very largely a consequence of the impossibility of the task he had set for himself. But a man of his generation and past could not be expected to realize that it was not possible to exorcise Stalinism from Soviet life without major political reforms; it could not be done merely by readjusting procedures and personnel. And, besides, for him as for many at home and abroad, the inherent crisis of Communism was obscured by the country's vigorous economic growth, the Kremlin's more humane ways, and the Soviet Union's growing military strength and prestige in the world at large. Few as yet saw the growing disunity of the international Communist movement as reflecting basic flaws in Marxist-Leninist philosophy. As is often the case with believers in historical determinism, Khrushchev saw the source of trouble there in personalities: Mao and his handful of "left-wing sectarians and dogmatists" in China, some unreliable leaders in Eastern Europe, and the Soviet Union's loss of prestige among the Western leftists. He chose to fight against the ghost of Stalin, rather than trying to excise what remained of Stalinism from the country's political and social structure, and eventually lost that struggle.

The Brezhnev era probably came closest to what might be described as a period of stability in Soviet history. "A future historian assessing the Brezhnev era may well have reason to conclude that it persisted in ignoring or sweeping under the rug the most perplexing problems of Soviet society and of world Communism, but as of 1976 one could not begrudge it credit for a large measure of success in the management of its domestic as well as foreign affairs."[4] In the international arena, the appearance of success was largely due to the travails of Moscow's rivals. The United States' foreign policy was in disarray in the backwash of the Vietnam fiasco and the constitutional crisis arising out of the Watergate affair. OPEC's exactions had shaken the entire West's economy. China had undergone the inanities of the Cultural Revolution; with Mao's death, it seemed on the verge of a new period of political and social turbulence. By contrast, the Soviet Union's foreign policy could be seen as set on an even keel: while still proclaiming its adherence to détente, the Kremlin was acquiring new clients in the Third World. Through patient diplomacy, the Brezhnev-Kosygin team achieved what the USSR had sought since 1945 (and what had, for all his pyrotechnics, eluded Khrushchev): virtual recognition of East Germany by the West and a formal confirmation of the Potsdam territorial settlements. Fissiparous tendencies within the "socialist camp" were sternly rebuked by the 1968 invasion of Czechoslovakia, but the Kremlin did not seek to revert to the pre-1953 manner of control of its junior partners.[5]

At home, the Soviet ship of state settled down to what still appears as the only viable pattern of Stalinism without an omnipotent dictator: an oligarcho-bureaucratic regime, severe on open dissent, but flexible in its methods of repression. The mainstay of the system, the bureaucrat (if not the average citizen), enjoyed what he had never had under Khrushchev and Stalin: security. In fact, one may speak of an unwritten compact between the elite of the elite, the Politburo circle, and the serried ranks of the *nomenklatura*. The former reserved to themselves all the policy and decision-making, while the latter (save in exceptional cases) were guaranteed their jobs and privileges without any purges, administrative innovations, or restructuring that would disturb their serene bureaucratic existence.

Why was the system—which, by the premises of those who ran it, worked so perfectly and which was so effective in suppressing or containing any disaffection and dissent—suddenly subjected to the turbulence and uncertainties of *perestroika?* Most contemporary analysts would attribute this sudden termination of the golden age of the Soviet ruling class to two factors: the personality of the man who took over the leadership of the Communist Party in March 1985, and to the slowing down (and, by the 1980s, the virtual stagnation) of the Soviet economy. But while the generational change and the troubles of Soviet industry and agriculture both helped to provoke the attempted reforms, neither furnishes a sufficient explanation of the astounding course of events of the last four years in the Soviet Union. The basic cause of the present vicissitudes of the Soviet system lies in the erosion of the ideological base of Marxism-Leninism.

II. Trying to Save Ideology

The first part of Marxism-Leninism has long lost any relevance to the politics of Communism. Classical Marxism is essentially a theory of the dynamics of capitalism, rather than a blueprint for a socialist society. What little guidance it provides for socialism lies mainly in its insistence on economic determinism—in its explicit warning (occasional utterances of Karl Marx to the contrary notwithstanding) that history cannot be hurried, that capitalism, for all of its inequities, cannot and should not be expected to leave the scene until and unless it has completed its mission: i.e., to fully modernize and industrialize the given society.

Lenin, of course, disregarded that warning, reiterated before October by Plekhanov and the Mensheviks. From 1914 until the seizure of power, what mattered most for him about Marxism was its revolutionary rhetoric and appeal, not its alleged historical laws and cautions. Russia, though not ready for socialism, was ripe for a revolution. Once in power, the revolutionary party would perform the task assigned by classical Marxism to capitalism—to industrialize and modernize Russia so that it would catch up with the advanced countries of the West and thus "start the movement toward socialism." This departure from the orthodoxy by one who before had condemned Trotsky's thesis of permanent revolution[6] was justified in his mind by the world war: a startling exposure of that rationalist and democratic tradition which, by the beginning of the century, had become the dominant tendency within the social democracies of Europe. The war for Lenin was a radical refutation of what Marx had said about the pacific nature of capitalism.[7] Marx had not realized that the inevitable corollary of capitalism, for all of its liberal and parliamentary accoutrements, was fierce competition of major nation-states, culminating in imperialist wars.

The logical consequence of Lenin's argument was to decouple the Marxian revolution from socialism. Communism would find at least as fertile a soil for growth in less-developed countries as in the highly industrialized ones. Russia, as of February 1917, was ripe for a *real*, not merely a bourgeois, revolution. "The complete hopelessness of the situation, having by the same token increased the strength of the workers and peasants tenfold opened for us the possibility of laying the foundations of a civilization in a different way from all other Western European nations," wrote Lenin in 1923—thus arguing that the war justified the Bolsheviks' seizure of power. And if those Marxist pedants had been shocked by his party's actions, let them but wait: "New revolutions in the much more populous and socially much different countries of the East will display even more singular characteristics than the Russian Revolution."[8]

The focus of gravity of revolutionary Marxism was thus shifted in the Bolsheviks' scheme from the internal mechanics of the capitalist system to the international scene. It was the propensity of capitalism to wage imperialist war rather than its great economic crises (though the latter will still occur) that would catalyze the progress of Communism and ultimately its triumph on the world stage.

By the time he penned those reflections, practically on his deathbed, Lenin had had good reasons to appreciate his Marxist opponents' criticism of the infant Soviet republic. The alleged workers' and peasants' state was rapidly and increasingly assuming an oligarcho-bureaucratic character; the Bolsheviks' arbitrary and violent ways had discredited militant socialism in the West in the eyes of many of its original supporters. But the founder of that state *had* to believe the current flaws of the Soviet system could be cured by the infusion of rank and file proletarians into the Party ruling apparatus, and that the eventual industrialization and modernization of Russia was bound to bring real proletarian democracy. If the revolutionary stirrings in the West had temporarily subsided, they were bound to recur with ever greater effectiveness in the colonial and semi-colonial areas. Whatever the present difficulties, the Bolshevik Revolution represented a giant advance toward world socialism and thus world peace.

Lenin's ideological legacy thus contained two promises which were to sustain the believers' faith into our own times. First, under Communism backward Russia would still be able to achieve a level of development materially, culturally, and morally surpassing that of the most advanced capitalist countries. Second, it would be the strength and attractiveness of this new socialist culture, rather than the economic breakdown of capitalism, that would make the Soviet model an object of emulation for other nations, including those which the old Marxist canon considered unready for socialism. Stalin's "socialism in one country" thus fitted Lenin's prescription much better than did Trotsky's counter-formula asserting that a revolution in a Western country had to precede the building of socialism in Russia.

Political manipulation and terror are not themselves sufficient explanations of why the despotic regime was able to survive. It had to draw its sustenance from real faith—even if it were only held by a small minority—and that faith would endure, because the events of twentieth-century politics seemed to confirm Lenin's prophecies and prescriptions. At each critical point, some grandiose feat of social engineering or a fresh danger to the "first socialist state in the world" obscured (and some thought justified) every new escalation of Stalin's tyranny. Belief became an incongruous companion of fear. In many, including some of its victims, terror bred not revulsion but enhanced faith in the historical mission of the party and the infallibility of the Leader. To believe otherwise would have meant to admit to oneself that the entire society has been gripped by mass lunacy. Ideology had been harnessed to terror. And that made it almost inevitable that once a revolution of common sense broke out in the USSR, first in 1956 and then more fully in 1985, it would be not only "the cult of personality" but also the entire paraphernalia of Marxism-Leninism that became discredited.

The post-1953 leadership was acutely aware of the danger of dissidence and ideological agnosticism resulting from merely a partial revelation about the crimes and abuses of the past thirty years (though Khrushchev, as we have seen, initially tried to confine his criticism to the period after 1934). The cult of personality, it was (and still is) stressed, was a perversion of Leninism, not in any sense a consequence or continuation of it. Even during the most harrowing times, Krushchev and his successors insisted, the Party preserved its integrity and continued to build socialism. This argument has ignored the obvious question: in view of this basic incorruptibility of the Party, how was Stalin able to achieve and to hold on to power? By 1964 it became clear to the Party elite that any further serialization of Stalin's crimes (so to speak) was bound, as it has since 1985, to undermine such feeble rationalizations. Following Khrushchev's removal, criticisms of Stalinism became muted. The new leaders obviously hoped that the passage of time would make the problem of a reexamination in moral and ideological terms of the 1924–53 period less and less important to the new Soviet generation. There were even discreet attempts to rehabilitate the past partially and to emphasize the allegedly positive aspects of Stalin's stewardship of the Soviet Union and world Communism, such as his wartime role.

The regime rested its main emphasis on proving the validity of the doctrine and maintaining the morale of its followers on the success of its policies to modernize Soviet society and to enhance the prestige and power of the USSR, and hence of Communism, in the world at large. The rising figures of steel production, the conquest of space, and the improving standard of life at home would eventually obliterate the painful memories of terror and famines. Krushchev's incautious promise that the Soviet Union would surpass the US in consumer welfare and enter the era of Communism by 1970 was a typical example of trying to endow ideological propositions with new life by now virtually meaningless proclamations—not only to the population at large, but even to loyal Party members.

Internationally, expansionist policies of course reflected the by then anachronistic imperialist strivings of the Kremlin, but they were still rationalized in the ideological idiom. For the Soviet citizen, each new client of the USSR's in the Third World and every fresh setback of the West in Vietnam, Algeria, or Latin America would provide additional proof that Communism was steadily advancing in power and world-wide influence, while the capitalist powers, for all their alleged freedoms, were in disorderly retreat—capitalism being, as Brezhnev said at the Twenty-Fifth Party Congress in 1976, a social system with no future.

Alas, by the 1980s, neither the domestic nor the foreign policies of the Soviet Union could be offered as convincing arguments for Communist doctrine. At home, the undoubtedly enormous material progress of the USSR since the war had failed to translate into a satisfactory rise in its people's standard of living. It became evident even to the rulers that the most troublesome features of the Soviet economy were precisely those that bore the heaviest imprint of ideology: the collective farm system and the rigidly centralized machinery of control and planning of industry and trade.

In the outside world, the seventies witnessed what could superficially be seen as Soviet advance and the West's disarray: "It is precisely during the past five years that the capitalist world has experienced an economic crisis, the seriousness and depth of which . . . can only be compared with the crisis of the 1930s," declared Brezhnev in 1976.[9] As against the ordeal of the entire capitalist system, "The Soviet people are proud of having given considerable help to Vietnam in its struggle against the imperialist intruders. . . . Laos and Cambodia have followed Vietnam in winning their freedom. . . . The sovereignty of the German Democratic Republic has been universally acknowledged [despite] the efforts of American imperialism . . . socialism has sunk its roots in Cuban soil."[10]

Yet such successes were of little or no interest to the average Soviet citizen, while those in the inner circles knew that the expansionist course of Soviet foreign policy was straining the country's resources, that the paralysis of American foreign policy in the wake of Vietnam and Watergate would be only temporary, and that further steps along the route of expansion could bring intolerable cost and risk. Toward the end of the decade, Brezhnev was to acknowledge that a nuclear confrontation would utterly devastate both the US and the USSR.[11] Until then, the Soviet leaders had insistently asserted that socialism could and would survive a nuclear war. That long-proclaimed, if feigned, equanimity in the face of a horrendous danger had been an important factor in the Kremlin's ability to intimidate the West and to make it acquiesce in the Soviets' encroachments. Though he himself was soon to launch upon an adventure in Afghanistan, the General Secretary's admissions led to the logical deduction that Moscow's foreign policy would have to be more prudent in the future: even a minor clash between the two superpowers might escalate to the ultimate horror.

In any case, whatever gains the Soviet Union registered abroad, they could hardly be credited to the doctrine. In fact, the recent course of events has vividly illustrated the inability of Marxism-Leninism to transcend and reconcile national differences and conflicts. The most seductive promise of Communism was the assertion that its eventual triumph would lead to a peaceful and stable world order. But that monolithic structure of world Communism and its submissiveness to Moscow's orders which had been virtually unchanged while the USSR was still a weak and vulnerable state came perversely to an end with the rise of other Communist regimes, even though by now the Soviet Union was infinitely more powerful than in the twenties and thirties. Yugoslavia's heresy in 1948 could still be considered an isolated case. But following Stalin's death, it became clear that Communism in Eastern Europe was staying in power only because of the presence or the shadow of Soviet tanks and bayonets. The trouble came not only because of the local nations' resistance to foreign domination, but also because the rulers of those countries—once faithful servitors of Moscow, like Tito—began, when in power, to crave its substance rather than the status of mere Soviet satraps. In Europe at least, proletarian nationalism was quickly unmasked as a euphemism for Soviet imperialism.

Even more important in exposing Communism's claims to be a supra-national ideology has been the case of China. The Sino-Soviet conflict, beginning in 1959–60, confirmed what one had suspected long before the rise of the People's Republic: Communism in power tends to stimulate, rather than reduce, the xenophobic instincts of a given society and its rulers. And even in states that could not aspire to the status of a great power, Communist rule has often brought with it an increased emphasis on militarism and territorial expansion. That acquisitive itch that, according to Marx, is so characteristic of the capitalist world has been very much pronounced in the various "people's," "democratic," and "socialist" republics.

All in all, Marxism-Leninism has not passed the test placed before it by the second half of the twentieth century. It was not only overt dissidents who, by the 1980s, had good reason to appreciate Solzhenitsyn's ruthless formulation of the dilemma caused by the continuation of ideological orthodoxy: "It is not authoritarianism itself that is intolerable, but the ideological lies that are daily foisted upon us. Not so much authoritarianism as arbitrariness and illegality, the sheer illegality of having a single overlord in each district, each province and sphere, whose will decides all things."[12] Previously, the gap between dogma and reality had been obscured by the ultimate in repression and by the virtual sealing-off of Soviet society from the outside world. Now that the people had come to fear less, they were becoming gradually emancipated from their awe of the official slogans and rituals. The state was still strong and repressive enough to prevent rebelliousness and to contain open dissent. But it could not cope effectively with a much wider covert and unconscious dissent which manifested itself in the malfunctioning of the economy, social afflictions such as the spread of alcoholism, and the growth of corruption within the *nomenklatura*.

Another psychological prop of the regime has also eroded: "Soviet patriotism." Ever since the early thirties, the Kremlin has presented Communism as being indissolubly bound up with the unity and greatness of the Soviet-Russian state. But in the popular consciousness, it was another Communist state which was now seen as posing in the long run the greatest threat to national security. Satisfying as it may have been to national pride at another time, acquiring client states in the Third World and standing armed guard over the faltering Communist regimes in Eastern Europe have come to be seen as of little relevance to the country's security in the nuclear age—and, indeed, as unnecessary burdens and potential sources of danger.

This is not to suggest that the regime would not have been able to continue in its old ways for a considerable time beyond 1985. But as has been the case with most political upheavals, the erosion of official ideology has been accompanied by a decline in the morale and sense of self-assurance of the ruling class itself. In foreign policy, this could be seen in the story of the Afghanistan war. A more self-confident regime would have flooded the unfortunate country with a much greater military force and striven more vigorously to intimidate Afghanistan's neighbors into ceasing their assistance to the guerrillas. Conversely, it would have broken off its armed intervention, rather than face a protracted and profitless conflict. In domestic affairs, except for some half-hearted measures in the beginning, the post-Khrushchev period saw no serious attempts to make Soviet economy more efficient. Nothing illustrates the old Kremlin team's diffident conservatism better than its assignment of the highest Party post in February 1984 to a man who, as was widely known, was physically debilitated and had not long to live.

III. Into Uncharted Waters

Paradoxically, the same conservatism was probably instrumental in helping to persuade the majority of the Politburo to choose Gorbachev. The twenty years of the Brezhnev era had led the old hands at the Kremlin to forget that, prior to it, each change in the top leader had been followed by consequences quite unforeseen not only by outside observers, but even by those who had supported him. The new General Secretary's age suggested that he might seek an escape from the pattern of *immobilisme* that had characterized the preceding period, but his entire background seemed reassuring: if a reformer, he would turn out to be a moderate and cautious one. And it must have been felt that the Party's prestige had suffered through its being headed by elderly invalids during the last ten years.

It is most doubtful that, at the time of his election, Gorbachev himself planned or foresaw anything like the full extent of reforms which he would attempt to carry out on his country during the next four years. He certainly could not have wished for or anticipated how much *perestroika* and *glasnost* would eventually endanger the two basic foundations of the system: complete domination of society by the Party and Moscow's absolute control of the Soviet Union's national subdivisions.

His initial goal was quite unrevolutionary: to cure the malfunctioning of the system by removing the flaws and replacing some parts in its existing machinery, rather than by tampering with the system itself. This framing of the needed reforms in purely administrative terms was accompanied by another equally traditional action for a new Soviet leader: measures and exhortations designed to enhance the work ethic and elevate the general morale of society.

Gorbachev's initial approach was thus basically not dissimilar from what he was to castigate as the sins of his predecessors: "The situation called for [basic] changes. [But] a strange psychology came to characterize policies of both the central and local authorities: one can achieve improvements without changing anything."[13] Measures to combat alcoholism, tighten labor discipline, and eradicate corruption in the state and Party apparatus were a continuation of the policies already initiated during Andropov's brief reign.

Without exception, every previous Soviet leader had attacked bureaucratic inertia and inefficiency and then attempted to overcome them . . . through fresh bureaucratic contrivances. And so, at first, did Gorbachev. At the Twenty-Seventh Party Congress in 1986, he paid lip service to the need for individual enterprises to be more self-regulating. But the General Secretary's main emphasis was still on central planning and control. "The Central Committee and its Politburo have specified the main thrust of the reconstruction of the economic mechanism. We are setting out to increase the activity of the central leadership of the economy, to strengthen the role of the center in the realization of the basic economic strategy of the Party and in deciding the pace and structure of the development of the national economy and of its separate parts."[14] New central economic organs were created, adding to the superfluity of the already existing committees and ministries which were often working at cross-purposes and getting in each others' way.

Believers in ideological orthodoxy (and what might be called the official myth-making orthodoxy) could also at first be reassured by Gorbachev's conduct. On the fortieth anniversary of V-E Day, he hailed the victory of the Soviet people and their army. It was achieved, as he specified, under the leadership of "the General Secretary J. V. Stalin." On his first visits abroad, he displayed considerable irritation when responding to questions about human rights and political persecution in the Soviet Union. The academician Sakharov was in exile, Gorbachev explained in answer to a provocative question by a French journalist, because he had violated Soviet laws.

It was mainly in foreign policy that one could notice departures from the orthodoxy in the first year of the new regime—indeed, one could see the beginning of what might be called a revolution of common sense. The theme that a nuclear war would be an unmitigated disaster had been sounded before, but it fell to Gorbachev to present it as the cornerstone of the new philosophy of Soviet foreign policy.

> At its [April 1985] meeting the Central Committee had analyzed again the character and potential scale of the nuclear danger. The nature of the existing weapons does not allow any state the possibility to defend itself through military-technological means, be its defenses the strongest possible . . . one can achieve security only through political means. Security cannot indefinitely be sought through [the opponent's] fear of retaliation. . . . Security, if one speaks about the relations between the USSR and the US, can only be mutual, and on the world-wide scale universal. . . . It is necessary that every state should achieve an equal feeling of security because the fears and terrors of the nuclear age give rise to the incalculability of policies in concrete situations.[15]

In a nuclear war, there could be no winners. What had been a reluctant and only occasionally enunciated admission of the late Brezhnev period now became the central motif of Gorbachev's policy.

But, a skeptical (i.e., Western) observer might note, the Soviets have always asserted that they are against war and that its danger comes exclusively from the imperialist side. So what has changed? An authoritative analyst of Soviet foreign policy, E. Primakov, sought to deal with that impolite question. In a rather tortuous argument, he came close to saying: before, we just talked about the peaceful coexistence, but now we really mean it.

> Up to quite recently, peaceful coexistence was thought by us as a respite, very likely to be broken by those who would once more try to destroy the first country in which socialism had triumphed . . . Today such opinions and interpretations have become clearly insufficient and inaccurate. The defensive potential of the Soviet Union remains of great importance, but what must take the first place is the search for preserving its security through political means . . . [Hence we need] an entirely new philosophy of and approach to internal problems.[16]

Quite apart from the question of how long-lasting the theory—and, what is more important, the practice—of this "new thinking" was likely to be, its very enunciation was of capital importance not only insofar as Soviet foreign policy was concerned but also to the whole nexus of Marxism-Leninism. It was not only Soviet expansion but also much domestic repression that had been rationalized in terms of the ineradicable hostility and danger from the capitalist world. Now *almost* explicitly, such expansion was condemned, for it increased the danger of war. "It is an imperative of the nuclear age, that propagation of revolutions abroad should cease."[17] If one must strive for peaceful relations with the capitalists, and such relations are necessary not just during an occasional respite but permanently, then Soviet society cannot be sealed off from all sorts of relations with the West. And if such intercourse indeed is desirable, then much of the rationale is undermined for the need for "vigilance"—i.e., repression—at home.

A Communist regime's friendlier relations with the West has not always been reflected by (or led to more liberal policies by) the Communist regime at home; if one has forgotten 1934–38 in the USSR, then one has recently been reminded of it in China. But both the international situation and the Soviet domestic scene after 1985 have combined to make détente both a companion and a further spur to *glasnost* and *perestroika.*

The main stimulus for enlarging the scope of reforms came from the realization by Gorbachev's team that administrative contrivances were by themselves incapable of curing the numerous ills afflicting the Soviet economy. By 1986–87, bracing slogans and exhortations had also proved to be ineffectual. Social and political revitalization of the system, rather than adjustment of its machinery, was now seen by the ruling team as an absolute imperative—both because, without it, the economy was unlikely to emerge from its stagnation and because the enlargement of the citizen's freedoms and interest in public affairs would provide him with some compensation for the queues, the shortages of goods, and the other manifestations of economic distress.

Gorbachev's domestic critics might well have taken as their motto the title of Lenin's essay, "Better Less but Better." Why not concentrate on improving the economy, without simultaneously embarking on hastily conceived constitutional and political experiments, enlarging the sphere of permissible discussion and criticism to the point where no aspect of the Soviet past or present remained sacrosanct? In view of the veritable flood of revelations about the horrors and criminal abuses of the Stalin era, whatever Khrushchev had to say on the subject now seemed mild and almost apologetic. The more recent past officially dubbed as "the period of stagnation" could not be painted in such lurid colors, but the public was still made privy to the appalling picture of the incompetence, complacency, and corruption of the ruling elite during the years. The ritual of confessions and recantations once imposed upon victims of the mass terror now appeared to have become the standard practice of Soviet Communism at large, the great difference being that this breast-beating disclosed real transgressions and crimes. By 1988 one could see criticisms of Lenin's policies in the press, something that would have been inconceivable during the previous sixty years.

To the conservative die-hards, this frankness in reexamining the past has posed a mortal danger to the very fabric of Soviet society. Their alarm and indignation was well expressed in a letter allegedly written by a rank-and-file Party member, Nina Andreyeva, but obviously inspired if not actually composed by someone much higher up: "I would very much like to know in whose interest and why it is that every leader of the Party and the Soviet government should with his tenure of office over be accused and discredited because of his real and imaginary mistakes? From where has come this passion for squandering the authority and dignity of the leaders of the first socialist country in the world?"[18] The letter recalled how Lenin demanded severe punishments for critics of the Soviet system "who by the way appeared quite inoffensive in comparison with some of those whose writings are being published today." What was the purpose of this entire slanderous campaign? Clearly its authors, "under the aegis of moral and spiritual 'cleansing' " sought "to erode the bounds and criteria of scientific ideology." Those who are abusing glasnost are propagating anti-socialist pluralism," concluded the author(s) of this Stalinist *cri de coeur.*

Few could have disputed one sentence in the letter: "The problem of the role and place of socialist ideology has today assumed a very sharp form." For the conservatives within the Party ranks, what is going on —if unchecked—could lead to the demolition, not just the restructuring, of the Soviet edifice.

What the conservative critics fear most are not so much the institutional changes but the phenomenon and the extent of *glasnost.* Yes, the Soviet system might hobble along with a real rather than a phony parliament. The collective farm structure could be loosened or even dissolved, and Communist rule would not necessarily be weakened. Even a measure of private ownership in the industry is tolerable. But Communism simply cannot coexist with the far-reaching freedom of speech and press. As Andreyeva's letter unwittingly argues, mythmaking is an essential condition of the preservation of "scientific ideology" (the letter admits that the previous leaders had committed "real errors"). The Soviet system is incompatible with a free critique of its past and present, for no matter how much such a critique may be justified by considerations of historical truth or morality, it tends to "erode the bounds and criteria" of Marxism-Leninism.

Those at the other end of the political spectrum see the pace of *perestroika* as too slow, and the regime's own reassessment of the past as still somewhat half-hearted. There is no doubt that Gorbachev has lagged behind the more advanced elements of public opinion when it comes to both the urgency of reforms and the willingness to reexamine ideological and historical dogma thoroughly. On the seventieth anniversary of the Bolshevik Revolution, what Gorbachev had to say about Stalin must have sounded rather strange to some of his listeners in view of what has now become the public image of the tyrant. Yes, said the

General Secretary, "the guilt of Stalin and his entourage . . . is enormous and unforgivable." But he also saw fit to praise Stalin on several counts. "Stalin's contribution to the struggle for socialism is from the point of historical truth unquestionable."[19] Among those alleged contributions was Stalin's stout defense of Leninism against Trotsky and other enemies of the correct Party "line" and most importantly, his leadership in the Great Fatherland War. "What also played a role in the achievement of victory was the enormous political decisiveness, persistence and clearness of purpose of J. V. Stalin, as well as his skill in organizing and disciplining people."

By the time this strange mixture of condemnation and eulogy reached the Soviet public, several journals had already published their own accounts of Stalin's life, which effectively exploded the legend of any redeeming features in his career. Even the last line of defense of Stalin's reputation, his wartime role, had been breached. New and uncensored versions of World War II generals' memoirs clearly revealed that, in addition to his prewar massacre of the officer corps, Stalin also damaged the Soviet Union's ability to defend itself by his persistent refusal to believe reports of the impending German invasion. And his "decisiveness and clearness of purpose" as the supreme commander was evidenced mainly in his scrupulous care that he himself should get the major share of glory for the victories won by his soldiers and marshals.

But Gorbachev's performance in this case was not atypical of the role that has been imposed upon him by the travails of *perestroika* and the rapidly shifting political climate in Soviet society. Early in his leadership, he must have realized that he could not carry out any substantive reforms just as a *Party* leader; he must have seen that he had to break Soviet society from its longstanding condition of passivity and intimidation. To work for reforms within the traditional framework of Communist politics would probably have led to his dismissal quite early in the game—hence his bid for the support of the intelligentsia and his sanctioning of what he may well privately consider excesses of *glasnost.* The resulting turbulence has shaken not only the authority of the Party but the integrity of the structure of the Soviet state as well. At this point it is still unclear whether the new constitutional framework can be reconciled with the monopoly of power by the Party and how the problem of non-Russian nationalities will be resolved. Until now, however, the vulnerability of the system has contributed to the strength of Gorbachev's personal position. His colleagues, horrified as most of them undoubtedly have been (if not by his policies, than by their consequences), realize that a coup like that of October 14, 1964 would risk turning the present turbulence into chaos. The General Secretary, then, has had to play a dual role: intermittently cheering on the one hand and censuring or curbing the tumultuous transformations on the other, at times appeasing conservatives and at other times authorizing new departures from the orthodoxy. He has been, so to speak, both leader of the opposition to the orthodoxy as well as its defender and guardian.

What is supposed to lie at the end of the road? Well, the Gorbachev faction must undoubtedly hope that the recently introduced institutional framework with eventual improvements in economic conditions would succeed in creating what would become—to paraphrase Khrushchev's phrase—the new barriers and retaining walls of Soviet society. The Party would still dominate the political landscape, but there would be a wide measure of social pluralism. Aspirations of the non-Russian nationalities would be partly appeased, but the USSR would not be allowed to become a confederation or the means to secession of a national unit. *Perestroika*—like transformations of other Communist regimes—would reconcile its peoples to their countries remaining within the socialist camp. Since they have both undergone painful trails, the Soviet Union and China would draw closer, and their eventual cooperation in the international sphere would allow Communism to recoup its former worldwide prestige and attraction.

There is, of course, a great deal of wishful thinking in that picture. Both conservative and progressive critics of the present course agree on seeing inherent contradictions in the vision of a Communist *Rechstaat.* The former long for a somewhat modified version of the pre-1985 setup. The latter chafe under the existing constraints on democratization; they would like to see the ultimate goal of *perestroika* as the adoption of a different model than a formal adherence to Marxism-Leninism, perhaps something similar to Sweden's. Few expect the economic picture to improve in short order without the adoption of drastic measures, and these in turn would greatly magnify the political dangers faced by the regime. And there are those who see the portent of the befuddled society's destination in phenomena such as Pamyat, with its retrograde, xenophobic, and quasi-fascist set of beliefs.

Still, *perestroika* has been a bold experiment to free the political and social atmosphere from the miasmas of the past. And Gorbachev, for all his obfuscation of some basic issues and for all his linking of the reforms to considerations of his personal power, has displayed considerable courage in steering the Soviet ship of state into uncharted waters.

We can be sure of one thing: Marxism-Leninism has lost any meaningful significance as the compass for the future course of Soviet state and society. The regime will continue to try to retain its liturgy and symbolism, but it has already found it irrelevant or counterproductive insofar as actual policies are concerned. But even such decorative use of ideology may prove to be a burden rather than a help when dealing with concrete challenges to the present order: pressures for political pluralism, fissiparous tendencies among the nationalities, and stagnation of the economy.

Some have pleaded, paraphrasing what has been said about Christianity, that the trouble with Marxism-Leninism lies in the fact that it has never been practiced. It has been argued that perestroika should be seen as the emergence of "socialism with a human face," rather than as a confirmation of the bankruptcy of the ideology. Yet "socialism with a human face" had, in fact, preceded the emergence of Communism—it is that social democratic tradition that Lenin abruptly jettisoned in 1914, but which was continued by the socialist parties of the West. Following World War II, however, almost all of them renounced their adherence to the dogmas of Marxism, since democratic socialism was in fact turning into what might be called latter-day liberalism.

Marxism has been found wanting, and not just because of its association with the repressive past features of the Soviet system. Perestroika and what goes on in other Communist societies have demonstrated the obsolescence of Marxism in general and of its Leninist offshoot in particular. "Gray is the dogma, but ever green is the tree of life," as Lenin himself liked to repeat after Goethe.

NOTES

1. E.g., the pre-1985 Soviet state being the executive committee of the exploiting class.
2. The euphemism used in the late 1940s and early 1950s for Jewish writers and scientists.
3. *Khrushchev Remembers—The Last Testament* (New York: Little, Brown & Co.: 1974), p.79. My italics.
4. Adam B. Ulam, *Dangerous Relations: The Soviet Union in World Politics. 1970–1982* (New York: Oxford University Press, 1983), p. 146.
5. When the Soviets ordained all the social and economic policies in the satellites.
6. Which would have a socialist revolution growing directly out of a bourgeois one.
7. "National differences and antagonisms between peoples are daily more and more vanishing, owing to the development of the bourgeoisie, to freedom of commerce, to the world market, to uniformity in the mode of production and in the conditions of life corresponding thereto." *The Communist Manifesto,* Marx and Engels, *Basic Writings on Politics and Philosophy,* ed. Lewis S. Feuer (Doubleday: Garden City, 1959), p.26.
8. V. I. Lenin, *Works,* (4th ed.; Moscow, 1954), vol. 33, p. 438–39.

9. L. I. Brezhnev, *Following Lenin's Path* (Moscow, 1976), vol. 5, p. 497.
10. *ibid.,* p. 454.
11. Saying what the Soviets had known all along.
12. A. Solzhenitsyn, *Letter to Soviet Leaders* (Collins: London, 1974), p.53.
13. From his speech at the Twenty-Seventh Congress, reported in Radio Liberty, *Digest of the Soviet Media,* pp. 93–96.
14. *ibid.,* pp. 93–139.
15. *ibid.,* pp. 94–111.
16. E. Primakov, "The New Philosophy of Foreign Policy," *Pravda,* July 10, 1987.
17. *ibid.*
18. Nina Andreyeva, "I Cannot Renounce My Principles," *Soviet Russia,* March 13, 1988.
19. *Izvestia,* November 3, 1987.

"The Captive Mind" Revisited: Intellectuals and Communist Totalitarianism in Poland

Andrzej Walicki

I. Introduction

In 1980 Czeslaw Milosz (born in Lithuania, 1911), an émigré Polish writer and a professor of Slavic literature at the University of California, Berkeley, was awarded the Nobel Prize in literature. This award consolidated his reputation as the greatest Polish poet of the living generation. For a long time, however, he was known in the West not as a poet, but as the author of *The Captive Mind* (1953), a book written, primarily with the Western reader in view, to explain some peculiar mechanisms of the totalitarian control over the minds and the consciences of the people. This semi-autobiographical book was hailed by philosophers (among them the great German existentialist, Karl Jaspers), sociologists, and political scientists as an enormously important contribution to the understanding of Communist totalitarianism.

Today *The Captive Mind* is regarded as one of the classical analyses of the totalitarian ambitions of the Communist regimes.[1] At the same time, however, some of its theses are thought controversial, or even simply outdated. This applies, above all, to its central thesis about the ability of the Communist parties to exercise thought control and to produce "captive minds." In most Communist countries (although not all of them, and not to the same extent), the grip of the officially proclaimed ideology has greatly loosened; the authorities have become skeptical, if not openly cynical, about the utopian aim of a total transformation of man; and the population has succeeded in liberating itself from "mental captivity." This change could be explained in different ways: as proof that totalitarian systems could, in fact, do without thought control and commitment to ideologically defined ultimate ends—or, conversely, as a proof that Communist regimes are not necessarily totalitarian. Some political scientists, mostly left-wing, have even tried to discredit the very notion of totalitarianism, claiming that the idea of establishing a control over people's minds was merely an anti-Communist myth, invented for cold war purposes.

The evolution of the Communist system was especially visible in Poland—a country whose population became openly anti-Communist and whose Communist rulers tried to preserve their power while getting rid of Communist dogma. Because of this, ironically, *The Captive Mind* has become almost unintelligible for the younger generation of Poles. They admire Milosz as a poet, seeing him (against his wishes)[2] as a sort of national bard, but they fail to understand his analysis of Communism as a powerful and fascinating "New Faith." Milosz's stress on the "power of attraction exerted by totalitarian thinking," as well as his view that Communist rule in East-Central Europe cannot be satisfactorily explained "in terms of might and coercion,"[3] run counter to their deeply ingrained inclination to treat "totalitarianism" as a purely coercive system, based on naked force alone. For the older generation, including the former Stalinists, *The Captive Mind* has also become difficult to accept. Some of them feel that Milosz's analyses are too "dialectical," too empathetic, and thereby embellish the reality of the Stalinist system which, in fact, had been brutally simple. Thus, for instance, at an academic conference organized in Warsaw to celebrate Milosz's Nobel Prize, Roman Zimand—a scholar with a Stalinist past—treated *The Captive Mind* as a book insufficiently critical of the "self-justifying mechanisms of capitulation."[4]

Of course, Milosz's prestige in contemporary Poland is so great that even an outspoken skepticism about the explanatory value of *The Captive Mind* does not assume the form of a direct attack on its author. Nevertheless, the reaction of many contemporary Poles to such elements of Milosz's view of Communism as its historical inevitability, or as a powerful "New Faith" and thus an antidote to the spiritual emptiness of decadent "bourgeois society," is, in substance, quite similar to the opinions voiced in the early 1950s by the majority of émigré Poles.[5] Admittedly, today nobody would dare to endorse the view that Milosz was making up complicated theories in order to conceal his own renegade behavior, or that he wrote *The Captive Mind* to propagate the secret charms of the Communist faith. But most young Poles are, nonetheless, similar to the old émigrés in their inherent inability to accept the view that Stalinism could have been experienced as a *spiritual* tyranny, and not merely an external coercion.

To fully understand the early Polish reactions to *The Captive Mind,* it is necessary to remember that its appearance was preceded by the publication of an article in which Milosz tried to explain the reasons for his defection to the West without making any concessions to the mainstream opinions of Polish political emigration.[6] He wrote in it that he had served the new regime in Poland, both as a writer and as the cultural attaché in the United States and France, out of deep conviction: because of his support for the sociopolitical reforms which had broken the "semi-feudal" structures of pre-war Poland, emancipating the popular masses and firmly setting the country on the path of industrialization. He even confessed that he treated the émigré politicians as "vaudevillian figures."[7] Small wonder, indeed, that the émigrés reacted with rage. On the other hand, Milosz's colleagues in Poland, who continued to collaborate with the Communists, could not swallow his exposure of their "mental captivity," Their reactions to his view of Stalinism as "spiritual tyranny" were, therefore, equally as hostile as the reactions of the émigrés. Let us quote a few samples.

Antoni Slonimski, an eminent poet, known before the war (and also after the "thaw" of 1955–1956) as a champion of liberal democratic values, used the official party organ for a personal attack on Milosz: "You instigate against planned labor, which is absorbing an ever greater mass of the Polish people, you attack the building of factories, universities and hospitals, and you are the enemy of workers, intelligentsia and peasants."[8] The great writer Jaroslaw Iwaszkiewicz, known earlier for his markedly aristocratic leanings, presented Milosz's defection as amounting to a betrayal and commented: "he immediately found himself in a neo-Nazi paper, on the same page as General Vlassov."[9] Roman Zimand, by then a young, militant party activist, summed up Milosz's case as follows: *The Captive Mind* is "a masterpiece of hostile propaganda . . . Milosz was and has remained a traitor" (1955).[10] And Kazimierz Brandys, who was then a leading representative of socialist realism, presented this case in a short story entitled *Before He Becomes Forgotten.*[11] This typical exercise in "ideologically committed literature" treated Milosz as a contemptible renegade and confidently predicted that even his name would be successfully exorcised from the memory of socialist Poland.

In fact, all these reactions in the milieu of young Communist intellectuals and older fellow-travelers in Poland could be seen as splendid confirmation of the correctness of Milosz's diagnosis.

None of the above mentioned Polish intellectuals was literally "coerced" to write what they had written, and none of them could be suspected of calumniating Milosz because of base, careerist motives. All of them felt sincerely indignant and wanted to express this feeling. At the same time, however, it is obvious that their feelings—or, at least, the form of their expression—would have been significantly different without the intense, organized ideological pressure that was characteristic of the Stalinist period. Slonimski and Iwaszkiewicz internalized this pressure only partially, with a certain mental reservation, but they were nonetheless forced to believe that they *had* to side with the Communists because the only alternative was the position of the notorious "enemy of the people," the "objective ally" of neo-Nazism. It is evident that this belief did not express their true selves and, in this sense, was not truly "theirs"; rather, it showed their loss of independent judgment, their surrender to organized psychic pressure, and, consequently, the degree of their "mental captivity." The case of Brandys and Zimand, who at that time genuinely identified themselves with Communism, was somewhat different, but they also exemplified, each in their own way, the phenomenon of the "captive mind." After the "thaw" of 1955–56, they came to their senses and distanced themselves from their past conduct. Brandys wrote a short story, *The Defence of Grenada,* whose hero (an alter-ego of the author) presents himself as a victim of a mesmerizing influence of "Doctor Faul," a clever manipulator, invoking such notions as "higher reasons," "the only choice," "historical necessity," and so forth. (It was clear that this was to be a portrait of Jakub Berman, the most influential member of the Stalinist Politburo, directly responsible for ideology, culture, and matters of security, removed from power in 1956 and in the next year expelled from the party.[12]) Zimand, an ex-member of the young (and aggressive) ideological vanguard, could not pose as somebody's victim. Hence, he broke with Stalinism, and soon afterwards with Communism in general, without attempting to justify his past commitments. This explains his later criticism of *The Captive Mind* for its alleged indulgence in the desire of self-justification.

Even more blunt criticism of *The Captive Mind* has been repeatedly made by Gustaw Herling-Grudzinski, a writer connected with the émigré monthly *Kultura* (whose editors published Milosz's books and defended him against his attackers).[13] He claimed that, in fact, Communism had no power to enslave human minds from within but could only apply physical terror and thus force people to lie. This similarity between the views of an ex-Communist (Zimand) and those of a sophisticated anti-Communist (Herling-Grudzinski) seems to be quite natural. Milosz's book concentrates on the phenomenon which the Russian dissidents have called "dual consciousness"[14]—that is, a state of mind characterized by both yielding to ideological pressure and defending oneself against it. From the point of view of both a consistent anti-Communist (immune to the temptations of the "New Faith") and a consistent Stalinist (a believer immune to doubts), the reality was simpler: either-or, choose for yourself and do not blame others. In fact, however, Zimand's biography provides, I think, an argument against Herling-Grudzinski's thesis that "mental captivity" was simply a product of physical terror. Physical terror did not last long enough in Stalinist Poland to become leveled against young Communist zealots; young Communists, like Zimand, could be used to intimidate others but had, as yet, no reason to feel terrorized themselves. And yet even those who, like Zimand, were endowed with a sound moral instinct and brilliant critical intellect behaved in such a way then as if their moral and intellectual qualities were stifled, if not fully paralyzed. They might not have been aware of this, but in fact they were not free; their minds and consciences were enslaved, victimized by a deliberately organized, hysterical "ideological mobilization." Their own enthusiastic participation in creating this collective enslavement does not change the fact that it was also *their own* enslavement. Therefore, Milosz's category of "captive minds" applies to them as well.

There are many reasons why Milosz's book needs to be recalled when discussing the current problems of Communist totalitarianism. Briefly, it provides powerful arguments against left-wing attempts to discredit the very concept of "totalitarianism"[15] but, at the same time, it warns us against the indiscriminate and ahistorical usage of this term. Above all, it analyzes the "ideocratic" dimension of the totalitarian phenomenon with exceptional depth[16] and thus helps us to see the fundamental difference between genuine totalitarianism and mere "partocracy." By the same token, it supports those conceptions of totalitarianism which see its essence in genuine commitment to a messianic ideology, the ability to exercise ideological control over the population, and the corresponding capacity to mobilize the masses for active, though strictly controlled, participation in the "building of a new life."[17]

We must realize that this is not the same as seeing the essence of totalitarianism in "the birth of a new ruling class—the political bureaucracy, the *nomenklatura*—that holds a monopoly on decision-making on all issues relevant to its interests."[18] Putting emphasis on the monopolistic rule of a "new class" is an attempt to redefine the notion of totalitarianism so that it minimizes the significance of the changes which occurred in the Soviet Union after Stalin and thus denies the very existence of the processes of "de-totalitarianization."

However, the logic of this view would require us to see the Soviet Union under Brezhnev as more totalitarian than under Stalin, which is obviously absurd. It was only under Brezhnev, the first Soviet leader who had silently abandoned utopian dreams, that the higher echelons of political bureaucracy received collective security of tenure and thus a position of power which enabled them to guide the party in accordance with their own material interests.[19] An idealistic revolutionary can perceive it as the final betrayal of the Revolution, but liberals should see it as a symptom of loosening ideological controls, weakening the "teleocratic" character of the system, and putting an end to the universal unpredictability and uncertainty characteristic of classical totalitarianism. The culmination of totalitarianism was the period of permanent purges, followed after World War II by the infamous "struggle against cosmopolitanism"; in these conditions, as Isaac Deutscher has said, the party bureaucracy was kept "in the state of flux, renewing permanently its composition" and not being allowed "to form a compact and articulate body with a sociopolitical identity of its own."[20] Thus, the fully-fledged *nomenklatura*—that is, something similar to a "new class" —was in fact a product of the post-ideocratic and (therefore) post-totalitarian stage of Soviet history.[21] If we doubt the validity of these distinctions, let us read Milosz's *The Captive Mind.* Is it not obvious that if Communist totalitarianism could be reduced to the class rule of the *apparatchiks,* this book could not have been written? Comparing the Communists to the "new Christians" makes sense only if the Communists movement is still in its totalitarian-ideocratic phase—committed to the messianic goal of a "new man" and a "new earth," seeing its leader as an embodiment of an all-embracing and world-changing knowledge, and basing its rule on a peculiar combination of terror and a measure of a skillfully manipulated popular support, drawn from the promises of a "radiant future." Only such a party (or, to be more cautious, a party capable of creating such an image of itself) could succeed in imposing its crude ideological rule on otherwise sophisticated intellectuals. Of course, I mean here the Soviet party under Stalin, since the Polish party was then perceived, quite correctly, as subordinate to it.

Today it may seem incredible, but Stalinist Communism—precisely because of its unrelenting totalitarianism—was able to exercise a powerful influence on intellectuals, East and West. Milosz was not alone in stressing that "the pressure of the state machine is nothing compared with the pressure of a convincing argument"; convincing logically (hence

Hannah Ardendt's proposal to define totalitarianism as "logocracy")[22] and, even more, by its effectiveness in producing a "mass hypnosis."[23] His friend and mentor, Tadeusz Kronski (whom he called "the Tiger"),[24] was not original in seeing Stalinism as the embodiment of the Hegelian *Weltgeist* and presenting its crimes as the manifestation of a cruel but rational historical necessity. Maurice Merleau-Ponty did the same, justifying Stalinism as "the dictatorship of the truth" and praising Marxist philosophy as "a theory of violence and justification of terror," which brings "reason out of unreason," distinguishing revolutionary violence from "regressive forms of violence," and thus making possible the belief in the rationality of history, the only remedy against nihilism and despair.[25] "In this sense," he wrote, "Marxism is not a philosophy of history; it is *the* philosophy of history and to renounce it is to dig the grave of Reason in history."[26]

The number of such testimonies is almost infinite. They show that susceptibility to totalitarian temptations was, as a rule, rooted in the intense need for meaning in human collective life. Leszek Kolakowski bore witness to this when he confessed, in one of his early essays, that the deeply experienced and fully assimilated Communist faith endowed the individual with *the most intense* feeling of meaningfulness in life.[27]

II. 'The Captive Mind' and the Polish Version of Totalitarian Ideocracy

Poland's experience with totalitarian Communism is often treated with neglect. It is widely believed that strong national feeling did not allow Stalinism to take deep roots in Poland, that the majority of Poles saw their Stalinist government as a mere puppet regime, a tool of Poland's traditional enemy, and that the Catholic Church, so powerful in Poland, saved its believers from internalizing Communist ideology. Even Milosz himself has become persuaded that his *Captive Mind* described a phenomenon which was universally significant but rather atypical for Poland. In his interview with Ewa Czarnecka, he said: "What I wrote was true with regard to a certain number of people in Poland. It's just that there were very few such people in Poland." He hastened to declare his full awareness of the fact that the issues dealt with in this book "ceased to be relevant in Poland." In Poland, he commented, everything "is much less complicated in that no one there believes in the magic power of Marxist philosophy."[28]

However, it was not always so. It is true that Poland has been the only country of the Soviet Bloc "in which Sovietisation was not fully implemented."[29] The attempts to collectivize the peasants were half-hearted, the powerful Catholic Church remained unbroken, and some groups among the older intellectuals did not yield to ideological pressure. But it is not true that Polish Stalinism completely failed to impose its rule on people's minds. Taking into account the hostile atmosphere in the country and the programmatic moderation in reeducating the intelligentsia by means of physical terror, its successes in the mass production of "captive minds" were quite impressive. This is now seen as an incomprehensible "domestic shame,"[30] but it was especially true about the intelligentsia. After the full-scale ideological offensive which followed the crushing of the so-called "right-wing nationalist deviation" in 1948, the majority of the Polish intelligentsia fell under the spell of the "New Faith." Admittedly, some peculiarly intransigent enemies of Communism remained unbroken and visible. There were also intellectual circles (mostly Catholic) which accepted the regime as a sort of "geopolitical necessity" while being immune to its ideology. Finally, one should distinguish between different forms and degrees of "mental captivity." Nevertheless, it was unfortunately a fact that two especially important groups —the majority of the so-called "creative intelligentsia" and the majority of the students —proved susceptible to Communist indoctrination."[31] Some of them embraced it enthusiastically; others surrendered to it without enthusiasm, as a result of organized pressure. On the whole, however, the success of indoctrination was remarkable. In the early 1950s, Milosz was not wrong in seeing Poland as one of the "converted countries."[32]

These preliminary explanations enable us to return to Milosz's *The Captive Mind.* To show its significance as a historical (and not merely personal) document, I shall also deal with a few other similar texts.

After five years of loyally serving People's Poland, Milosz decided to break with the Stalinist regime and to remain in the West. In his article "No" (1951),[33] he distanced himself from the stereotype of a Communist who became disappointed and chose freedom. He explained that he had never been a Communist. If Communists could be called "the new Christians," his relation to them was that of a "good pagan"—somebody attracted by the "New Faith," willing to serve it, but not truly converted. Like other progressive Polish intellectuals, he was profoundly disgusted with "God-and country" nationalism—the dominant ideology of prewar Poland—and aware of the need for deep social reforms. He believed in the historical necessity of the "New Christianity," and he was willing to serve its cause. Nonetheless, he refused to become "baptized." The "pagan" values were a part of himself, and he was unable and unwilling to renounce his identity. The priests of the "New Faith" solved all problems for the writers—both moral and material. They offered them great prestige and carefree, privileged existence.[34] But for this they demanded the renouncement of freedom and truth. Their dialectical method (which Milosz otherwise found very convincing) proved that lies could serve the cause of truth, and that true freedom consisted in the scientific understanding of necessity. Milosz was not indignant about this theory; he was simply unable to cross this threshold in practice. He chose the West with fears of committing suicide as a poet, expecting only feelings of loneliness.[35] The alternative, however, was a worse sort of moral suicide: speaking with an alien voice and thus ceasing to belong to himself. In this situation, Milosz chose the proverbial "lesser evil." He wrote: "If freedom is to consist exclusively in understanding necessity, then I, miserable worm, stand in the path that history must take, in the thunderings of tanks and the flutterings of banners, and it is a matter of no interest to me that I shall be called the slave of my superstitious and inherited habits."[36]

In the same year, 1951, an economic historian, Witold Kula (who was to become one of the greatest Polish historians of this century), wrote an interesting text entitled "Wizardry"[37]—an autobiographical document written for his small daughter, to enable her, at some point in the future, to understand her father. Its form is a correspondence between two ancient Romans of the end of the fifth century, Claudius and Lucius. Both of them are pagans, deeply critical of the injustices of the old pagan Rome, but firmly rooted in its culture, now threatened from two sides: by the Northern Barbarians and by the Christians. Together with the latter the Romans have defended their fatherland against the former; they now witness its growing domination by Christianity. Claudius cannot accept it. He prefers being an iconoclast than a blind believer. He is appalled by the aesthetic taste of the Christians, by their narrow dogmatism and absurd belief in the infallibility of their Church, so crudely expressed in their favorite book, *The Apostolic History,*[38] their absolute intolerance and disrespect of individual freedom, their attempts at imposing thought control, extracting confessions of sins and throwing anathemas on the unrepentant. Lucius shares all these feelings but tries to overcome them as culture-bound and supporting the decadent, evil world. The Christian Church, he argues, organizes the masses to struggle for the new world; therefore it is true that the Church is always right, even when it is plainly wrong.[39] Christianity is a world-historical force, hence even its errors have to be accepted as helping, in a mysterious way, to realize the Kingdom of God on earth. *The Apostolic History* is indeed crude, but it helps millions of former slaves to create a new and better world. Aesthetic tastes are relative; what now seems appalling might appear great to future generations.

Anyhow, the present epoch is a magnificent turning point in history. The world will become Christian, whether we want it or not.

At the end of this correspondence, an unexpected element appears. Claudius receives an invitation to come to Alexandria to take part in the enterprise of translating the Scriptures from the Hebrew, Aramaic, and Greek into Latin. Despite his criticism of Christianity, he sees this as a great scholarly opportunity and asks Lucius to join the project. Lucius, however, refuses. Despite his praise of Christianity, his deep roots in the pagan culture make him *unable* to cooperate with the Christians. Nonetheless, he once more declares his love for the culture of the future whose foundations are now being laid by the Church. The world of the future deserves to be loved, he says, even if it remains alien, incomprehensible, and unimaginable.[40]

Apart from the historical parallel with the breakdown of the ancient world, two important motifs are common to Kula, Milosz, and Kronski (who also compared Communists to the early Christians and interpreted Marxism as the secularization of the chiliastic element in the Judeo-Christian tradition).[41] The first can be defined as a peculiar variety of dialectical catastrophism. What made it dialectical was the perception of catastrophe not as a mere disaster, the end of one's world, but also as a regenerative event, "a new beginning." ("Dialectical, or catastrophic? It is not quite the same, but almost"—wrote Milosz, in connection with "the Tiger.")[42] And what made it "peculiar" was the fact that catastrophe was not a matter of historical prophecy, a presentiment of the future, but the historical reality, the definition and dialectical interpretation of the present. This interpretation—and here we have the second common element—had to involve a historiosophical justification which would enable intellectual reconciliation with reality.

Such a stance, although not yet a commitment, was by no means value-free. Defining a given situation as a "dialectical catastrophe" was equivalent to seeing it as historically legitimate, "deserved" by the sinful "old world," and necessary for earthly salvation. Nazism could never claim such a status, at least outside Germany.[43] In Poland it was only perceived as an episode: mad, terrifying, but inescapably temporary, short-lived. This is an important argument against the view that the Stalinist "New Faith" was simply a rationalization of "interiorized terror." Not every terror gives birth to an "ideocratic fear"; the content of its legitimizing ideology also counts. Nazi terror in occupied Poland gave rise only to a desire to fight, and often also provoked jeering and ridicule. The strength of Communism as an ideology of expansionist totalitarianism was inseparable from its appeal to universalist values.

In this connection, Milosz made an interesting observation about himself and "the Tiger": "We were not like the Russians, because there was no blessed patriotic cloud to obscure our consciousness. While we sought escape in justification, we could not escape into the most convenient one, which the power of one's own country always affords, even though acquired at an indecent cost."[44]

I think that this observation can be generalized. Polish conversions to totalitarian Communism (especially after 1948) were peculiarly interesting—peculiarly "pure," as it were—because they were not contaminated by anything like "national bolshevism." It is significant that the chauvinist, anti-Semitic "struggle against cosmopolitanism," which raged at that time in the Soviet Union, had no equivalent in Stalinist Poland. We know now that this restraint in imitating the Soviet "anti-cosmopolitan campaign" was a deliberate policy of Jakub Berman, who was rightly afraid of setting free Poland's "nationalist demons."[45] As a Jew, he rightly felt that he might become a victim of it himself. Whatever its reasons, this policy gave Polish Stalinism the appearance of doctrinal purity, which made it more attractive for Polish left-wing intellectuals like Milosz, Kronski, Kula, Kolakowski,[46] and so many others.

Another peculiarity of those Polish intellectuals who found themselves within the orbit of the mesmerizing influence of the "New Faith" was their relative lack of naive illusions. Milosz explained: "We were also different from Western Leftists because they were still tending a legend. For us, months and years of that legend carved our very flesh."[47] In other words, Polish intellectuals from Milosz's generation had, as a rule, enough knowledge of the cruel history of their part of Europe and, therefore, faced the task of *explaining the contrast* between ideal and reality. This task, similar to that of theodicy (or, rather, historiodicy), led them to think in historiosophical terms and especially to the widespread use of the Hegelian category of "historical necessity." Milosz called it "the Hegelian bite"; young Kolakowski, at his "revisionist" stage, referred to it as "the opiate of the demiurge." The exoteric side of the "New Faith" were the ideas of a "better world" and "radiant future," but on a deeper level it stressed the Engelsian (and Hegelian) "conscious recognition of necessity." The ideological functions of the idea of necessity were many. It could be therapeutic, through providing historiosophical consolation and bringing about a philosophical reconciliation with reality. In the case of failure to produce such a serene state of mind, it served as "an instrument of moral masochism,"[48] through creating an inner pressure to accept the unacceptable. As a rule, it combined therapy with intimidation: people in its grip were "paralysed with fear" of finding oneself "on the wrong side" and landing in "the rubbish bin of history."[49] And in all cases it provided powerful—not merely opportunistic, but historical, philosophical, and moral—arguments for "swimming with the current" and thus accepting the power of those who seemed, and pretended, to embody historical Reason. As Milosz later wrote:

> "He who has power, has it by historical logic.
> Respectfully bow to that logic."[50]

Those who actually had power sincerely believed that they had it "by historical logic." Even at the very end of his life, after the Solidarity revolution and the martial law which followed, Jakub Berman, the veteran of the Communist Party of Poland (whose prewar leaders had been humiliated and killed by Stalin), expressed unshakeable belief that history was on his side, that it was a historical law that the minority, the avant-garde, always rescued the majority, and that the Polish nation would, sooner or later, abandon the "lunatic" idea of national independence and "mould itself into its new shape."[51] He ended his interview with Teresa Toranska with the following words:

> . . . I am nonetheless convinced that the sum of our actions, skilfully and consistently carried out, will finally produce results and create a new Polish consciousness; because all the advantages flowing from our new path will be borne out, must be borne out, and if we're not destroyed by an atomic war and we don't disappear into nothingness, there will finally be a breakthrough in mentality which will give it an entirely new content and quality. And then we, the Communists, will be able to apply all the democratic principles we would like to apply but can't apply now, because they would end in our defeat and humiliation. It may happen in fifty years or it may happen in a hundred, I don't want to make prophecies, but I'm sure it will happen one day.[52]

But let us return to the period when people like Berman were in power and tried to realize their aims as quickly as possible.

What happens if those in power believe that they owe their position to historical necessity and pretend to have a monopoly on the "correct understanding" of this necessity? Their interpretation of the "laws of history" becomes the sole and sufficient legitimation of their authority—a legitimation that does not admit any limitations on power, since (as has been rightly observed) "to rule in the name of history is to rule completely."[53] He who carries the only true knowledge of the meaning and laws of history has the right, and even the duty, to carry historical necessity into effect without any scruples as to the choice of means and even in the teeth of everybody else.

However, the victory of socialism was not to be a result of the Hegelian cunning of historical Reason which acts behind our back and achieves its ends irrespective of our will and consciousness; neither was it conceived as a necessary outcome of a "natural" evolution of society. The doctrine of "necessity understood," especially in its Leninist interpretation, made it dependent on a "subjective factor": correct *understanding* of, and active cooperation with, necessity—in other words, adequate consciousness and organized will. It was so because socialism was to put an end to *blind* necessity and lead humankind to the "kingdom of freedom." And if socialist freedom was to consist in a correct *understanding* of necessity, then mass indoctrination was obviously an indispensable precondition of it. The correct, adequate consciousness, Lenin taught, could not be expected to appear spontaneously; hence it must be instilled from without. And since the victory of socialism demands total mobilization of the "subjective factor," the indoctrination—i.e., raising human consciousness to the adequate level—must be total as well, detailed and complete, leaving no room for doubts, which characterize the Hamlet-minded bourgeois intellectuals.

This logic brought about the state of affairs in which historiosophical acceptance of socialism was not enough. Milosz feared this when he asked himself: "If we swim with the current, what kind of conditions must be met?"[54] It turned out that these conditions included not only "the recognition of necessity" but also the acceptance of and the active participation in the most crude and mendacious propaganda. It could have seemed that accepting Communism as a rational historical necessity was the maximum concession. In fact, however, such a stance aroused suspicions that it was a way of accepting the new order only conditionally, relativizing its values and thus not surrendering one's inner freedom and separate identity. And indeed, it was perfectly possible to regard the old world as doomed but nonetheless containing certain values which the new world would sometimes rediscover and assimilate—just as Christianity had assimilated the cultural legacy of pagan antiquity. Such a position justified secret adherence to "pagan values" in order to preserve them for future generations, and this could not be tolerated. Ideological mobilization could not be based on frankly telling the sad truth and explaining it, historiosophically, as the necessary price for progress. It required concealment of truth, enthusiastic belief in propagandistic lies, and active participation in collective brainwashing. It aimed at creating "social and political conditions in which man ceases to think and write otherwise than necessary."[55] The means for achieving this was a combination of physical and psychic terror: the first "to destroy the fabric of human society" and to change "the relationships of millions of individuals into channels for blackmail,"[56] and the second to subject atomized individuals to a system of ideologically conditioned reflexes which would control them from within, thus depriving them of their own minds and consciences.

Milosz observed this in Poland. He felt the hostility of the terrorized population, participated in the congresses of artists and writers, saw them surrendering to the doctrine of socialist realism imposed on them under pressure, and realized that his own fate might be the same.[57] At this stage he said his "No" and wrote *The Captive Mind*.

Twenty years after this book, when issues raised in it had long ceased to be relevant in Poland, a Russian *samizdat* writer, Dmitrii Nelidov, wrote an interesting analysis of the "ideocratic consciousness" and the phenomenon of "doublethink" (or "dual consciousness") in the Soviet Union.[58] He defined "doublethink" as the submission to "the socio-ideological mannequin,"[59] installed in everybody's mind through "ideocratic" pressure, which allows people to separate themselves from it by stepping back and looking at themselves from the outside. According to the author, every person in his society (if not "blessed with a special inner power for resistance") was forced in some measure to accept "the mannequin," to "make it one's self."[60] But there were different degrees of possible separation from it. At one pole there was "ideological infantilism"—the minimal degree of separation; on the other, cynicism—or the maximum degree of distancing oneself from the externally accepted rules of the game. Cynics usually feel themselves to possess inner freedom, but in fact they are also held on an ideological leash—although a longer one than in the case of others. They see no alternative to the official ideology and, in fact, serve it more effectively than the "infantile believers." Despite their ability to indulge in irony, they also voluntarily submit to the "ideological mannequin," becoming accustomed to it and correcting themselves in accordance with "the mechanics of the reflexes elaborated in it."[61]

Against this background, we can see the originality of Milosz's contribution to the analysis of "doublethink." In contrast to Orwell and Nelidov, he has brought attention to a form of dual consciousness in which the separation from the automatic reflexes of the imposed ideological self (or, to use a Freudian term, the totalitarian "super ego") is not merely passive (observing oneself from outside) or cynical, but involves a form of active, although desguised, resistance—a "game played in defense of one's thoughts and feelings."[62] He found an analogy to it in the Islamic civilization of the Middle East, where it developed into a sophisticated technique called Ketman: a technique of mimicry and deception bound up with a form of positive self-assertion which functioned by interpreting the obligatory faith in one's own special way and thus saving one's separate identity. People playing Ketman were afraid of the mullahs, but they felt superior to them and found an immense pleasure in deceiving them.[63]

According to Milosz, a similar Ketman developed in the people's democracies, where the response to totalitarian indoctrination was "a conscious mass play rather than automatic imitation."[64] His analysis of what happened to these countries—or, rather, to their intellectuals—employs three crucial terms: the "New Faith," the Murti-Bing pill, and Ketman. It is too complicated to be presented here in all its detail but sufficiently clear to allow a brief and yet (I hope) undistorted summary.

The idea of the Murti-Bing pill was created by S. I. Witkiewicz, a Polish catastrophic writer who committed suicide when the Soviet army invaded Poland in 1939. In his fantastic novel *Insatiability* (1932), he described the two contrasting worlds: the decadent Western world, with intellectuals tormented by "the *suction* of the absurd,"[65] and the Sino-Mongolian Empire, whose inhabitants have swallowed the pill invented by a Mongolian philosopher Murti Bing, acquiring thereby an organic world-view which made them "serene and happy."[66] (Perhaps not as much as that, Milosz commented, but at least attaining "a relative degree of harmony."[67]) The incompatibility of the two worlds led to a war in which the Western army quickly surrendered.

The Sino-Mongolian army occupied Europe and helped to build there "the new life." The Western intellectuals, eager to get rid of their tormenting problems, offered their services to the new society. Instead of dissonant music and abstract paintings, they now produced marches, odes, and "socially useful" pictures. But they did not succeed in changing themselves completely, and therefore became schizophrenics.[68]

Milosz saw this vision as a prophecy which was being fulfilled in much of Europe. In his view, the "cultural revolution" in East-Central Europe—i.e., embracement of Soviet Marxism and "socialist realism"—could not be explained in terms of physical coercion alone. For many reasons (such as disappointment with right-wing ideologies and regimes, disappointment with the West, fear of nihilism, and social alienation and desire to feel useful), the intellectuals and artists of these countries were, as a rule, prepared to accept the "New Faith." Nevertheless, they proved to be too firmly rooted in their cultures to accept it *entirely*, in its primitive Soviet form. Their conversions, even the most sincere, did not end in swallowing the Murti-Bing pill in its *entirety*. And this enabled them to defend their identities through playing the game called Ketman.

The number of varieties of this game was "practically unlimited." Milosz chose to analyze the following.[69]

"National Ketman," widespread in the masses and appearing even in the upper brackets of the Party. Genuine commitment to the "New Faith" combined with "an unbounded contempt for Russia as a barbaric country." A means of secretly qualifying the obligatory allegiance to Soviet Communism and pledging loyalty to one's own national identity.

"Ketman of Revolutionary Purity," a rare variety, more common in Russia than in the people's democracies. Hatred towards the Great Leader, as the butcher of nations, combined with a fatalistic conviction that in the given circumstances it is necessary to support him. A means of combining loyalist behavior with independent moral judgement.

"Aesthetic Ketman," or loyalty to the "New Faith" combined with preservation and cultivation (in private) of one's own aesthetic taste.

"Professional Ketman," or paying lip service to the official ideology while not allowing it to interfere in one's professional work.

"Skeptical Ketman"—a purely external conformism, justified by prudential reasons.

"Metaphysical Ketman," characteristic of countries with a Catholic past, especially Poland. Justifying the "New Faith" on the grounds of the old, Christian faith ("perhaps the New Faith is an indispensable purgatory; perhaps God's purpose is being accomplished through the barbarians," etc.), trying to penetrate it, influence its evolution, and so on. In other words, trying "to swindle the devil who thinks he is swindling them."[70]

Finally, "Ethical Ketman," not rare among the highly placed figures in the Party, especially in the people's democracies—i.e., in the countries where the Communists did not rule long enough to become corrupted. A form of compensation for cruel and plainly immoral methods of exercising power by clinging to severe, puritanical morality in private life.

It is somewhat surprising that this list does not include the form of Ketman which was particularly important in Milosz's case: the "Hegelian" or "historiosophical Ketman." Probably he could not write about it without portraying "the Tiger," who was then a philosophy professor in Warsaw and would not have liked to become "unmasked" in this way. After Kronski's premature death, Milosz hastened to write on him in his *Native Realm,* returning on this occasion to the problem of Ketman. Hence the chapters on "the Tiger" from *Native Realm* should be regarded as an important supplement, if not an organic part, of *The*

Captive Mind. They show Kronski as a master of dialectics, a true Hegelian for whom the notion of historical necessity was a double-edged weapon: justifying the existing reality but also helping to see it as historically transient and to distinguish its essential and inessential features. Owing to this, he remained free "in his inner self"[71] and saw a positive mission for people like himself: "to carry the precious values of our European heritage across the dark era."[72] But he was also "filled with a great dread,"[73] and this was to increase after his visit to Moscow (in 1950), where he saw the most advanced stage of the Orwellian world. Unfortunately, even the Polish thaw of 1956 did not liberate him from this fear, while adding to it another one: the fear of setting free Poland's reactionary forces. Hence, he disappointed his friends by proclaiming the thaw as going too far and not entirely consonant with the *Weltgeist.*

The intellectual portrait of "the Tiger" also provides a better understanding of Ketman as a general phenomenon, correcting, as it were, certain passages in *The Captive Mind.* It defines Ketman as similar to the Jesuit *reservatio mentalis* and quite different from mere hypocrisy or cynicism[74] (which amounts to the elimination of the "skeptical Ketman," if conceived as purely external conformity, "allowing for complete cynicism").[75] This in turn modifies the statement that "he who practices Ketman lies."[76] In his remarks on Kronski's speeches, Milosz takes care to indicate that he was not a simple "liar": his words carried a double meaning—the literal meaning and the meaning for the initiated—and thus aimed at expressing what he saw as truth.[77] This is, of course, a more subtle and more adequate description of Ketman, as distinct from other forms of prudential mimicry. After all, the essence of Ketman is not just mimicry, but *such* a form of mimicry which allows for resistance and self-expression.

Nevertheless, Milosz's Ketman was a risky game. Like Hegelian historiosophy, it was a double-edged weapon. Although intended to serve as a cunning way of defending one's identity, it also involved an attempt to adapt oneself to the system, to reconcile oneself with it through acknowledging (despite everything!) its historical legitimacy. There is no doubt that for many readers of Milosz's book, this second aspect of Ketman overshadowed the first one. In the dominant perception, *The Captive Mind*—in accordance with its title—is a book about surrendering to "mental captivity," not about defending oneself against it. On the whole, this is not entirely false: the stories of the four Polish writers who became victims of their "playing with the devil," plus the last two chapters of the book, show Milosz's profound pessimism about the chances of living under Communism and avoiding the fate of "captive minds." But it does not follow that he saw Ketman as a mechanism of cowardly self-surrender. On the contrary, he defined it as a means of self-realization *against* external pressure.[78] He simply thought that the "New Faith" was able to exert a much stronger ideocratic pressure than the traditionalist Islamic theocracy. Hence, he was pessimistic about the outcome of the play, but he did not condemn the players. Neither did he recommend other, more effective ways of resistance.

In other words, Milosz saw Ketman not as a mechanism of self-enslavement but rather as an insufficiently effective means of self-protection. He distinguished between Ketman and swallowing the Murti-Bing pill; the very existence of the former was for him a proof that the struggle for the defense of inner freedom had not yet been lost. If he criticized Ketman, he did it from within, not from an external, ahistorically-moralistic position.

The young Polish intellectuals, who want to see Milosz as a paradigmatic moralist and intransigent anti-Communist, are often insufficiently aware that the technique of Ketman, so different from moralistic straightforwardness, was something in which he himself had excelled. They can hardly understand how a man like Milosz could have engaged in a game involving "cunning" and even a seeming "insensibility to totalitarian atrocities";[79] how it was possible that he regarded Communism as a historical necessity; and why a refusal to recognize this necessity was for him a symptom of madness.[80] But Milosz did not conceal these facts. He analyzed them in depth in his *Native Realm* in the chapters on his friendship with "the Tiger." And he dotted the "i" by stating: "we were firmly lodged inside a totalitarian system."[81]

This statement, however, needs to be qualified. A fully-fledged Communist totalitarianism, like the Siviet Union under Stalin, aimed at, and succeeded in enforcing, much more than being recognized as a historical necessity. Accepting Stalinist Communism as a necessity was a way of saying that it is *not* accepted unreflectively, unconditionally, and enthusiastically. The Hegelian *Weltgeist* provided a justification of evil, but it did not demand closing one's eyes to its very existence. It justified totalitarian cruelties—not as good in themselves, but only as the tragic price for historical progress. From the point of view of a fully-entrenched Stalinism, this was an unaffordable intellectual luxury, if not plain rottenness.

In explaining his "Hegelian bite," Milosz compared himself to the Russian nineteenth-century Hegelian, Vissarion Belinsky, who "made use of Hegel during a certain phase of his life, to deify czardom."[82] "A man," he wrote, "cannot bear the thought of being crushed by physical compulsion; therefore he deifies the force that rules over him, investing it with superhuman traits, with omniscient reason, with a special mission; and in this way he saves a bit of his own dignity."[83] This severe judgment emphasizes the Freudian "rationalization" of a moral surrender. But the problem should be reduced to this: it was not only concern about a dignified form of surrendering but also a means of actually saving one's dignity. The Hegelian language made it possible to avoid Orwellian Newspeak. Saying that Stalinism represented historical necessity was, after all, completely different from praising Stalin as the "Father of all nations" and the greatest benefactor of humanity. Paradoxically, the internalization of the belief in the historical necessity of Stalinism made it possible to accept it without accepting its horrendous lies. Milosz went as far as that, but no further; when pressed to make a step further—i.e., to participate in the glorification of the "new reality"—he responded with a categorical "No."

Interestingly, young Leszek Kolakowski also turned attention to Belinsky's case and found it very relevant for the moral problems of his generation. He pointed out that the "morally sensitive Communists" used to espouse the idea of historical necessity as "an attempt to resolve the conflicts between their conscience and the social reality" in which they found themselves.[84] And he commented: "In innumerable instances Stalinism has repeated the spiritual history of young Belinsky, who believed that Russian czardom embodied the spirit of history and that one should not resist history for foolish personal reasons but assent to its basic course despite the anxieties and resistance of the individual conscience."[85]

Kolakowski's testimony is very important. It confirms Milosz's view of the peculiar importance of the belief in historical necessity for the Marxist and 'Marxisant' intellectuals in Stalinist Poland. It rightly shows that this belief appealed mostly to the "morally sensitive" members of the Party—that is, to those who accepted moral evil only on the grounds of its alleged necessity. By the same token, it also explains why Marxist revisionism, which was to be born among those people, attached such importance to the struggle against "deterministic metaphysics."[86]

Of course, we must not forget the other functions of the idea of historical necessity. For the holders of political power, it was the source of their absolute certainty about the rightness of their cause. It is important to stress that such people could be found among the rulers of Stalinist Poland. They were Stalin's puppets, but they played this role as true, incorruptible Communist believers. Owing to the depth of their convictions, they were able to speak with authority and command respect.[87] For the intellectuals' perception of the Party, this element of fanatical self-confidence was of crucial importance: if it had not existed, it would have been impossible to see the Communists as the "new Christians" and to explain their rule in terms of rational, although cruel, historical necessity.

III. An Autobiographical Digression

At this juncture, I will render a brief account of my own experience with Polish Stalinism.[88] It seems proper to do so for at least two reasons. First (and above all), because my reactions to totalitarian pressures confirm the accuracy of Milosz's analysis—although I experienced these pressures as a young and needy student, not as a member of a highly privileged cultural elite. Second, because the forms of pressure to which I was subject were, of course, much more crude than the "terror of the dialectical method" described in Milosz's book; hence the possibility of showing some mechanisms of the system in a more concrete, empirically tangible way. Let me elaborate:

(1) Like Milosz, I did not see Stalinism as a system of purely physical terror, based on "naked force." I experienced it as a system of constant psychic pressure, combining intimidation with a highly effective technique of indoctrination, capable of exercising control over human minds, thus enslaving people from within and finally forcing them to surrender their identities and actively participate in building their common prison. The "naked" physical terror, which I had witnessed in Nazi-occupied Poland, was something completely different: it threatened my very survival but left my inner freedom intact.[89]

In an autobiographical book, which revolves around my intellectual encounters with Milosz, I summarized this experience as follows:

"Stalinism was for me the worst evil, for it enforced not only the toleration of lies, but also active participation in lying, and attempted to deprive me (to use Mickiewicz's words) of "the very last freedom, which is respected by all tyrannies, the freedom to remain silent." This was a threat to the innermost essence of my being, and it is therefore not surprising that I experienced my delivery from it as an authentic liberation."[90]

I was fully aware that many people in Poland, even from my own generation, were shielded from such an experience, and perceived Stalinism as just another form of external coercion. But the fact was that I belonged to those members of the intelligentsia who wanted to accept the "new reality," even if it involved a painful process of psychic adjustment. I was sensitive to the appeal of the idea of progress; I did not want to be thrown to the "dustbin of history." I was deeply attached to the values of traditional Polish patriotism, but I was not totally unimpressed by voices which declared them to be anachronistic. Sometimes I was genuinely concerned with my spontaneous hatred of the Communist ideology: I was afraid that it might reflect my class prejudices—that is, a certain blindness from which I ought to liberate myself. I clearly saw the evils: the mass arrests (my own father, a university professor, was imprisoned for his patriotic activities during the war within the ranks of the underground Home Army), mock trials, ideologization of science and liquidation of cultural freedom, purges of the 'bourgeois professors', increasingly aggressive language of the propaganda—in a word, the Sovietization of the country, accompanied by the grotesque cult of Stalin. But at the same time, I persuaded myself that, in order to oppose the evil, it was *necessary* to take a stand on the ground of the "new reality."[91]

In this way, while only a high school student, I began my flirtation with the idea of historical necessity. It enabled me to reconcile contradictory elements in my attitude to People's Poland—to accept it as a necessity and *only* as a necessity, thus avoiding the hard choice between its total acceptance or total rejection. I do not think that this was merely a convenient rationalization of opportunism. I wanted above all to avoid the hostile and impotent alienation in society, while simultaneously preserving a certain philosophical distance from it.

Things greatly changed when I began my university studies, especially after I moved from Lodz to Warsaw (1950). Because of my "social and family background" (my father in prison), I was only allowed to take Russian Studies, a department which had been created *ad hoc* and had a serious shortage of candidates. Naturally enough, it was probably the most thoroughly Stalinist department of Warsaw University. Its main party activist, a woman much older than other students, was a prewar Communist turned into a Stalinist fanatic; the entire program of studies was based on Soviet books and the level of indoctrination was pretty much the same as in Moscow. The literature which was to shape my mind was truly horrifying. I was appalled and, in a sense, amused by the unheard-of vulgarity and crudeness of Soviet Marxism (in comparison with which official Polish Marxism looked almost sophisticated). I was shocked by the utter stupidity and obscurantism of the *zhdanovist* "struggle against cosmopolitanism"; I felt an authentic sense of dread when I realized that this curious mixture of Leninist dogmas with crude anti-Western and anti-Semitic chauvinism was not a "lunatic fringe" but a methodically conducted campaign, a systematic forgery of historical facts, backed by the repressive apparatus of a totalitarian state. I was equally shocked and amused by the language of this campaign, by the obligatory use of such expressions (defining its targets) as "a title-bearing flunky of the bourgeois," "self-prostration and kowtowing before the West," "a rabid dog of imperialism," "reactionary obscurantist who attacks socialism with foam in his mouth," and so forth. And I was truly horrified by the scope of obligatory unanimity: all Soviet books on a given topic had to be as alike as peas in a pod—the same standardized interpretation (in terms of "reactionary vs. progressive" and "materialist vs. idealist"), the same thunderbolts launched against Western scholarship and native "cosmopolitans," the same quotations from Lenin and Stalin, the same general conclusions. It was possible to relax by making fun of it; I enjoyed listening to a colleague of mine, Janusz Szpotanski (now a well-known satirist), who excelled in presenting Stalinist Marxism and Zhdanovist "anti-cosmopolitanism" as a gigantic grotesque or farce. But the terrible thing was that I would not have dared to openly disclose my thoughts in writing, in the classroom, or even in the presence of more than one member of the "student collective."

My main means of adapting myself to this situation were the same as described (later) in Milosz's *Captive Mind*: the idea of historical necessity and "ketman." At the beginning, historical necessity was a consolation for me (a belief that the further development would lead to something better) and a sort of "deeper initiation" (interpretation of Stalinism as a tragic price for socialist progress in Russia); with the passage of time, however, its repressive function came to the fore, forcing me to increase control over my spontaneous reactions and thus to prepare myself for a long journey through darkness. Sometimes it even drove me to complete hopelessness by suggesting that totalitarianism might turn out to be a historical destiny of all humanity.[92]

My favorite thinkers were Belinsky and Hegel.[93] When I came across Belinsky's "reconciliation with reality," I was startled by the innumerable parallels between his problems and mine. On the whole, the evolution of his views helped me to resist despair. My first article on him, dealing mostly with the relationship between ethics and historical necessity (written in 1953, published in 1954), was immediately noticed by Milosz; he saw in it one of the first symptoms of "thaw."[94] The reaction of Milosz's former mentor, "Tiger," was somewhat different: like myself, he was fascinated by Belinsky's "reconciliation," but did not share my suggested conclusion about the possibility of following the Russian thinker in his later rejection of alleged "necessity." I heard from him: "They are horrible, but the *Weltgeist* is on their side!"[95]

My conception of "ketman" (whose very name was not yet known to me) was activist; I tried to defend my true thoughts and feelings through actively resisting the suppression of intellectual freedom. Of course, I had to act in disguise. One method of doing this was to pretend to adhere to the official ideology while in fact attempting to make it more inclusive and more flexible, or even to smuggle into it some clearly unorthodox ideas. (Thus, for instance, during the celebrations of the 100th anniversary of Gogol's death, I made use of the Russian formalists' interpretations of his works in an attempt to show that their technique of literary analysis was not necessarily incompatible with "Marxist scholarship.") Another method consisted in turning attention to our own predicament by using the "Aesopian language" of historical analogy (for instance, in discussing Belinsky's "reconciliation with reality").

Owing to inconsistencies in the Stalinization of Poland, I scored some successes in using both these methods in my early publications in political-cultural weeklies. But I was not so successful in my university milieu—the thoroughly Stalinized Russian department. There I was quickly "unmasked" and properly punished.

(2) How did the mechanisms of the totalitarian system work? In order to keep this paper within manageable proportions, I shall limit myself to a simple enumeration of the methods applied and the effects achieved.

An organized campaign against me at the so-called "productive sessions" (at which the "student collective" received instructions from the Party-organization) *and at the meetings of the ZMP—the Union of Polish Youth.* The latter were particularly difficult to bear, because there I was castigated by my classmates, even those who were "privately" friendly towards me and were afterward ashamed of their conduct. I was chiefly accused of individualism, of holding aloof from the collective, of an unhealthy enthusiasm for individual study and evading "group" study. To make me more collective-minded, I was made responsible for the academic results of three of the weakest students and forced to work with them. Of course, I was reproached with reading the wrong things (e.g., "decadent" poetry, Dostoevsky, the "formalists," "bourgeois philosophers," and so on). My "class background" was constantly exposed, I was required to break with "hostile elements" (i.e., with the majority of my friends and acquaintances outside the Russian Department), and I was constantly pressed to tender "self-criticism." On one occasion I yielded to this demand, but this only gave rise to accusations of "insincerity" and that I was covering up my sins.

Intimidation through "private" conversations with the Party activists. Their "private talks" with me consisted mostly of direct threats. My colleagues were told "in private" that I was the son of "an enemy of the people," that it was necessary to isolate me, and that the consequences of falling under my influence might be very unpleasant. They were instructed to disregard my publications: if "people like Walicki" were still being published, it was only because we were still in a transitional period, but soon all roads would be closed to people of this kind. My classmates were obviously not prohibited from reporting to me the content of these "private talks." More subtle were the talks with my girlfriend, who was repeatedly "advised" to break with me (which she finally did).[96]

Organized collective enthusiasm. In his *The Captive Mind,* Milosz called it "collective *warmth,*" "the great longing of the 'alienated' intellectual." My experience confirms his observations: my (deliberately created) alienation was especially painful when confronted with "crowds, red faces, mouths open in shouts, arms brandishing sticks."[97] During the May Day holiday, the sight of the enthusiastic crowds (among them my colleagues from the Russian Department singing revolutionary and youth songs in Russian) aroused a hopeless sense of solitude in me, and the longing to lose myself in that marching mass. In this way a collective superego was created, which meant that even individuals who thought critically were able to sink into the atmosphere of enthusiasm—which, while it was admittedly artificially created, was in no way simulated! I did not "lose myself" in the crowd, but it roused mixed feelings in me: some sense of my own superiority, but also more guilt that I was unable to break out of the shell of "bourgeois individualism."[98]

Finally, *permanent "ideological mobilization."* Although (unlike Milosz) I was not very impressed by the "scientificity" of Stalinist Marxism, I was nonetheless vulnerable to the constantly repeated argument about the historical rightness of the "new reality." I heard in every quarter: the future belongs to socialism, socialism means Stalinism, there is no other way,[99] nothing is politically neutral, you are doomed if you think otherwise, how lucky we are that Poland has already chosen the right side and has a secure place in the camp of the victors. And so forth. I was able to take a critical stance, I ridiculed and satirized (in private) the monstrous cult of the Leader of Nations, but nevertheless (to use Milosz's words) "the harpoon had hit its mark."[100]

All these factors together created an incredible and increasingly internalized pressure. My consciousness and conscience were becoming split; a part of myself was no longer myself. The event which best illustrates this process took place in 1952, during the elections to the People's Diet. Students had been used to canvass the workers, to persuade them to go to the polls, but the ZMP authorities had decided to "punish" me by denying me this "honour" and "privilege." And I did in fact feel that I had been punished! I went to the Faculty ZMP board and said that while I fully understood the lack of trust towards me, I nonetheless requested to be allowed to join in the campaign. I was treated with magnanimity: I was allowed to become, for a while, a cog in the machine of political propaganda.[101]

And yet, despite such defeats, my will to resist survived; this made my persecutors furious, since they wanted to see me entirely broken. As a result, I fell into a nervous illness and was sent for several months to a sanatorium for nervous diseases. Of course, the Party activists in the Russian Department accused me of "provocative simulation" of nervous illness and began to mount a new campaign against me. Happily, I also suffered from tuberculosis and had to be treated in tuberculosis sanitariums. There I could relax, analyze the situation, formulate my diagnoses in writing, and prepare myself for further struggle. My diary and private letters of that time show that I was fully aware of being subject to two types of coercion: external coercion—i.e., drastic external limitations of freedom—and an inner, moral coercion. My utmost concern was the latter, because it involved my self-identity, my soul. In April 1953, I defined the state of my mind as follows:

> This inner moral compulsion does not—in my case—stem from the conviction that the people who form the "other camp" within that same camp (i.e., Stalinists in the camp of the advocates of socialism) are right, but from the fact that they are stronger, and because without them we could not win what is today an historical necessity. They are not stronger numerically, but in their resoluteness, which results from a certain limitation. Some individuals break loose from this principle, but even they can see that we cannot be counted on, because we are too weak. It is difficult to pass from the kingdom of necessity to the kingdom of freedom. And anyway, I do not always believe in the latter. But I do believe deeply in my own usefulness in various areas. I also believe in the following words of Belinsky:
>
> "Something which is not successful, which achieves nothing, which is not a step forward, may also constitute progress. And the other way round: progress may sometimes consist in lack of success, decline, a step backwards. That is what happens with historical progress. There are unhappy epochs in the life of nations and of mankind, in which whole generations are in a way sacrificed to future generations. But when the dark hour is past, good comes out of evil."[102]

This quotation, otherwise yet another attempt at achieving a sort of "reconciliation with reality," clearly shows the limits of my readiness to accept the Stalinists: I could persuade myself to see them as indispensable *tools* of a higher necessity, but I was unable to accept their claim of being "right," as possessing the only true *understanding* of this necessity. By the same token, I refused to submit to them morally.

This might seem to be very little, but my Stalinist persecutors, in fact, were right in seeing me as an enemy. My stoic reconciliation with reality contained mental reservations which could at any time be transformed into a stepping stone for a counterattack on my part. And this was bound to happen. A year later—in the early spring of 1954—I was no longer concerned with adapting myself to alleged "necessity." I turned against Hegelian "necessitarianism" and liberated myself from the spell of the "New Faith." Instead, I defined Stalinism as "totalitarianism," in many respects similar to Nazism.[103]

How did it come about, and why? I experienced this change as an inner process of self-liberation, caused by critical self-analysis and catalyzed by intensive reading. (Especially important for me were Thomas Mann, Dostoevsky, and Berdyaev's interpretation of Dostoevsky's *Oeuvre*.) I would retrospectively attach crucial importance to the death of Stalin. True, the Stalinist system in Poland remained institutionally unchanged—attempts were even made to strengthen it—but the self-confidence of its supporters was shattered and their "ideological offensive" became less brutal. For people like myself, this was a perceptible and significant change of political climate. Because of this, I could afford to reconquer the part of myself which had already been under partial control of the missionaries of the "New Faith." In other words, a slight relaxation of ideological pressure enabled me to get rid of the symptoms of "dual consciousness."

Soon afterwards, at the end of 1954, everything in my life began to change for the better. I unexpectedly received a stipend for doctoral studies in the Polish Academy of Sciences, although a year earlier my application had been, of course, rejected. In 1955 the intellectual "thaw" was gathering momentum in the scholarly discussions and in the press, and I could participate in this movement. Symbolically, it was Milosz's friend, "the Tiger," who provoked me to settle my accounts with Hegelian justifications of ideological coercion.[104]

And then came the historic year of 1956. After this turning point many people, even some of my former persecutors, congratulated me for "never being deceived by Stalinism." But I always corrected them by pointing out that, despite appearances, I had not belonged to the truly "clear-headed" and "morally intransigent" anti-Stalinists. It was true that I had never been a Stalinist believer, but it was no less true that I had experienced Stalinism *from within*; I was a victim of it, but not a total outsider. Thus, without yet knowing of Milosz's *The Captive Mind*,

I stressed my belonging among those intellectuals for whom Communist totalitarianism was not merely a matter of *external* coercion.

I was aware that my attitude toward Stalinism was peculiarly complex. Simpler attitudes, such as "sincere belief," "total rejection," or "purely external conformity," were certainly more widespread. But I also felt that these "simpler attitudes" did not allow an adequate insight into the essence of totalitarian enslavement. So I valued my experiences as a sort of cognitive privilege. After the final victory of the "thaw," I drew from them the following conclusions:

"That the most important and most elementary freedom is inner freedom, freedom of conscience, independence of judgement.

That the most terrible thing is ideological totalitarianism, a new theocracy (or "ideocracy") which takes us captive from within, demanding that an individual should submit to it totally, utterly."[105]

IV. Problems of Definition

What, exactly, is totalitarianism? The most essential and distinctive feature of totalitarianism was best defined by George Orwell. For him, the uniqueness of totalitarianism consisted in its attempt to coerce people from within, through controlling their thoughts and feelings. "It is important to understand," he stressed, "that the control of thought is not only a negative feature, but a positive one as well. It not only forbids you to express, or think, certain thoughts; it also dictates to you what you have to think, it provides you with an ideology, it tries to govern your emotional life and it establishes a code of behavior."[106] In this way a total unanimity was to be created—"the moral and political unity of society," as the Stalinists used to call it.

Milosz's *The Captive Mind* confirms this Orwellian diagnosis.[107] Russian dissidents' analyses of "doublethink" and "ideocratic consciousness" confirm it too. And my own experience does not allow me to doubt its correctness.

However, enforcing unanimity was not an end in itself. In contrast to the traditionalist, custom-based unanimity of a primitive tribal society, it was to be a *revolutionary* unanimity, a unanimity of the revolutionary collective will, subordinating everything to the not-yet-achieved ultimate goal. Hence the importance of the utopian element in its ideology. Totalitarian ideology is not merely a secularized religion; it is a secularized form of *chiliastic* religiosity. Totalitarian hierarchy does not aim merely at self-reproduction or self-preservation. It derives its legitimacy from a commitment to aggressive action, aiming at a total transformation of society; it even aims to transform the very nature of man. Abandoning these ambitions, yielding to the temptation of a stabilized existence, in fact amounts to a desertion of the totalitarian ideal and entails a long and tortuous process of detotalitarization.

This perspective explains my agreement with those theorists who saw the most distinctive feature of totalitarianism in its "ideocratic" dimension—that is, in the paramount importance of ideological coercion. It seems justified to say that in the 1950s, this was a matter of almost general consensus. Despite all their differences, both theoretical and political, theorists of totalitarianism were, as a rule, acutely aware of the "ideocratic" ambitions of totalitarian regimes and of their converse—the "Orwellian" features of totalitarian societies. In other words, they paid due attention to such uniquely totalitarian and interconnected phenomena as "thought control" and the ruthless pursuit of a positively formulated single goal.[108] Hence it is legitimate to conclude (retrospectively) that they saw totalitarianism as "the ugly spawn of the fusion of a messianic ideology and modern techniques of communication, command, and control."[109]

However, the processes of "de-Stalinization" in the Soviet Union and in the countries of the Soviet bloc undermined this broadly defined consensus. It was increasingly evident that the model of totalitarianism, as elaborated in the 1950s, was too static to explain these changes. "Within the confines of the so-called totalitarian model," wrote Chalmers Johnson, "it is hard enough to conceptualize development and its consequences . . . It is even harder to conceptualize the resulting unintended changes in the social structure and the consequences of those changes."[110] As a result, the majority of scholars came to the conclusion that "totalitarianism as a concept had lost its explanatory power; that it is oversimplified; that it is too narrow in focus; that it unduly magnified Soviet peculiarities such as Marxist ideology."[111] Some of them went even further, treating the theory of totalitarianism as a product of the Cold War and rejecting it altogether.

Of course, wholesale rejections of the notion of totalitarianism are, as a rule, politically motivated: for left-wing radicals it is convenient to get rid of a concept which has, in their view, too often been used for right-wing purposes. But the same is true, as a rule, about the defenders of this concept, at least those for whom the main thing is to prove that the Soviet Union and its allies still deserve to be classified as "totalitarian." The disappointments with the détente of the 1970s and, later, the suppression of Solidarity in Poland visibly increased the number and intensity of such efforts. Personally, I am ready to credit them with positive achievements for dispelling many dangerous illusions. Nevertheless, I strongly feel that the significance of the processes of de-Stalinization should not be minimized and that the "really existing socialism" of the last two decades must not be equated with totalitarianism. Otherwise the original meaning of the term "totalitarianism" is completely lost, and adequate understanding of the distinctive features of genuinely totalitarian regimes (and societies) becomes impossible.[112]

As yet, the attempts to modernize or redefine the concept of totalitarianism did not yield convincing, theoretically coherent results. It is possible, however, to discern two characteristic fallacies in the contemporary usages of this concept: the "democratic fallacy" and the "liberal fallacy." A brief discussion of them will show their uselessness for understanding genuine totalitarianism, as defined by Orwell and experienced (intellectually and morally) by Milosz.

The "democratic fallacy" consists in conceiving totalitarianism as the opposite of political democracy. This leads, of course, to the conclusion that the monopolistic rule of one party, having no popular mandate to rule, must be a paradigmatic case of totalitarianism. From the democratic point of view, a non-democratic regime is better (more consistent with the popular will) if its social base is large and if it can rule with the tacit consent of the majority; the worst thing appears to be the rule based upon "naked force" and forcibly imposed on an openly hostile population. This explains why the Polish underground and émigré press described Poland after martial law was imposed as a country with a particularly oppressive totalitarian regime, and why this view found a wide and easy acceptance in the West.

In fact, however, this reasoning is deeply flawed. Totalitarian rule, as Milosz tried to explain, cannot be reduced to the rule of force. "Naked force," as it is applied in ordinary police states, aims only at the preservation of "law and order" (i.e., outward conformity) and has neither the capacity nor the ambition to create a "new man," enthusiastically supporting (or, at least, forcing himself to support) all the aims and ideals of the rulers. Lack of consent is not typical of totalitarianism, because a truly totalitarian regime can enforce much more than merely passive consent; the relationship of "open hostility" means that the ruled have liberated themselves from both fear and indoctrination, which marks the end of totalitarianism.

A drastic curtailment of nonpolitical civil liberties is not necessarily a step towards reestablishing totalitarianism. "The extinguishing of civil liberties in order to maintain and strengthen the regime," wrote Leszek Kolakowski, "does not amount to totalitarianism unless accompanied by the principle that every activity—economic, cultural, etc.—must be completely subordinated to the aims of the state; that not only are the acts against the regime forbidden and ruthlessly punished, but no political actions are neutral and the individual citizen has no right to do anything that is not part of the state's purpose; that he is the state's property and is treated by it as such."[113]

General Jaruzelski did not try to justify martial law in terms of Marxist ideology.[114] His speech explaining it was remarkably free of Orwellian language. His government stressed many times that it did not need to be loved; it wanted only to be recognized as a "lesser evil," a geopolitical necessity, thus deriving its legitimacy from a certain understanding of the national interest at the given moment, and not from any universalist ideology. The utopian vision of the "radiant future" completely disappeared, giving way to a rather gloomy realism; the authorities carefully avoided excessive optimism in assessing the situation because they now know how dangerous it might be to allow the rise of popular expectations and then to prove unable to fulfill them. The existing system was no longer praised as the best possible; on the contrary, the ruling group tried to exculpate itself by putting all the blame on anonymous systemic mechanisms. The totalitarian aim of "political and moral unanimity" was officially abandoned: it was replaced by a policy of so-called "socialist pluralism" which required only a necessary *minimum* of national consensus. Political mobilization of the masses became conceivable only as a popular crusade *against* the regime; hence, paradoxically, the party began to encourage apoliticism. Comparing this situation with the world described in Milosz's *Captive Mind* showed a remarkable reversal of roles. Under Stalinism it was the authorities who used and abused political-moral pressure, while now it was the opposition who organized such pressure in the name of national unity, enforcing non-collaboration with the authorities and silencing dissidents within its ranks. "Dual consciousness" was now the lot of many party-members, still loyal to the party but, nonetheless, exposed to the "moral terror" of its enemies. Gone and forgotten were the times when the party was able to impose Communist ideals on intellectuals and artists; now intellectuals and artists engaged in actively delegitimizing the system through both the political content of their works and the ostentatious refusal to cooperate with official institutions.[115] The ideological legitimation of the system ceased to be treated seriously even by otherwise staunch supporters; isolated attempts to revive it appeared ridiculous, and public declarations in favor of Communism required more civic courage than public attacks on it.

Thus, in contrast to totalitarian regimes, the Polish regime of the 1980s (1) did not derive its legitimacy from an all-embracing ideology; (2) did not commit itself to "a single positively formulated goal," emphasizing instead legal rules and even espousing the idea of a "socialist constitutionalism"; (3) did not attempt to politicize all spheres of life, especially intellectual and cultural; and, finally, (4) did not try to encourage and organize a controlled political activization of the masses, clinging instead to the traditional policy of keeping the masses away from politics. In other words, it became similar to traditional authoritarian regimes. This was not a sudden *volte-face,* but the final outcome of a process which had already begun in 1956. Nevertheless, it is important to stress that what had been under Gierek (December 1970–November 1980) a mostly unintended result of the increasing deideologization and corruption of the party, became a consciously adopted policy under martial law. In fact, the final abandonment of totalitarianism in favor of a self-limiting and consensus-seeking authoritarianism was the gist of Jaruzelski's political program. It was not enough as a program of reform, adequate to Solidarity's challenge, but it was nonetheless a programmatic retreat. It could be called "totalitarian" only by those who had forgotten, or never known, what totalitarianism was really like. Very often calling it "totalitarian" was simply an act of political struggle, signalling that the authors using it were totally and intransigently opposed to Communism.[116]

Let us now examine the "liberal fallacy." The word "liberalism" is used here in its classical sense—that is, as a concept very different from that of "democracy." Democracy defines the *source* of political power, while liberalism is concerned with limiting its *scope*. There is no necessary connection between the democratic ideal of "popular sovereignty" and the liberal ideal of "limited government."[117] One can easily imagine democracy without liberalism (for instance, primitive tribal democracy) or liberalism without democracy (for instance, classical constitutional and parliamentary monarchies under which only a small percentage of the population had the right to vote). According to F. A. Hayek, "the difference between the two ideals stands out most clearly if we name their opposites: for democracy it is authoritarian government; for liberalism it is totalitarianism."[118]

This conceptual distinction enables us to understand the epistemological reasons for the "democratic fallacy." From the point of view of popular sovereignty—that is, freedom as *collective* self-determination—the difference between authoritarianism and totalitarianism is difficult to perceive; it can even be said that a *successful* totalitarianism—that is, a totalitarian regime supported by "the people's will"—is more acceptable from this viewpoint than an unpopular and socially alienated authoritarian regime, even a mild one which respects the laws. Liberalism provides the opposite and much better perspective: its main concern is *individual* freedom. From this point of view, the problem of the scope of political power is more important than the problem of its source. For a liberal, therefore, the difference between totalitarianism and authoritarianism should be crucially important and clearly visible.

Why, then, the "liberal fallacy"? First, because contemporary Western liberals take the separation between political and spiritual power for granted; second, because the problem of the scope of political power is associated in their minds almost exclusively with the scope of governmental interference in the economy. The first prevents them from fully appreciating the fundamental importance of the freedom of conscience, nonexistent under totalitarian "ideocracy," thereby making them insensitive to the entire "Orwellian" problematic. The second leads them to classify all regimes with nationalized economies as "totalitarian," and thus to ignore the difference between classical totalitarianism and post-totalitarian authoritarianism.

It is very characteristic that in Hayek's *Constitution of Liberty* the problem of religious freedom—freedom of conscience—is completely ignored,[119] although, historically speaking, its importance for generating modern liberalism is crucial. Equally important is his endorsement of E. Brunner's thesis that "the totalitarian state is simply and solely legal positivism in political practice."[120] Indeed, legal positivism ignores the problem of limits of political power, makes organs of the government the only source of law, and sanctifies subjecting all spheres of life to legal (and thereby governmental) regulation. Admittedly, this is bad enough, but it is not yet totalitarianism. In contrast to totalitarianism, legal positivism rejects the idea of an "ideological state" and carefully distinguishes between law and morality. Hence "legal positivism in political practice" would not lead to such typically totalitarian phenomena as thought control, organized moral pressure, ideological crusades, public shows of enthusiasm, and (last but not least) compelling intellectuals and artists to think and create in accordance with positively formulated ideological prescriptions. A "legal-positivist regime" would be legalistic in spirit (although it would ignore the distinction between laws and administrative regulations), lacking "collective warmth," concerned with bureaucratic rationalization, and therefore not employing "political mobilization of the masses." It is difficult to imagine a legal positivist state subordinated to a hierarchically organized and militantly ideological party—a party penetrating everywhere and interfering not only with the private lives of citizens but also with the everyday work of the administration. In other words, a consistently implemented legal positivism would create not a "new theocracy" (in the form of totalitarian "ideocracy") but rather the Weberian "iron cage of bureaucracy."

The proper name for such a regime has been proposed by Bruno Rizzi: "bureaucratic collectivism."[121]

But why insist on a generic distinction? Would it not be better to classify "bureaucratic collectivism" as a form or stage of totalitarianism—for instance, as its "mature" and "routinized" stage, as opposed to its revolutionary and ideological formative period?

As a rule, I do not quarrel about taxonomy. The main thing is not the choice of terms, but rather their precise definition and thus the avoidance of the usual confusion which follows when one uses the same term with many different meanings. Nevertheless, I am not a total relativist in these matters; I strongly feel that some terminological choices are better than others. So I have to explain why I reject the Hayekian equation of totalitarianism with "unlimited government," and why I do not think that even a consistent "bureaucratic collectivism" would have been essentially identical with totalitarianism.

Liberals are entitled (and even expected, I would say) to classify political regimes from the point of view of individual freedom. The word "freedom" has many meanings, but it is reasonable to assert that individual freedom must include so-called negative freedom, which is inversely proportional to the scope of political power. Hayek has the merit of powerfully reminding us of this, but his philosophy of individual freedom is nonetheless inadequate. As a liberal economist, he specially emphasizes economic freedom and property-rights; this is understandable and legitimate, but it should not be forgotten that the liberal principle of "self-ownership" above all includes the ownership of one's self—that is, one's mind and conscience. Hence, moral and intellectual freedom have to be seen by liberals as more basic, more fundamental, than economic freedom. After all, a partial limitation of economic freedom may be compatible with liberal principles; a partial suppression of political freedom, or any sort of freedom of action, including even the freedom of speech, may also be justified (as a temporary measure) on liberal grounds. But is it possible to imagine a liberal state in which freedom of conscience would be partially (let alone completely) suppressed? Of course not, because this would encroach upon our innermost property—our self-identity. A state cannot be liberal if it does not adhere to programmatic neutrality in all matters pertaining to "the meaning, value, and purpose of human life."[122]

The same reasoning applies to "bureaucratic collectivism" (which is otherwise a purely theoretical model, since social life under "really existing socialism" escapes effective bureaucratic control).[123] Liberals should become aware that even the broadest scope of bureaucratic regulation is not the worst sort of coercion;[124] that the notion of the scope of coercion refers not only to the broader or narrower sphere of regulation but also above all to the intensity and depth of sociopolitical and moral pressure to conform.

The most distinctive feature of totalitarianism is not the unlimited scope of bureaucratic regulation and effective control over the economy (otherwise Soviet Russia at the time of the Stalinist "revolution from above" would have to be regarded as less "totalitarian" than, say, the German economy at the time of World War I). Totalitarianism should be defined in terms of the scope of enforced conformity. A society is totalitarian if it aims at absolute, total conformity—not only external but internal as well—and tries to achieve this goal by means of a deliberately organized, constantly exercised, all-pervasive and *direct* political-moral pressure, supported by physical and moral intimidation.[125]

In a recent book on the possible future of the Soviet Union, we find a definition of a totalitarian system as "one in which the top role controls all the subsystems of the society, subject only to environmental constraints."[126] According to this criterion, "there has been only one system that can be called totalitarian—the Soviet System, at least under Stalin."[127] But is it really certain that Stalin was always able to exercise effective control over all "subsystems" of Soviet society? If he embarked on such a mad task as forcible collectivization of the peasantry, it was because the rural economy and the peasantry as a class had *not* yet been subject to his control. Does it mean that on the eve of the collectivization the Stalinist regime had not yet been totalitarian? It seems, rather, that only a fully totalitarian regime could have carried out such a violent experiment in "social engineering" and survive its fatal, unintended consequences for the economy. Or would it change our view of Stalinism if it were established that all his five-year plans had been fulfilled on paper only? This would have meant that "the top role" in the system had only an illusionary control over the economy, but it would not give us any reason to doubt that the Stalinist system was the closest approximation of totalitarianism in the Orwellian sense of this term.

Another example of the inadequacy of the criterion of "total control" is Stalinist Poland. Milovan Djilas expressed the view that "it would not be incorrect to conclude that Poland was never a totalitarian state."[128] From the point of view of the actual achievement of total control it was really so, and not just because of the power of the Catholic Church and the predominance of private ownership in agriculture. Polish Stalinists were struggling for maximum control, but not on all fronts at the same time. This is even more true of their struggle for *ideological* control: some segments of Polish society (such as the clergy, the peasantry, many intellectuals of the old generation, officially sanctioned enclaves of the lay-Catholic activists, and so on) remained untouched by Stalinist indoctrination, while others were fully "Stalinized." (As I already pointed out, the Russian Department of Warsaw University was a true bastion of full-fledged, Soviet-style totalitarianism.) On the whole, however, Bierut's regime in Poland (1948–1956) was unmistakably totalitarian, although not entirely successful in molding the society on its own image. The majority of the Polish intelligentsia have passed through the experience of Stalinism and (as *The Captive Mind* convincingly testifies) experienced it as a sort of "mass hypnosis,"[129] not merely an external coercion. This is why Czeslaw Milosz could have written (and felt compelled to write) *The Captive Mind;* it has been rightly observed that "after all, it was a non-fictional report on a really *lived* experience."[130]

The gradual dismantling of Stalinist totalitarianism in Poland, which officially began in 1956 (and unofficially somewhat earlier), was a long and difficult process in which both "leaps forward" and partial reversals occurred. Today's Poland is undoubtedly the most detotalitarianized country of the Soviet bloc. After the historic compromise between the government and the Solidarity-based opposition announced in April 1989, it quickly passed from liberalizing authoritarianism to a higher stage of detotalitarianization: a controlled parliamentary democracy (conceived as a transition to unrestricted democracy in the nearest future). The party has accepted not only limitation of its power (i.e. the narrowing of its scope) but also sharing it with other political forces. Political pluralism has been proclaimed to be an organic part of socialist democracy; General Jaruzelski has told the party-members that opposition in Poland "was, is, and will remain."[131] The June elections of 1989 brought the landslide victory of Solidarity and paved the way for a government in which the non-Communists, for the first time after the war, have an overwhelming majority. This is a very hopeful outcome. *Perestroika* in the Soviet Union and the changes in the other countries of "really existing socialism" (especially Hungary) support this hope by allowing us to see the case of Poland as an extreme case of a general trend.[132] Anyhow, the most determined pessimist could not believe that totalitarianism is humanity's inevitable destiny. As a prophecy, Orwell's *1984* remains happily unfulfilled.

But this does not mean that Orwell was wrong in his insight about the nature and intentions of totalitarian regimes in the heyday of their power. The fact that these regimes proved relatively short-lived does not warrant the conclusion that "totalitarianism is not a regime" and that it should not be given "a permanent place in the typologies of political science."[133] On the contrary! For all those who are interested in the fate of human freedom (and unfreedom), it is necessary to pay special attention to the regime that tried (and still tries in some countries) to achieve a "coerced unanimity of the entire population."[134] It did so by using both most primitive means (direct personal pressure, as in the primitive tribal societies) and modern techniques (such as the mass media); it aimed at creating conditions in which everything not explicitly allowed would be prohibited—and even "the allowed" would be a constantly shifting category, with people condemned today for what was allowed yesterday.

There are also very practical reasons for preserving the notion of totalitarianism as an important typological category. The countries which are now undergoing the process of detotalitarianization are struggling, and will have to struggle for a long time, with the remnants of their totalitarian heritage, both perceived and unperceived, both defined and hidden (in a more or less residual form) in the mentality of the people. Hence, in order to help the process of detotalitarianization—and to properly understand this process—we must have an up-to-date theory of totalitarianism. Most recent attempts to theorize about totalitarianism (such as the "new-class theory" or "monopolistic rule theory") are inadequate and misleading;[135] their authors wrongly assumed that the Soviet Union, the paradigmatic exemplification of totalitarianism, could not really change, and for that reason they either ignored the changes or theorized about totalitarianism on the basis of what really was an early stage of detotalitarianization (whose very possibility—without a violent overthrow of the regime—was dogmatically denied by them).[136] Therefore, the best starting point for understanding the totalitarian phenomenon is still the theories elaborated in the 1950s. It is true that they are static and do not explain further developments, so they must be supplemented (and correspondingly modified) by a theoretical explanation of the subsequent changes.[137] The main problem is how to conceptualize these changes: as changes "within the system" (for instance, a development towards a "mature" totalitarianism) or as leading beyond totalitarianism towards a qualitatively different and yet-unnamed socio-political reality. The first approach leads inevitably to minimizing the importance of the changes; in addition, it diverts attention from classical totalitarianism, totalitarianism in its heyday, and thus (unintentionally) prevents the younger scholars from fully understanding the horrors of a truly totalitarian regime. On the other hand, it prevents us from understanding the spectacular dismantling, or collapse, of the main quasi-totalitarian regimes in East-Central Europe. What happened to them in 1989 shows that their ideological zeal—the quintessence of a genuine totalitarianism—had been dead for a long time and that their externally totalitarian features had become reduced to an empty and fragile shell.

For all these reasons, it is necessary to develop a theory of detotalitarianization. Some steps in this direction have already been made. The early stages of detotalitarianization have been convincingly analyzed by Richard Löwenthal.[138] More recently, on the eve of the events of 1989, Zbigniew Brzezinski created an ambitious theory of the phases a country might go through to retreat from Communism. According to him "communist totalitarianism" is being replaced by "communist authoritarianism," then "post-communist authoritarianism," and finally "post-communist pluralism."[139] The first phase (totalitarianism) is exemplified by Albania, North Korea and Vietnam; Romania, East Germany and Czechoslovakia represent the transition to "communist authoritarianism" (the Soviet Union has already accomplished this transition); Hungary and Poland pass from "communist authoritarianism" to the post-communist one, while "post-communist pluralism" remains a theoretical possibility. Obviously the sudden acceleration of political change would have to modify these classifications. Thus, for instance, Poland and Hungary are now in the pluralist phase, while East Germany and Czechoslovakia are heading in the same direction, trying to skip the authoritarian phase. On the whole, however, Brzezinski's theory of "the retreat from communism" has been brilliantly vindicated by events.

In closing, I would like to add a remark as to the usefulness of the liberal perspective in elaborating such a theory.

In his review of Hayek's *The Road to Serfdom,* Orwell wrote: "In the negative part of Professor Hayek's thesis there is a great deal of truth. It cannot be said too often—at any rate, it is not being said nearly often enough—that collectivism is not inherently democratic, but, on the contrary, gives to a tyrannical minority such powers as the Spanish Inquisition never dreamed of."[140]

I fully agree with this wise judgment: a great deal of truth, but not the entire truth. I have explained above why some essential features of totalitarianism cannot be grasped within the theoretical framework of Hayek's *Road to Serfdom* thesis. Now I want to point out the relevance and enormous usefulness of Hayek's explanation of the economic reason for detotalitarianization. His theories enable us to understand why a marketless, centrally planned economy cannot compete with a market economy and why, in the long run, it is bound to destroy itself. This is, I think, crucially important for understanding why totalitarian systems could not achieve stabilization, why they had to fail, and why the idea of "total control" over the economy had to produce total economic chaos. Nowhere has this become so obvious as in Poland. Small wonder, therefore, that Hayek's ideas have found many enthusiastic and intelligent followers among Polish intellectuals, including even some Party members.[141]

October 1989

NOTES

1. The adjective "Communist" is very important in this context, because people like Milosz have been absolutely immune to any influence from a nationalist variety of totalitarianism. Milosz's case strongly supports Richard Löwenthal's disagreement with Carl Friedrich's formula that Communism and Nazism could be described as "basically alike." See R. Löwenthal's "Commentary," *The Soviet Union and the Challenge of the Future, Vol. 1—The Soviet System: Stasis and Change,* eds. A. Shtromas and M. A. Kaplan (New York: Paragon House, 1988), p. 36.
2. See E. Czarnecka and A. Fiut, *Conversations With Czeslaw Milosz.,* tr. R. Lourie (San Diego-New York-London: Harcourt Brace Jovanovich, 1987), pp. 326–29.
3. C. Milosz, *The Captive Mind* (Harmondsworth: Penguin, 1985) pp. viii, 6.
4. See A. Walicki, *Spotkania z Miloszem* (Encounters with Milosz) (London: Aneks, 1985), p. 11.
5. For further details see *ibid.,* pp. 10–11. The character of the émigrés' attacks on Milosz is evident from the titles of their articles such as: "Converted—but not entirely" (A. Bregman); "Milosz—the former fellow-traveller" (S. Piasecki); "A Stakhanovite in exile" (A. Pragier); "Captive mind, or corrupted character" (Z. L. Zaleski); and so on.

   For a critical view of Milosz's *The Captive Mind,* typical of the young generation in contemporary Poland, see Z. Rafalski's review of my *Spotkania z Miloszem* in the underground monthly *Kultura niezalezna* (Independent Culture), no. 33 (September 1987), pp. 30–49.
6. See C. Milosz, "Nie" ("No"), *Kultura,* no. 5 (Paris, 1951). Reprinted in *Krytyka,* no. 13–14 (Warsaw, 1983). A Western edition was published by *Aneks* (London, 1984), pp. 206–16.
7. *ibid., Aneks* edition, p. 208.
8. A. Slonimski, "Odprawa" ("Rebuff"), originally published in *Trybuna ludu* (November 4, 1951), reprinted in the issue of *Krytyka* quoted above, pp. 242–43.
9. Quoted from J. Andrzejewski, "Milosz '51," *ibid.,* p. 206. A. A. Vlassov (1900–1946) was a Soviet general who decided to cooperate with Nazi Germany and organized for this purpose a volunteer Russian army. The participants in Vlassov's movement believed that the defeat of Stalin's regime would lead to the emergence of a non-Communist Russian state, formally allied to Germany but substantially independ-

ent of it. After the war, most of them (including Vlassov) were executed as traitors.

10. Quoted from Walicki, *Spotkania z. Miloszem,* p. 11.
11. K. Brandys, *Nim bedzie zapomniany* (Warsaw, 1955).
12. An interesting interview with Berman has been published in T. Toranska, *"Them." Stalin's Polish Puppets,* tr. A. Kolakowska (New York: Harper and Row, 1987), pp. 201–354.
13. Compare Czarnecka and Fiut, *Conversations,* p. 147.
14. See M. Meyerson-Aksenov and B. Shragin, *The Political, Social, and Religious Thought of Russian "Samizdat." An Anthology.* (Belmont: Buchervertriebsanstalt, 1977), pp. 22, 131–32, 135, 230, 256–65, 274–78, 286–89. The concept of "dual consciousness" is a modified version of George Orwell's "doublethink" (See *ibid.,* pp. 131–32, footnote).
15. Compare Sheila Fitzpatrick, "New Perspectives on Stalinism," *The Russian Review,* Vol. 45, No. 4 (October 1986), pp. 357–58.
16. The concept of totalitarianism as "ideocracy" (first introduced by N. Berdyaev) has been widely used in Russian dissident writings (see M. Meyerson-Aksenov and B. Shragin, "Samizdat," pp. 19–22, 25, 262, 265–70, 287). See also W. Gurian, "Totalitarianism as Political Religion," ed. C. J. Friedrich, *Totalitarianism* (Cambridge: Harvard University Press, 1954), pp. 119–29. He defines "ideocracy" as "secularized socio-political religion" (*ibid.,* p. 123).
17. See, for instance, C. J. Friedrich, "The Unique Nature of Totalitarian Society," ed. C. J. Friedrich, *Totalitarianism,* pp. 47–60, and H. J. Spiro, "Totalitarianism," in *International Encyclopedia of the Social Sciences,* vol. 16 (New York: Free Press, 1968), pp. 106–12.

    After Khrushchev's "thaw," Friedrich expected the increase of "psychic" (or "psychological") terror as a replacement for the reduction of "physical terror." (See Friedrich, "The Evolving Theory and Practice of Totalitarian Regimes," in C. J. Friedrich, M. Curtis, B. R. Barber, *Totalitarianism in Perspective: Three Views* (New York: Praeger, 1969) pp. 123–54.) Happily, this diagnosis proved to be mistaken: the weakening of totalitarian power (let alone the process of "detotalitarianization") involves the loosening of ideological controls. There are, of course, some important exceptions to this rule, like Romania, North Korea, and People's China.
18. See M. Voslensky, "The Soviet System," ed. Shtromas and Kaplan, *The Soviet Union,* vol. 1, p. 8.
19. According to Zhores Medvedev, this was a long step towards the "new class," as described by Milovan Djilas. (See Z. Medvedev, *Gorbachev,* (Oxford: Basil Blackwell, 1986), p. 120.)
20. L. Deutscher, *The Prophet Outcast: Trotsky, 1929–1940* (London and New York: Oxford University Press, 1963), pp. 306–7.
21. See R. Löwenthal, "Beyond the 'Institutionalized Revolution' in Russia and China," ed. Shtromas and Kaplan, *The Soviet Union,* pp. 13–34 (especially pp. 23–5).
22. See Friedrich (ed.), *Totalitarianism,* pp. 133–34 (the discussion of W. Gurian's article).
23. Milosz, *The Captive Mind,* pp. 6, 12–13.

24. The Hegelian philosopher, Tadeusz J. Kronski (1907–58), was described by Milosz in his *Native Realm* (London-Manchester: Sidgwick and Jackson/Carcanet New Press, 1981), pp. 258–300. See also the chapter on him in Walicki, *Spotkania,* pp. 47–71.
25. M. Merleau-Ponty, *Humanism and Terror. An Essay on the Communist Problem,* tr. J. O'Neill, (Boston: Beacon Press, 1969) p. 92, 98. The French original was published in 1947.
26. *ibid.,* p. 153.
27. L. Kolakowski, *Światopoglad i życie codzienne* (The World-View and Everyday Life) (Warsaw, 1957), p. 194.
28. Czarnecka and Fiut, *Conversations,* pp. 147–48. The next sentence reveals the ambiguous character of this comment, since it says: "On the other hand, in the world as a whole, nothing could be more relevant for a great many people who are just learning to read and write than their genuine concern with Marxism."
29. M. Hirszowicz, *Coercion and Control in Communist Society. The Visible Hand in a Command Economy* (New York: St. Martin's Press, 1986), p. 22.
30. See J. Trznadel, *Hanba domowa. Rozmowy z pisarzami* (Domestic Shame. Conversations with Writers). (Paris: Instytut Literacki, 1986). An anthology of interviews concerning the Stalinist period in Poland.
31. According to J. M. Rymkiewicz, "Almost all young intelligentsia had been caught." (See Trznadel, *Hanba domowa,* p. 141.)
32. Compare Milosz, *The Captive Mind,* p. 6.
33. See C. Milosz, "Nie."
34. See *Krytyka,* 13–14, *Aneks* edition, pp. 208–9.
35. *ibid.,* pp. 206, 216.
36. *ibid.,* p. 215.
37. Printed after the "thaw" of 1956 in W. Kula, *Rozważania o historii* (Reflections on History) (Warsaw, 1958), pp. 225–93.
38. *ibid.,* p. 267. This was, of course, an allusion to the official *History of the Communist Party of the Soviet Union (Bolsheviks).*
39. *ibid.,* p. 253.
40. *ibid.,* pp. 288–89.
41. See Milosz, *Native Realm,* p. 271.
42. *ibid.,* p. 262.
43. Of course, it claimed to lead the Germans to the fulfillment of their historical destiny and presented itself as an embodiment of the National Spirit *(Volksgeist).* As such, it could influence even those Germans who were otherwise appalled by its practices.
44. Milosz, *Native Realm,* p. 298.
45. Compare Toranska, *"Them,"* pp. 320–21.
46. In his interview for *Tygodnik Powszechny,* Kolakowski stressed the role of anti-clerical and anti-nationalist motives in his youthful conversion to Communism. See "Marksizm, Chrześcijanstwo, Totalitaryzm," *Tygodnik Powszechny* (February 12, 1989), pp. 1–2.
47. Milosz, *Native Realm,* p. 298.
48. L. Kolakowski, "Responsibility and History," *Toward a Marxist Humanism,* tr. Jane Zielonko Peel, (New York: Srove Press, 1968), p. 126.

49. In his *Native Realm* (p. 277), Milosz pondered: "What is this monster, historical necessity, that paralysed my contemporaries with fear?"
50. Milosz, "Child of Europe," in Milosz, *Selected Poems.*
51. See Toranska, *"Them,"* pp. 257, 334, 353.
52. *ibid.*, p. 254.
53. E. Kamenka, "Human Rights and the Soviet Future," in Shtromas and Kaplan, *The Soviet Union,* p. 92.
54. Milosz, *Native Realm,* p. 289. This question is preceded by a statement about "salvation": "It is impossible if we wear ourselves trying to swim against the historical current, because then we fall victim to illusions."
55. Milosz, *The Captive Mind,* p. 12.
56. Milosz, *Native Realm,* p. 281.
57. Compare Milosz, *The Captive Mind,* p. 13.
58. See D. Nelidov, "Ideocratic Consciousness and Personality," ed. Meyerson-Aksenov and Shragin, *The Political, Social and Religious Thought of Russian "Samizdat",* pp. 256–90.
59. *ibid.*, pp. 274–77.
60. *ibid.*, p. 277.
61. *ibid.*, pp. 275–76.
62. Milosz, *The Captive Mind,* p. 57.
63. *ibid.*, pp. 57–60.
64. *ibid.*, p. 55.
65. *ibid.*, p. 9.
66. *ibid.*, p. 4.
67. *ibid.*, p. 23.
68. *ibid.*, p. 5.
69. *ibid.*, ch. III (pp. 54–81).
70. *ibid.*, pp. 72–3.
71. Milosz, *Native Realm,* p. 288.
72. *ibid.*, p. 269.
73. *ibid.*, p. 270.
74. *ibid.*, p. 269.
75. Compare Milosz, *The Captive Mind,* p. 72.
76. *ibid.*, p. 80.
77. Milosz, *Native Realm,* p. 270.
78. Milosz, *The Captive Mind,* p. 80.
79. Milosz, *Native Realm,* p. 269.
80. *ibid.*, p. 278.
81. *ibid.*
82. *ibid.*
83. *ibid.*
84. Kolakowski, *Towards a Marxist Humanism,* p. 120.
85. *ibid.*
86. See L. Kolakowski, *The Main Currents of Marxism* (Oxford, 1981), vol. 3, p. 462.
87. Toranska's *Them* provides many proofs of this. See especially her interviews with Edward Ochab, Roman Werfel, Stefan Staszewski and Berman. Jan Bujnowski, the author of the introduction to the Polish edition of this book, stressed their ability to defend themselves

with conviction and in a dignified way. (See Toranska, *Oni,* Aneks (London, 1985), p. 23.) Of course, I am fully aware of the possibility of quite different impressions—especially among the younger generation, for whom the mentality of authentic Communists has become incomprehensible.

88. For a detailed presentation and analysis of my experiences and thought of that time see my *Spotkania z Miloszem* (an intellectual autobiography revolving around subjects raised in my correspondence with Milosz). Milosz's letters to me are printed as a separate appendix to this book.
89. Compare Walicki, *Spotkania z Miloszem,* pp. 15–16. Needless to say, it would have been different if I were a German.
90. *ibid.,* p. 177. The quoted words of the Polish romantic poet, Adam Mickiewicz, refer to his experiences with the messianic sect of Andrzej Towianski.
91. *ibid.,* pp. 17–21.
92. *ibid.,* pp. 23–28.
93. *ibid.,* pp. 23–25, 35–40.
94. *ibid.,* p. 162 (Milosz's letter to me of November 4, 1960).
95. *ibid.,* p. 62.
96. *ibid.,* pp. 28–35.
97. Milosz, *The Captive Mind,* p. 8. (Milosz stresses that Stalinism, in contrast to rightist totalitarianism, added to this the appeal of communicating with the masses in the language of a "scientific" doctrine.)
98. Walicki, *Spotkania z Miloszem,* p. 29.
99. This expression appears in Milosz and in Kolakowski *"But there is no other way.* That much is clear" (Milosz, *The Captive Mind,* p. 20). Cf. Kolakowski's "anti-clerk": "He knows, too, that in political contests, any third force is merely a sham, a fraud, and that an attack can be launched from only one position . . . Since history acts brutally, he is prepared to accept its terms consciously" (Kolakowski, *Toward a Marxist Humanism,* p. 89).
100. Milosz, *The Captive Mind,* p. 13.
101. Compare Walicki, *Spotkania z Miloszem,* pp. 35–36.
102. *ibid.,* p. 35.
103. *ibid.,* pp. 37–38.
104. See my polemic against Kronski's Hegelianism in "Two Metaphysics," *Przeglad Kulturalny* (December 7, 1955), reprinted in *Spotkania z Miloszem,* pp. 51–58.
105. Walicki, *Spotkania z Miloszem,* p. 26 (written in August 1957).
106. George Orwell, *Collected Essays* (New York, 1968), vol. 2, p. 135.
107. Leopold Labedz has rightly noticed that Milosz's book "powerfully supplemented *1984.*" See L. Labedz, "Appreciating Milosz," in his *The Use and Abuse of Sovietology,* (New Brunswick and Oxford: Transaction Publishers, 1989), p. 206.
108. I mean, above all, the works of Hannah Arendt, Sigmund Newman, Franz Neuman, Barrington Moore, Karl Popper, Carl J. Friedrich, Zbigniew Brzezinski and Jacob L. Talmon. A good summary of their contributions has been made by J. J. Spiro in his "Totalitarianism." See also B. R. Barber, "Conceptual Foundations of Totalitarianism,"

in C. J. Friedrich, M. Curtis, B. R. Barber, *Totalitarianism in Perspective.*

109. Terry McNeill, "Images of the Soviet Future: The Western Scholarly Debate," in Shtromas and Kaplan, *The Soviet Union,* p. 316.
110. C. Johnson, "Comparing Communist Nations," ed. C. Johnson, *Change in Communist Systems,* (California, 1970), p. 2. See also C. J. Friedrich, M. Curtis, B. R. Barber, *Totalitarianism in Perspective.* B. R. Barber concluded: "A carefully and critically nurtured language of comparative political analysis will leave little room for concepts like totalitarianism" (p. 39). According to M. Curtis (whose contribution bears the title "Retreat From Totalitarianism"), "the concept of totalitarianism is no longer the most useful classificatory device for the study of current communist systems" (p. 112). Only C. J. Friedrich defended the concept. According to him, "totalitarianism, a novel form of autocracy, appears to be a highly dynamic form of government which is still evolving. Socialist legality may have an important role to play in the ritualization of its ideology as well as in the routinization of its inspirational appeal" (p. 154).
111. T. McNeill, "Images of Soviet Future," p. 318.
112. In many cases the word "totalitarianism" is being applied to the Soviet Union under Gorbachev, or to Poland under General Jaruzelski, without any attempt to justify this practice. Sometimes it amounts to a deliberate manipulation of language: a word with strongly negative connotations is used to evoke hostile reaction in the reader, although there is in fact no justification for its usage. Many left-wing authors do the same when, for instance, they use the word "genocide" in discussing the American war in Vietnam, or apply the term "fascist" to all right-wing opponents of democracy. I strongly feel that liberal political culture should energetically defend itself against such practices.
113. L. Kolakowski, *Main Currents of Marxism,* vol. 2, p. 514.
114. The significance of this fact has been noticed by Kolakowski in his "Totalitarianism and the Virtue of the Lie," ed. Irving Howe, *1984 Revisited,* (New York: Harper and Row, 1983), p. 135. For a detailed analysis of the situation in Poland after the crushing of Solidarity see my articles: "The Main Components of the Situation in Poland: 1980–83," *Politics* (Journal of the Australasian Political Studies Association), 19, no. 1 (May 1984); "The Paradoxes of Jaruzelski's Poland," *Archives Europeennes de Sociologie,* 26, no. 2, (1985); and "Liberalism in Poland," *Critical Review. A Journal of Books and Ideas,* 2, no. 1, (Winter 1988).
115. For a detailed and colorful presentation of these activities see "Independent Culture in Poland," in *Uncaptive Minds. A Journal of Information and Opinion on Eastern Europe,* 2, no. 1, (1989), pp. 25–32. (The title of the journal is an allusion to Milosz's *The Captive Mind.*)
116. For a presentation of arguments which were being used against this practice (mostly by people defining themselves as liberals), see my "Liberalism in Poland," pp. 15–17.
117. See I. Berlin, "Two Concepts of Liberty," *Four Essays on Liberty* (Oxford: Oxford University Press), 1969 especially pp. 121–22 and 162–66.

118. F. A. Hayek, *The Constitution of Liberty,* (Chicago, 1960) (Phoenix Edition 1978), p. 103.
119. Characteristically, the only reference to tolerance appears in Hayek's book not in connection with struggles for the freedom of conscience but in the following context: "There must be, in other words, a tolerance for the existence of a group of idle rich." (*ibid.,* p. 127.)
120. *ibid.,* p. 499, no. 83. The quoted words belong to E. Brunner, *Justice and the Social Order* (New York, 1945), p. 7.
121. Bruno Rizzi, *La bureaucratisation de monde,* 1939. Reprinted as *Il collectivismo burocratico,* Imola 1967. Se M. Krygier, "The Revolution Betrayed: From Trotsky to the New Class," ed. E. Kamenka and M. Krygier, *Bureaucracy. The Career of a Concept,* pp. 98–99.
122. Cf. John Rawls, "The Priority of Rights and Ideas of the Good," *Philosophy and Public Affairs* (Fall, 1988), vol. 17, no. 4, p. 256.
123. Hence the term bureaucracy, as used in this context, does not have the Weberian connotation of "rationalism" and "efficiency."
124. Ralf Dahrendorf rightly remarked: ". . . whatever the miseries of the "cage of bondage" of bureaucracy, they are different from totalitarianism, if only because they are not based on either total mobilization or total control." (R. Dahrendorf, "Totalitarianism Revisited," *Partisan Review*, 1988, LV, no. 4, pp. 549–50).
125. Direct political-moral pressure should be sharply distinguished from manipulation through mass media. Turning off a TV set does not entail any penalty, while refusal to take part in a collective brainwashing does.
126. Morton A. Kaplan, "A Commentary," ed. Shtromas and Kaplan, *The Soviet Union,* p. 43.
127. *ibid.,* p. 44. It needs to be repeatedly stressed that "unlimited power" and "effective control" are two different things. In many respects, the capitalist countries are paragons of effective control in comparison with the countries of "really existing socialism." Thus, for instance, financial control, or control over the quantity and quality of work, is, of course, incomparably stronger under capitalism. On the other hand, it is obvious that totalitarian governments have not succeeded in doing away with the problem of unintended consequences of their actions. Therefore, it is deeply misleading to define totalitarianism as a system in which everything is firmly "under control."
128. M. Djilas, "Disintegration of Leninist Totalitarianism," in *1984 Revisited,* p. 145.
129. Milosz, *The Captive Mind,* p. 13.
130. Labedz, *The Use and Abuse of Sovietology,* p. 206.
131. See *Polityka,* Warsaw (March 25, 1989), p. 2 ("Z kraju").
132. President George Bush said on this occasion: "The totalitarian era is passing, its old ideas blown away like leaves from an ancient leafless tree." See "Excerpts From Speech by Bush on Polish Aid," *The New York Times,* April 18, 1989, p. 8.
133. M. Walzer, "On 'Failed Totalitarianism'," in *1984 Revisited,* p. 119.
134. Z. Brzezinski, *Ideology and Power in Soviet Politics* (rev. ed.; New York: Praeger, 1967), pp. 46–47. The best example of a regime which still successfully implements the totalitarian idea of a "coerced unanimity" is to be found in contemporary North Korea.

135. Since there is nothing *distinctively* totalitarian about class rule or monopolistic rule. In Poland the spread of the tendency to equate all forms of one party rule with totalitarianism was obviously (and understandably) an emotional reaction to martial law. It is important to note that the opposition in other countries of "really existing socialism" was more cautious in using the term "totalitarianism." Even Czechoslovakia, where the process of detotalitarianization is much less advanced than in Poland, was described by its leading dissident, Vaclav Havel, as a "post-totalitarian" country. See V. Havel, "Sila bezsilnych" ("The force of those who lack force") in *Krytyka,* N 5, Warsaw 1980 (reprint by *Aneks,* London, 1982).
136. For an exemplification of the first choice (ignoring the changes, or minimizing their importance) see M. Heller, *Cogs in the Wheel: The Formation of Soviet Man* (New York, 1988). Despite its profound pessimism as to the chances of detotalitarianization, this book provides an excellent analysis of the "Orwellian" features of Stalinist totalitarianism in the Soviet Union. The best-known representative of the other method of supporting the "totalitarian image" of the Soviet Union is Alain Besancon, professor at the Ecole des Hautes Etudes in Paris. He acknowledges the existence of "the real crisis" in the Communist party of the Soviet Union but at the same time tries at all costs to deny the possibility of a genuine systemic change. See his "Gorbachev Without Illusions," *Commentary,* Vol. 85, no. 4 (April, 1988), pp. 47–57.
137. Of course, the only totalitarian regimes which existed and further developed in the later period represented *Communist* totalitarianism. Hence, the theory of detotalitarianization can be elaborated only as a part of comparative study of Communist party dictatorships.
138. See especially the works of Richard Löwenthal: "Development vs. Utopia in Communist Policy," ed. C. Johnson, *Change in Communist Systems,* pp. 33–116; "Beyond Totalitarianism?", in *1984 Revisited,* pp. 209–67, and "Beyond the 'Institutionalized Revolution' in Russia and China," eds. Shtromas and Kaplan, *The Soviet Union,* pp. 13–34.
139. Z. Brzezinski, *The Grand Failure* (New York: Scribner's, 1989), p. 255.
140. Orwell's review of Hayek's *The Road to Serfdom,* in *The Observer,* (April 9, 1944). Quoted from Labedz, *The Use and Abuse of Sovietology,* p. 201.
141. Compare my "Liberalism in Poland."

Totalitarianism, Reform, and Civil Society

John Gray

What must be true for post-totalitarianism to be a possibility? This question—a question as to the conditions under which totalitarian political orders may mutate, or successfully transform themselves, into orders, authoritarian, liberal, or otherwise, in which the constitutive features of totalitarianism have been transcended or suppressed—presupposes a conception of totalitarianism itself. The history of the idea of totalitarianism, however, is a history of controversy. Presented initially by theorists and practitioners of Italian fascism as a positive notion,[1] the idea of totalitarianism acquired an unequivocally pejorative connotation in postwar literature,[2] being used to capture the common features of National Socialism and Soviet Communism in their worst and most terroristic periods. It was later subject to criticism and attack, both by Marxists and by others,[3] who sought to deny its theoretical coherence and utility and who tried to represent it as an ideological construct of liberalism and conservatism deployed for the purposes of the Western powers during the Cold War period. My inquiry is based on the rejection of this latter view and on a commitment to the validity and usefulness of totalitarianism as a central category in contemporary social and political theory. This does not mean that I endorse the conventional conception of totalitarianism as developed in the postwar Anglo-American literature. Legitimate as this conception may be, it obscures a number of interesting questions. Is totalitarianism necessarily or inherently terroristic, or is terror a developmental phase which some totalitarian orders pass through? This is a question with obvious relevance to the possibility of post-totalitarianism, since it allows that a totalitarian regime may sustain and reproduce itself by other means than the threat of violence.

Can the institutions of democratic capitalism be characterized as encompassing a totalitarian order, as Marcuse and others have alleged?[4] Is totalitarianism a uniquely modern phenomenon, or are there instances of it in ancient times? Can post-totalitarian orders in which civil societies have clearly emerged be subject to successful retotalitarianization? Or is the move from totalitarianism typically irreversible?

What of the cultural roots of totalitarianism: is it alien to the Western tradition, an aberration within it, or a development of elements of the most central, ancient, and fundamental Western tradition? I shall approach these and related questions by way of a critique of the received notion of totalitarianism and of its standard applications to the Soviet case. The standard conception of totalitarianism equates it with such phenomena as mass terror and a charismatic leader with a cult of personality. It suggests that, in the absence of clear evidence of these phenomena, we have a post-totalitarian regime. By contrast, the conception of totalitarianism I shall advance enables us to recognize as neo-totalitarian the forms of social and political control that have emerged recently in the Soviet Union, and to distinguish such a neo-totalitarian regime from the genuine post-totalitarianism that exists in Poland, Hungary, and (more precariously) in the Baltic states.

The danger of the conventional conception is that it may blind us to the varieties of totalitarianism. This is not to say that totalitarianism is a sort of cluster-concept, with the variety of totalitarian regimes being unified only by a pattern of family resemblances. For I shall maintain that the totalitarian project is constituted by a single objective—that of merging state and society in a new order from which the conflicts of interest, purpose, and value which are found in all historic societies have been extirpated. This definitively totalitarian objective may be stated with greater precision. *The totalitarian project is the project of suppressing civil society—that sphere of autonomous institutions, protected by the rule of law, within which individuals and communities possessing divergent values and beliefs may coexist in peace.* Implementing this project involves another project, one even more stupendous: that of remaking the identities of those who have come within the sphere of totalitarian power. A number of theorists, such as Heller,[5] have seen the most essential, definitive feature of totalitarianism in this project of making over human nature on a new model. I shall argue that, whereas the totalitarian project has in many instances succeeded in destroying civil society, it has nowhere forged a new humanity. I shall take the destruction of civil society to be the chief historical result of totalitarianism. Indeed, on the view I shall defend, the suppression of civil society is not so much a consequence or side-effect of totalitarianism as its very essence.

It is for this reason that I shall affirm the radical modernity of the totalitarian phenomenon. Totalitarianism is uniquely modern—not only because it presupposes a contemporary technology of repression, but chiefly because it expresses a revulsion against the distinctively modern institutions of civil society. It did so even in China, where Communism sought to legitimate itself as a project of modernization. I shall affirm the radical modernity of totalitarianism as a political order, even though I will maintain that its cultural origins are in elements of the most ancient and central Western values and ideas (and not, for example, in the traditional cultures of Russia and China).

In particular, interpretations of the Soviet Union in terms of the antique categories of tyranny or empire miss the mark by invoking concepts to capture realities of which Montesquieu or Aristotle could have had no conception. When Pipes argues that "the techniques of police rule, introduced piecemeal by the Russian imperial regime, were first utilized to their fullest potential by their one-time victims, the revolutionaries,"[6] he neglects the very radical discontinuities between the magnitude of repression between the Tsarist and Bolshevik regimes (which I shall spell out in detail below); above all, he passes over the fact that the Tsarist secret police was never employed to liquidate entire social groups.

The claim that totalitarianism existed in ancient times is equally far from the mark. When Barrington Moore cites the adoption in ancient China of "the famous pao-chia system of mutual surveillance, which resembles and long antedates modern totalitarian procedures," he confuses totalitarianism with a technique which has been adopted by a variety of types of government. When he goes on to refer to "the hsiang-yueh system of periodically lecturing the population on Confucian ethics" as another "revealing precursor of modern totalitarian practices"—all of which, he says, "demonstrate conclusively that the key features of the totalitarian complex existed in the premodern world"[7]—he neglects the revolutionary character of totalitarian ideological indoctrination.

Totalitarian ideologies are instruments of social transformation; they seek to displace traditional systems of belief. That is why the academic canard, that Communism is a modern secular or political religion, is true only in the sense in which occultism and theosophy are religions—the sense in which all are modernist projects of supplanting the mysteries and tragedies of inherited faiths with gnostic techniques of liberation, represented as applications of scientific method. There is an inherent paradox in totalitarianism in that it deploys modern ideology in the service of an antimodernist project. Because it embodies a revolt against modernity, totalitarianism can only be its shadow. If totalitarian orders are to be reformed, accordingly, such reform can be achieved only by way of a rediscovery of the most distinctive institutions of the modern world—the institutions of civil society.

The question of the possibility of post-totalitarianism, accordingly, is the question of whether totalitarian regimes may so alter their nature as to allow the reemergence or reinvention of those institutions of civil life to whose destruction they had been committed. Indeed, since the emergence of civil society encompasses a mutation in the very nature of totalitarianism, a question inevitably arises whether totalitarian orders are capable of reform—and, if they are not, how are current developments to be understood?

It is enmity to civil society, with its constituve institutions of private property and the rule of law, rather than opposition to liberal democracy which is most nearly definitive of totalitarianism. "Civil society" here refers to the domain of voluntary associations, market exchanges, and private institutions within and through which individuals having divergent conceptions and diverse and often competitive purposes may coexist in peace. It is this conception, I believe, that is held in common by such otherwise very different theorists as Locke and Hegel. In the mind of both, civil society is distinguished sharply from the state. But each recognizes that the institutions of civil society need definition and protection by law, and so cannot flourish without the shelter of government. There are many types of government, however, under which a civil society may exist—there are as many varieties of authoritarianism, for example, as there are of democracy. Only the unlimited government of totalitarianism is incompatible with civil society. For this reason, non-totalitarian (and, indeed, post-totalitarian) regimes may come in a variety of forms, of which liberal democracy is only one. In all of its varieties, however, post-totalitarianism represents the inversion of the totalitarian order, not a terminal phase in its development. For a totalitarian regime to cease to be such, it must be able to recall the civil life it has lost, or else to fashion anew the institutions of civil society. My purpose in this paper is to speculate about the conditions under which actually existing totalitarian regimes might successfully negotiate this transformation and so resurrect or adopt a civil society.

In fact, my project here will be the more limited one of conjecturing as to the prospects of such a metamorphosis in Soviet-bloc regimes. I pass over as not centrally germane to my purpose the example of Nazi Germany, in which a totalitarian regime perished through military defeat, and all of the Fascist states, none of which was genuinely totalitarian (even where, as in Italy, it claimed to be). I pass over these other potential instances of totalitarianism, primarily because the Soviet example constitutes the paradigm case. In terms of chronology, the Soviet Union was the modern world's first totalitarian state. Further, its example animated every subsequent totalitarian (or would-be totalitarian) state. As Schapiro has said:

> The originator of the technique of mass manipulation, in modern times, was Lenin; not only Stalin, but Mussolini certainly and Hitler (through the German communists) indirectly, learned it from him . . . Lenin never became (or ever wanted to become) a Leader such as Hitler or Stalin; but in the course of building up his technique of mass manipulation as part of the process of ensuring victory for his party he provided a model for these very different men.[8]

Lenin initiated not only totalitarian techniques of mass manipulation, but also most of the other distinctive institutions of totalitarianism—such as the concentration camp and the extralegal powers of the secret police. As Nolte has argued, there is also a case for ascribing the responsibility for pioneering the techniques of mass extermination to the Bolsheviks, whom the Nazis later emulated in their genocides.[9] For these reasons, then, I feel justified in focusing on Soviet-type instances as paradigm cases of totalitarianism. For a different reason, lack of space, I do not discuss in any systematic fashion the potentially important case of Communist China other than by brief comments on the contrasts between traditional forms of despotism in China and Chinese Communist totalitarianism and a short comparison of the prospects of economic reform in China and the Soviet Union. I restrict the scope of my inquiries to the topical—but also globally decisively important—question: can the reform movements within the Soviet bloc—such as *perestroika* in the Soviet Union, Solidarity in Poland, and the various experiments in multi-party pluralism in Hungary and in the toleration of oppositional movements in the Baltic states—succeed to the extent of reestablishing civil societies, or something akin to them? My project here is not the hazardous one of prediction, though I will speculate as to the likely failure of *perestroika,* but that of theorizing the conditions of (and constraints upon) the emergence of post-totalitarian regimes within the Soviet bloc. Pursuing this theoretical goal entails making significant distinctions between circumstances and prospects in different countries, particularly as to the causal origins of the various reform movements. It also necessitates an attempt to specify those features of Soviet totalitarianism which give it its essential character and are most relevant to the possibilities of post-totalitarianism.

Here I shall make little use of the famous five-point syndrome of totalitarian regimes proposed by Carl Friedrich in 1954,[10] since it conflates historically contingent aspects of Soviet-style totalitarianism with its constitutive features. I shall focus instead on what I shall maintain are the three key features of totalitarianism—its suppression of the institutions of civil society (and especially of the rule of law), the central planning of the economy, and the character of the totalitarian regime as a *Weltanschauung*-state. I shall submit that current movements for reform, such as *perestroika* in the Soviet Union, are responses to the ruinous failure of the command economies—a failure that has left even the servile *nomenklatura* of these regimes under-rewarded. The tactical objective of the Soviet reform process is the refinancing of the system by Western credit. The strategic objective is the stabilization of the Soviet totalitarian order—which incorporates the goals of engineering a shift in the distribution of military power in Europe and the forging of subsidy relationships between the EEC and the Comecon countries. In all important respects, Soviet *perestroika* embodies an authentically Leninist strategy which includes a significant component of strategic disinformation. The crucial question—which I shall address towards the end of this paper—is whether the new Leninist strategy of the Soviet leadership risks unleashing uncontrollable forces in the Soviet bloc and in the Soviet Union itself which threaten the system's very existence, or whether, despite its colossal failures, the Soviet system can again renew itself through a combination of selective repression and Western aid. There is also the question of whether, even granted massive doses of Western capital and technology, the Soviet system can do anything more than temporarily stave off the prospect of a catastrophic economic collapse, with all the unpredictable political consequences that would have. In any case, we need to ask what the implications are for the prospects of post-totalitarianism in Poland, Hungary, the Baltic states, and elsewhere in the Soviet bloc. Before we can even approach these questions, however, we need to consider the constitutive features and decisive episodes in Soviet totalitarianism.

I. Theorizing Soviet Totalitarianism: The Conventional Methodology

We may begin by making some cautionary remarks on the methodology of conventional Soviet studies. The conventional wisdom among Sovietologists is that the Soviet state is a state like any other, whose distinctive features are derived from Russian political and cultural traditions. According to this dominant view,[11] the Soviet state is a tyranny, in whose formation Muscovite traditions of authoritarian rule are at least as significant as Marxist-Leninist ideology. If this is so, then the methods appropriate to the study of the Soviet state are no different from those used with any other state—the methods of standard political science, such as theories about political culture, the study of interest groups, analysis of institutions, and so on. It is no exaggeration to assert that this methodology has been thoroughly unproductive (and, indeed, counterproductive) in its impact on Western perceptions of the Soviet Union. It is radically defective for a number of reasons. In the first place, this conventional methodology is bound to exaggerate grossly the importance of cultural factors in explaining Soviet totalitarianism. That this is so is demonstrated by the profound similarities between Soviet-type regimes having very different cultural traditions. Despite their diverse political traditions, the East European states during the Stalinist period exhibited structural affinities—such as the campaign against religion and the attempt to impose a single *Weltanschauung,* the attack on the peasantry, show trials, a terroristic secret police and the regimentation of intellectual life—which are explicable only by reference to their being modeled on the Soviet totalitarian state. Again, the structural affinities between the periods of socialist construction in the Soviet Union and in Communist China—the reliance on slave labor in a vast Gulag, the catastrophic waste and malinvestment generated by a command economy which promoted rapid industrialization at the expense of the ruin of agriculture, and repression of minority peoples—overwhelm any divergences between the two regimes which their different cultures may account for. Indeed, Communist regimes remote from the Soviet Union, arising from radically different cultures, have emulated Stalinist policies aimed at the destruction of peasant life—as in Ethopia, where the Communist government goes so far as to call its policy for the forcible resettlement of the peasantry by the same term, "systematization," used for the policy in today's Stalinist Romania. Other examples—from (for instance) Cuba, Mozambique and Angola—could easily be used.

Finally, whatever their cultural contexts, all Communist regimes at present display decisive common features—the existence of an extensive parallel economy, the allocation of such goods as education and housing by a corrupt and exploitative *nomenklatura,* and a consequent pattern of extreme social stratification—which dominate their respective cultural inheritances. This may be affirmed, even if it be readily allowed that there are distinctive cultural factors—in Russia, Poland, and Bohemia, for example—which have modified the development of the totalitarian regimes there.

My strategy of argument will be, first, to subject the conventional methodology of Soviet studies to an historical critique by confronting it with six aspects of Soviet totalitarianism that it systematically neglects or underestimates: the economic, political, and cultural achievements of late Tsarism; the dependency of the Soviet economy on Western capital and technology; the central role of Marxist-Leninist ideology in Soviet development; the specifically Leninist origins of Soviet totalitarianism; the economic functions of the forced labor camps in the period of socialist construction, and the genocidal character of the policy of agricultural collectivization; and the use by the Soviet leadership of techniques of strategic disinformation. Having illustrated the poverty of the conventional methodology of Soviet studies by these examples, I shall proceed to more positively theorize Soviet totalitarianism by reference to the three characteristics that most radically distinguish it from a civil society—the first two being its lack of the institutions of market exchange and of their indispensable matrix, the rule of law, and the continuing identification and legitimation of the Soviet state by reference to the ideology of Marxism-Leninism. Soviet totalitarianism is not a despotism or a tyranny, but an economic chaos contained in a political state of nature. Only by so understanding it can we grasp its ruinous poverty as well as its awesome capacity for self-reproduction. We understand it adequately, finally, when we see the necessity to the Soviet regime of its third feature—its legitimation by a Marxist-Leninist ideology that at once animates the present policy of *perestroika* and prohibits the only real reform: the reappearance of civil society.

The alternative methodology that I adopt is distinguished by its taking seriously the role of Marxist-Leninist ideology in accounting for Soviet policy. It postulates that the Soviet state has no legitimacy, and (aside from the KGB) barely an existence, apart from that system of ideas. It focuses on the features that distinguish the Soviet system from authoritarian states—in particular, its control of information and its involvement of its subjects in the processes and practices whereby it reproduces itself. In seeking a better understanding of the Soviet system than that found in the conventional methodology, I shall make use of two bodies of theory whose salience to the Soviet phenomenon is persistently neglected by the conventional wisdom: Austrian economic theory and Virginia Public Choice theory. Applying these bodies of theory to the Soviet system generates an alternative perspective in which its most distinctive features are captured and rendered intelligible. This alternative methodology does not deny that the phenomena studied in the standard approaches exist within the Soviet system—it acknowledges that there are competing interest groups, just as it emphasizes that there are markets, and it does not deny that native Russian traditions are to be found within the Soviet system—but it affirms that these phenomena tend to reinforce the stability of the Soviet totalitarian order (often by being manipulated by it) rather than weaken it. By its virtual elimination of the private sphere within which such phenomena arise and flourish in pluralist and authoritarian states, Soviet totalitarianism drastically modifies their typical effects. It creates an altogether novel political order—a lawless Leviathan whose subjects are victims of a recurrent Prisoner's Dilemma in which they are constrained to reproduce the system that enslaves them.

II. The Achievements of Late Tsarism

The dominant methodology involves a massive distortion of Russian history. It neglects the emergence, during the last half-century of the Tsarist regime, of a strong and resilient (if never wholly dominant) tradition of liberal legal and political philosophy, whose development has been definitively analyzed by Walicki,[12] which made an important contribution to the constitutional reforms of the regime's last two decades. It grossly exaggerates the character of late Tsarism as a police state (as Norman Stone and others have shown)[13] and underestimates the many characteristics it had in common with other authoritarian states in Europe, such as Prussia. And the conventional wisdom which represents the Soviet Union as the continuation of Tsarist traditions disregards evidence of the extraordinary economic, cultural, and social progress which occurred during the last decades of Tsarism. Let us be specific. In a book published six months before the outbreak of the First World War, the French economist Edmond Thery notes that in the five-year period from 1908–1912, coal production increased by 79.3 percent over the preceding five years; iron by 24.8 percent; and steel and metal products by 45.9 percent. Even allowing for inflation, the output of heavy industry increased by 74.1 percent from 1900 to 1913. Again, between 1890 and 1915, the rail network almost tripled.[14] As to the magnitude of foreign investment in Russia—frequently (if often inconsistently) cited as evidence of Russian backwardness—Norman Stone has noted that, on the eve of the First World War, foreign investment in Russia had declined as a proportion of total investment by one-half in 1900 to a fifth in 1914. By 1909 Russia had already become the world's fourth industrial power.[15]

Nor was progress confined to industry. Thery reports that, in agriculture, wheat production between 1908–1912 rose by 37.5 percent over the preceding five years; rye by 24 percent; barley by 62.2 percent; oats by 20.9 percent; and corn by 44.8 percent. With good harvests, as in 1909 and 1910, Russian wheat exports made up 40 percent of world wheat exports; even in bad years, they amounted to 11.5 percent. In social policy, spending on education doubled in the decade between 1902–1912. By 1915, over half of all children between eight and eleven years of age were in school, and 68 percent of all military conscripts were literate. Welfare legislation in Russia followed a Bismarckian pattern, although in Siberia conditions approximated more closely to laisser-faire. As in Bismarck's Prussia, various schemes of workers' insurance were introduced, and late Tsarist Russia followed Prussia in pioneering the rudiments of the twentieth-century welfare state.[16] As Dominic Leven has noted, Russia also followed Prussia in having a civil service that in the last decades of the nineteenth century "approached the Weberian ideal type."[17] Although development was uneven in many areas, Tsarist Russia in its last half century was not the autocratic, Asiatic despotism caricatured in conventional theturography, but instead a dynamic, progressive European state.

During its last half-century, Russia experienced an explosion of cultural energies, achieving a flowering in the arts—in literature, painting, dance, and religious thought, for example—which has rarely been matched in European cultural history. The last decades of Tsarism saw much policy that was clumsy, ill-conceived, or repressive—particularly in the policies of Russification of the national minorities and discrimination and persecution against Jews. The rapid progress achieved in the economy, in cultural life, and in some aspects of policy (but not, alas, in constitutional affairs, where policy was lagging and faltering), is nevertheless especially impressive, given the demographic explosion and consequent urban problems which government confronted. As Heller and Nekrich observe, the statistics for these years are revealing—and when the October Revolution occurred, it was a direct result of World War One.[18]

Perhaps the most striking discontinuity is in the area where the conventional methodology finds most similarity between the late Tsarist and the early Bolshevik regimes—that is, the discontinuity between the repressive activities of the Okhrana and the Cheka-GPU-OGPU. The most obviously demonstrable discontinuities, detailed below, are in the magnitude, scale, and intensity of repression. However, the *quality* of repression is also crucial: the Okhrana, unlike any of the Bolshevik security services, did not act extralegally but within a rule of law, and it did not seek to liquidate whole social categories. It is against this background that the quantitative comparisons made by Dziak are to be assessed:[19]

LATE TSARIST PERIOD (1826–1917)

Executions

1826–1906:	894
1866–1917:	14,000 approx.
1866–1900:	142
1906 (six months of the Stolypin military field tribunals):	950
1907:	1,139
1908:	1,340
1908–12:	6,000
"Following the 1905–7 Revolution":	11,000
"Eighty years that preceded the Revolution in Russia":	17/year (average)

Deaths from Executions, Pogrom Murders, and Deaths in Prison

1867–1917:	25,000

Convicts at Hard Labor

1913:	32,000 (year largest numbers were reached)

Political Exile without Confinement

1907:	17,000 (year largest numbers were reached)

Maximum Number Imprisoned (Criminals and politicals)

1912:	183,949

EARLY SOVIET PERIOD (1917–24)

Executions by Cheka and Tribunals

1917–23:	200,000
1918 & 1st half of 1919:	8,389

1917–20:	12,733
"Civil War":	50,000
1918–19:	1,700,000
1918–23:	2,500,000 per annum

Deaths Caused by Cheka

1917–22:	250,000–300,000

Deaths from the Suppression of "Rebellions" and from Prison and Camp Treatment

1917–24:	300,000

Executions in the Crimea Following General Wrangel's Defeat and Evacuation

1920–21:	50,000–150,000

Hostages and Prisoners in Camps and Prisons (1917–23)

1918:	42,254 hostages/prisoners in camps and prisons
1919 (to July):	44,639 hostages/prisoners in camps and prisons
1918:	47,348 hostages/prisoners in camps and prisons
1919:	80,662 hostages/prisoners in camps and prisons
1920 (late):	25,336 camp inmates plus 24,400 Civil War prisoners; 48,112 prisoners in RFSFR NKYu prisons; 60,000 NKYu prisoners according to commissar of justice
1921 (Jan.):	51,158
1921 (Sep.):	60,457
1921 (Dec.):	40,913; 73,000 prisoners in NKYu prisons
1922 (Oct.):	60,000
1923 (Oct.):	68,297

It is unequivocally and undeniably clear from these figures that, in addition to the arbitrary and extralegal character of the Bolshevik terror, the quantitative increases in the various kinds of repression in the Bolshevik regime, as compared with those of late Tsarism, are so enormous as to themselves amount to a qualitative transformation in the nature of the regime—from authoritarian to totalitarian.

It is not only that, as Dziak has put it, "an unbroken patrimony between Tsarist repression and Soviet terms cannot be claimed." It is not even that, as he also observes, "even at the height of its repression against revolutionaries, Tsarist courts offset Okhrana and Gendarme actions, thereby exercising a restraining hand. In Lenin's system the courts were either ignored, or became creatures of the Cheka."[20] The crucial point is that the extrajudicial coercion and terror of the Cheka were directed against whole social groups, and primarily against the peasantry and workers. According to Soviet statistics used by Dziak, of the forty thousand NKVD inmates for December 1921, almost 80 percent were illiterate or nearly so, and so were from peasant or worker stock. As Dziak decisively concludes: "It simply was not Tsarist policy or practice to exterminate whole categories of people. . . . The Cheka's class war certainly was an 'aristicide' of the leading sectors of tsarist society, but its more numerous victims were the very classes it claimed to represent and serve."[21]

There is, finally, the evidence of the *size* of the two security services, with Richard Pipes noting that in 1895 the Okhrana had only 161 full-time personnel, supported by a Corp of Gendarmes amounting to less than 10,000 men, while the Cheka by mid-1921 accounted for approximately 262,400 men, *not counting* Red Army, NKVD, and militiamen.

The external counter-intelligence activities of the Tsarist police were restricted, as Pipes notes, virtually to a single institution, the Russian Embassy in Paris, which employed a handful of people to keep surveillance on politically active Russian émigrés.[22] A comparison of the Tsarist external counter-intelligence commitment with that of the Soviet KGB is impossible, but given the vast magnitudes of difference in scale that everything we know suggests, it is also unnecessary. The Western conventional wisdom, so deep-rooted in academic folklore as to be probably unshakeable, that Bolshevik terror was nothing but a continuation of a tsarist police-state, is controverted by all available evidence. On the contrary, all the evidence supports the view of late Tsarist Russia as a civil society on the European model, which it was the historic role of the Bolsheviks (animated, ironically, by a European ideology) to destroy. Before it was destroyed by the Bolsheviks, the late Tsarist regime was one that compares favorably with the great majority of governments that exist today. It is highly probable, in fact, that were the Soviet Union now what Russia was in 1913, it would come within the twenty states that are most liberal and least oppressive in today's world.

III. Soviet Dependency on the West

In truth, the conventional image of late Tsarism better fits the early decades of the Soviet Union in certain important respects. Throughout its history, the Soviet Union has been crucially dependent on Western capital and technology. Indeed, Western aid may well have secured the survival of the regime during its periods of worst crisis. As Besancon has said, "international society has on several occasions saved the Soviet regime in moments of crisis. I need only mention Herbert Hoover's American Relief Administration mission, which saved between five and six million peasants starving to death during the famine of 1921, and American aid in World War Two. Even during the most desperate War Communism—the War Communism of the first Five Year Plans—the West sent the Soviet Union considerable sums of money, technology and engineers."[23]

Western aid, however, was no less important in the construction of Soviet power than in preserving it from collapse. The Treaty of Rapallo, signed between Germany and Soviet Russia in April 1922, was decisively important in promoting both the economic and the military power of the Soviet state. It provided for the establishment of joint Soviet-German industrial and commercial firms, with more than two thousand German technicians arriving in the Soviet Union in the wake of the signing of the treaty. The Treaty of Rapallo also initiated an important period of Soviet-Germany military cooperation, enabling the Germans to circumvent the Treaty of Versailles and rebuild the German army with state-of-the-art weapons manufactured and tested in the Soviet Union in return for the provision of training facilities for Red Army officers in Germany. The intimacy of this connection may be gauged from the fact that German and Russian chemists collaborated in the production of experimental poison gases.

This period of Soviet-German cooperation came to an end in 1927 with the Shakhty trial of German engineers,[24] after which the Soviet Union turned to the United States for assistance. Heller and Nekrich report that, whereas in mid-1929 the Soviet Union had technical agreements with twenty-seven German firms and fifteen American firms, by the end of 1929 forty American firms were cooperating with the Soviet Union. They go on:

> The five-year plan could not have been implemented without foreign assistance. In 1928 a group of Soviet engineers arrived in Detroit and requested that Albert Kahn and Company, an eminent firm of industrial architects in the United States, design plans for industrial build-

> ings worth 2 billion dollars . . . According to an agreement with the Supreme Economic Council of the USSR, the American firm agreed to design all aspects of Soviet industry, heavy and light. Foreign designers, technicians, engineers, and skilled workers built the industrial units of the first five-year plan. Primarily they were Americans, who pushed the Germans out of first place in 1928; after them came the Germans, British, Italians and French. The dam on the Dnieper was built by the firm of Colonel Hugh Cooper, a prominent American hydraulic engineer; the majority of the largest Soviet power plants were equipped by the British firm Metropolitan-Vickers; Western companies designed, built, and equipped Magnitogorsk and Kuznetsk, the Urals Machinery Works, the Kaganovich Ball Bearing Plant in Yaroslav, among others . . .
>
> The full extent of Western economic and technological aid to the Soviet Union will not be known until the Soviet archives are opened up. The Western firms that collaborated with Moscow have concealed the information almost as carefully as their Soviet partners. Nevertheless, the American historian Anthony Sutton has come to the conclusion, on the basis of German and English archives, that 95 percent of Soviet industrial enterprises received Western aid in the form of machines, technology, and direct technical aid.[25]

Such direct Western aid to the Soviet power is a recurrent, almost continuous feature in its development. In recent times, it has included economic and military assistance to Soviet satellite powers, as in the case of British commercial and governmental aid to Marxist Mozambique. Side by side with direct aid, there has been the explosive growth in recent decades of Western bank lending to the Soviet bloc, with Western credits amounting to 50 billion dollars by 1978. By the eighties, the Soviet Union was financing Western development of its resources with Western credit. West European capital financed the construction of the gas pipeline from the USSR to Western Europe, assuring an annual profit of 5-8 billion dollars to the Soviet Union, and in 1981 the Deutsche Bank and the Mannesman A. G. Steel Corporation arrived at a contract worth 16.5 billion with the Soviet government to develop its Siberian energy resources.[26] By the end of 1988, Soviet foreign debt was estimated at about 43 billion dollars, much of it loaned to the Soviet Union by Western banks at lower interest rates than those offered to blue-chip multinational corporations such as IBM or Shell.[27] It is difficult to resist the conclusion that the Soviet Union, in its demonstrated dependency on Western capital, technology, and (let us not forget) food imports, resembles the conventional caricature of Tsarist Russia as an underdeveloped, backward power far more closely than did the reality of late Tsarism.

IV. The Centrality of Marxist-Leninist Ideology in the Development of the Soviet Union

The dominant methodology of conventional Western Soviet studies demonstrably exaggerates the continuities in political culture between late Tsarism and the Soviet state and has passed over or suppressed the many evidences of the Soviet Union's dependence on Western aid throughout its history. In its attempts to apply the categories and techniques of Western political science to Soviet political life, the conventional discipline of Sovietology has systematically neglected, or attempted to interpret away, the decisive role of Marxist-Leninist ideology in explaining the strategies and tactics of Soviet leaders, and has consigned to an Orwellian memory hole the formative impact of ideology in constituting and reproducing the most distinctive institutions of the Soviet state.

Perhaps the most fundamental of the blind spots of the conventional methodology concern the experiment in War Communism, the origins of the Gulag, and the functions of the Gulag in the period of socialist construction, in each of which ideology played a decisive part. War Communism was the project Lenin initiated in the spring of 1918 of realizing the utopian fantasies of his *State and Revolution,* written just before the October Revolution. The conventional view, whose dominance was secured by the work of Maurice Dobb and E. H. Carr,[28] is that War Communism was forced on the Bolsheviks by the exigencies of civil war. More recent studies by Paul Craig Roberts, Thomas Remington, and Silvana Malle have demonstrated that War Communism was not an emergency measure, but a policy with the conscious goal of abolishing market institutions.[29] This policy, like many other aspects of Leninist totalitarianism (including the institution of forced labor), has a direct ancestry in the thought of Marx himself, for whom socialism and communism were, first and last, the abolition of commodity production and market exchange. In accordance with this Marxist project, a great leap forward was attempted, in which money was suppressed, private trade banned, compulsory labor service introduced, and grain requisitioned from the peasants at fixed prices. The results of this experiment were catastrophic. Famine broke out in the cities, industrial production collapsed, and in 1921–22 famine followed the collapse of food production in the countryside. But the most significant collapse during the experiment in War Communism between 1918–1922 was that in population itself. According to Soviet sources, over five million lives were lost as a result of the famine of 1921–1922. In addition, at least ten million lives were lost in the course of the Civil War. While it may be questionable to attribute the resultant total entirely to the experiment in War Communism, the human cost in lives in this period of social revolution and revolutionary war is fully comparable to that of the later period of Stalinism—and perhaps serves as a better illustration of the practical consequences of Communism in the full rigor of its doctrinal purity.

War Communism exemplifies a decisive characteristic of the Soviet state from its inception in the Bolshevik dictatorship—its character as a *Weltanschauung*-state. Tsarist Russia was a monarchy in which the head of state was also head of the Church—as in the case of the United Kingdom to this day. It was never a state dedicated to the revolutionary transformation of its subjects' beliefs and the inculcation of a new orthodoxy. Nor were its policies, foreign or domestic, governed primarily or consistently by an ideology. The Bolsheviks, by contrast, were guided primarily by ideology from the start. As Dziak has observed in regard to the terror of these years of War Communism: "The Cheka operated under an all-embracing plan, simple though it was: the bourgeoisie were to be exterminated. That this mass extermination was premeditated, and not merely, as Soviets claim, a response to White reaction and foreign intervention, is seen by its continuance well after the defeat of the Whites and the withdrawal of foreign forces, that is, well into the 1920's."[30]

The War Communism power exemplifies the totalitarian origins of Soviet Communism in all three respects—in the institution of a *Weltanschauung*-state, in the destruction of the rule of law by an extrajudicial secret police, and in the attempt to eradicate the institution of market exchange. These are features of the Soviet state that it has exhibited throughout its history, and which persist to the present day.

V. The Leninist Origins of Soviet Totalitarianism

Another distinctive feature of the Soviet state, ignored by the dominant methodology, is the origin of the terroristic secret police and the concentration camp system in Leninist theory and practice. This was a development fraught with significance for the future, since it heralded the emergence of one of the constitutive features of Soviet totalitarianism—the omnipresence of extralegal coercion and the creation of a lawless state of nature at the political level. Credit for the first use of the term 'concentration camp' goes to Trotsky, but the idea of establishing forced labor camps as part of a project of socialist reeducation originates with Marx, and the institution was established by Lenin. Shortly before the October 1917 coup, Lenin declared that he would adopt the institution of compulsory labor, which would be more potent than the guillotine; the guillotine merely terrorized and broke active resistance, while forced labor would break passive resistance, particularly among proletarians.[31]

Mass terror was characteristic of the Soviet state from its inception, with Dzerzhinsky giving unlimited "extra-judicial" powers—including powers of execution—to all regional Chekas in September 1918. In January of 1918, Lenin had agreed that the Cheka might appropriately be renamed "The Commissinat for Soviet Extermination," but judged it impolitic to do so.[32] In 1921 the Cheka assumed responsibility for the problem of the millions of homeless children in Russia, taking direct control of the camps and homes where many of them were sent. In 1922 the GPU, the Cheka's successor, acquired further extrajudicial prerogatives, which were further expanded in 1926. The GPU also inherited the notorious Solovetsky concentration camps from the Cheka, whose existence and character were revealed to an indifferent public in the West by survivors in the 1920s. The institutional framework of Soviet totalitarianism was constructed by Lenin—a fact which has been studiously ignored under *glasnost.* The suppression of Lenin's patrimony of Stalinist totalitarianism under Soviet glasnost to the present time is, in all probability, inevitable, since acknowledging this unbroken historical continuity would be a death-blow to the legitimacy of the Soviet system. One may state the same point in other words, by affirming that the acid test of Soviet glasnost will come when it proceeds to demythify Lenin and Leninism and recognizes in them the origins of the current pathology of the Soviet state.

VI. The Functions of Forced Labor Camps in the Soviet Economy

A further blind spot of the dominant methodology is the economic role of the Gulag, which is evaded or distorted in conventional Soviet studies. It is represented as peripheral in importance or as an aberration of socialist planning, rather than as an indispensable instrument of Soviet power during the period of the Five Year Plans. A classic example of this interpretation is found in Nove's *Economic History of the USSR*. In this book of over three hundred pages, there are only a few scattered remarks on the subject of the camps. We are told, for example, that "in this period (the period of the Great Leap Forward) prisoners and deportees, especially the latter, emerged as a significant factor in the life of the country. For example," Nove goes on, "only a small portion of the inhabitants of the new town of Karaganda went there of their own volition."[33] Later, Nove refers to the human cost of the period of socialist construction " in the diversion to camps of unknown millions, of whom a high proportion were above average in intelligence, energy and technical knowledge." And he admits that "especially after 1936, officials of the NKVD . . . exercised important supervisory functions through the economy, and they also ran a big economic empire using forced labor, until the break-up of this empire after Stalin's death."[34] Nove comments on the human cost of collectivization—in terms of deaths caused by famine and deportation—that "the Soviet population in 1926 was 142 millions, and for 1932 it was officially estimated at 165.7, since it had been increasing at the rate of about 3 millions a year. In 1939, seven years later, it was only about 170 million. Somewhere along the way well over 10 million people had demographically disappeared. [Some, of course, were never born.]"[35] Nove concludes, judiciously: "Perhaps it is Russia's tragedy . . . and a measure of her achievement that, despite all that happened, so much has been built, and not a few cultural values preserved and handed on to a vastly more literate population."[36]

An incomparably more accurate account of the economic significance of the Gulag and of the human costs of collectivization is given by Nekrich and Heller. As they put it:

> As early as 1929 all the camps had been placed under the direction of the OGPU, which for years had directed the archetypal camp at Solovki. The OGPU became the country's largest construction company. With a virtually limitless supply of unskilled labor at its disposal, the OGPU conducted massive arrests of engineers and technicians to manage the unskilled laborers. A new, purely Soviet institution arose, the *sharashka*: a prison in which engineers, scholars, and researchers worked in their fields of specialization for the interests of the state. At the large-scale building sites, in the super-factories, the specialists were monitored by armed guards. The largest construction site of the First Five-Year Plan, the Baltic-White Sea Canal, was built by prisoners under the leadership of 'engineer-wreckers'. Trotsky's dream of 'militarized labour' became a reality under Stalin in the form of the 'penalization of labour'. The gates of the camps were adorned with Stalin's words; "In the Soviet Union labor is a matter of honor, power and heroism."[37]

The reliance on slave labor has continued to be a stable feature of the Soviet system, as is demonstrated by the use of North Vietnamese conscripted labor in the construction of the Siberian gas pipeline over the past decade and in the Soviet policy with respect to nuclear accidents (such as that at Chernobyl, where Estonian conscripts were deployed).

On the genocidal character of agricultural collectivism, Nekrich and Heller write:

> The full story of this first socialist genocide has yet to be written. Chronologically, the first genocide of the twentieth century was that of the Armenians by the Turks. The massacre of Don Cossacks by the Bolsheviks during the civil war likewise approached genocidal proportions. The Turks destroyed a population of a different faith and nationality; the Cossacks suffered during a fratricidal civil war. The genocide against the peasants in the Soviet Union was unique not only for its monstrous scale; it was directed against an indigenous population by a government of the same nationality, and in time of peace.
>
> In 1945, after the defeat of Nazi Germany and the public disclosure of all its crimes, jurists, sociologists, psychologists, historians, and journalists began the inevitable controversy over whether the German people had known about the Nazi crimes or not. There is no question that the Soviet city people knew about the massacre in the countryside. In fact, no one tried to conceal it. Stalin spoke openly about the "liquidation of the kulaks as a class," and all his lieutenants echoed him. At the railroad stations, city dwellers could see the thousands of women and children who had fled from the villages and were dying of hunger. Kulaks, "dekulakized persons," and "kulak henchmen" died alike. They were not considered human. Society spat them out, just as the "disenfranchised persons" and "has-beens" were after October 1917, just as the Jews were in Nazi Germany.[38]

Again, it must be observed that the political creation of an artificial terror-famine with genocidal results is not a phenomenon restricted to the historical context of Russia and the Ukraine in the Thirties, but is a feature of Communist policy to this day, as evidenced in the sixties in Tibet and now in Ethiopia. The socialist genocide of small, "primitive" peoples, such as the Kalmucks[39] and many others, has been a recurrent element in policies at several stages in the development of Soviet and Chinese totalitarianism. Once again, communist policy in this respect faithfully reproduces classical Marxism, which had an explicit and pronounced contempt for small, backward, and reactionary peoples—no less than for the peasantry as a class and a form of social life. And the reliance on forced labor camps, like agricultural collectivization, was an inexorable consequence of the Marxist-Leninist project of eradicating one of the constitutive institutions of civil society, market exchange, together with its legal matrix in the institution of private property.

VII. Soviet Totalitarianism and Strategic Disinformation

The conventional methodology neglects or suppresses the economic role of the Gulag in the period of socialist construction, and it is silent as to the genocidal character of the policy of collectivization. This is so, in part at least, because of the high degree of control over information achieved under Soviet totalitarianism, and also because Western observers have often been reluctant to publicize information in their possession about the worst failings of the Soviet system. Thus the famine in the USSR in the early Thirties was little reported in the Western media, and Eugene Lyons writes in Chapter Fifteen of his autobiography, *Assignment in Utopia,* "The Press Corps Conceals a Famine," of his own participation in the suppression of what was then known of the millions of deaths the famine was causing.[40] The collaboration of the Western media with the Soviet authorities in concealing their worst atrocities is further exhibited in the silence which reigned in the Western media for about a quarter of a century as to the forcible repatriation and subsequent fate of over two million people claimed by the Soviet Union after the Second World War.[41] It is likely that Soviet responsibility for the Polish Katyn massacre will be admitted, under *glasnost,* by the Soviets themselves, before it is admitted by the British Foreign Office, which continues to adhere to the fiction of Nazi responsibility for that atrocity. The history of Vlasov's Russian Liberation Army (ROA), its role in the liberation of Prague, and its statement of enmity to Nazism and Stalinism in the Prague Manifesto have only recently been given an accurate historical statement.[42] Western authorities have colluded with Soviet authorities in concealing nuclear disaster and the existence of the nuclear Gulag.[43] It is only as a result of Soviet *glasnost* that the almost-apocalyptic ecological catastrophes in such areas as that surrounding Lake Aral have been publicized in the West. One of the many ironies of the present Soviet policy of *glasnost* is that, in focusing on aspects of Soviet history which in the West have been discussed only in rare, obscure, and neglected émigré journals, it has served to reveal the scope and limits of Western *glasnost.*

The dominant Western methodology goes most seriously astray in its neglect of the Soviet use of strategic disinformation. This blind spot in Western perception and theorizing is particularly disquieting, given the similarities evident between the current strategy of *glasnost* and the highly successful disinformation exercise conducted during the period of the New Economic Policy. Under the NEP, market relationships were partially restored in the economy; peasants in particular were free to charge market prices for their products, and so to enrich themselves. (When the NEP was ended by Stalin, the peasants found their new wealth liable to confiscation—a fact directly relevant to present Soviet experiments with cooperatives.)

This disinformation exercise was inaugurated along with the NEP in 1921 inside the USSR by the OGPU's formation of a false anti-Bolshevik organization, the Monarchist Alliance of Central Russia, otherwise known as the Trust, and operating under the cover title of the Moscow Municipal Credit Association, which replaced an earlier and genuine group destroyed by the OGPU in 1920. Unimportant in themselves, the historical details of the Trust are illuminating in revealing the mechanism of what Dziak has called "the prototypical deception and provocation operation in the Soviet repertoire."[44] The Trust operation had been proceeded by an earlier deceptive operation, usually known as Sindikat 1, in which the OGPU attempted to penetrate the organization of Boris Savinkov, former War Minister in the Kerensky government and a friend of the Polish leader Pilsudski and of Winston Churchill. A second operation, Sindikat 2, ran concurrently with the Trust, and successfully lured Savinkov back into the Soviet Union. Perhaps the first of the Soviet deception operations was that against the British agent, R. H. Bruce Lockhart, in the summer of 1918. It is possible that, at the same time, the British agent Sydney Reilly was "turned." In any case, Reilly claimed later to be convinced of the authenticity of the Trust; and like Sarinkov, he was persuaded to return to the Soviet Union, where he probably perished.[45]

The primary objective of the Trust was to weaken, divide, and neutralize the powerful anti-Soviet émigré movement that had arisen in Europe in the wake of the great Russian diaspora after the Civil War. Numbering over a million, of whom a quarter were White officers or men, the anti-Bolshevik émigrés constituted a threat the Soviet government could not afford to ignore. A secondary goal of the Trust was to persuade the governments and intelligence services of the Western powers that the revolutionary socialist government of the Bolsheviks was on the brink of a metamorphosis, of which the NEP was only an intimation, into a traditional Russian regime which could safely and easily be integrated into the international community.

The formation of the Trust was accompanied by the OGPU's capture of two important émigré movements, the "Changing Landmarks" movement and the "Eurasian" movement. Apparently originating as early as 1918 among the old intelligentsia in Russia, the movement found expression in several voices in 1920. In the summer of that year, a former Cadet leader and lawyer, Professor Gredeskul, undertook with the approval of the authorities a speaking tour of the Soviet Union. "Slavic Dawn," a Prague émigré newspaper, in a statement characteristic of the movement, affirmed that the Bolsheviks were now defenders of the Russian national interest. In the autumn of 1920 a collection of articles entitled *The Struggle for Russia* appeared in Harbin, Manchuria, which amounted to a seminal statement of "changing landmarks" ideology. Written by six members of the émigré community, of which Nikolai V. Ustryalov (a former Kadet and supporter of Admiral Kolchak) was most prominent, the collection appeared subsequently in Prague in 1921 under the title *Smena Vekh.* The theme of the collection—which was taken up by sympathizers within the conservative intelligentsia such as Shulgin, Efimovsky, and Klyuchnikov—was that the Bolshevik government was in the process of mutating into a nationalist dictatorship along the lines theorized in the writings of reactionary thinkers such as Konstantin Leontiev and Joseph de Maistre.

The movement received substantial unofficial support from the Soviet government, which facilitated the publication in Prague and Paris of a weekly magazine, *The Change of Signposts,* and a journal in Berlin called *On the Eve (Nakanune).* In 1922 the Soviet government allowed the movement to publish the journals *New Russia* and *Russia* in Leningrad and Moscow. *Smena Vekh* journals also appeared in Riga, Helsinki, Sofia, and Harbin. *Nakanune* survived with Soviet subsidies until it was closed in June 1924. A year and a half later, the Changing Landmarks movement was suppressed in the USSR. As Dziak comments: "*Nakanune* faithfully reflected the Soviet party line and was of immense value to Moscow as an émigré instrument of conversion in the Soviet cause . . . like the Trust, when it [the Changing Landmarks movement] had served its purpose it was eliminated."[46]

The Eurasian movement followed a similar pattern of evolution. In 1921 an anthology was published in Sofia entitled *Exodus to the East (Iskhod k Vostoku)* advocating Russian nationalism, the idea that the political culture of Russia was as Asiatic as it was European and speculating that the Bolshevik regime might be a proto-version of an appropriate authoritarian system for Russia. *Exodus to the East* was followed by a further seven volumes, the last appearing in 1931. A *Eurasian Chronicle* appeared in twelve volumes between 1925 and 1937. The Eurasian movement flourished until 1928, when it split and began to decline, but its importance continued well into the Thirties, when it was influential in gaining the collaboration of sympathetic émigrés with the Soviet government.

Between 1921 and 1927, the Trust organization achieved major successes in its campaign of disinformation. Leading émigré leaders such as Boris Savinkov and Generals Wrangel and Kutepov were contacted by Trust agents and convinced of the Trust's authenticity. The émigré leaders, in turn, were decisive in convincing Western intelligence services of the genuineness of the Trust. By the mid-1920s, it seems that no less than eleven Western intelligence services were heavily dependent on the Trust for information about developments in the Soviet Union.[47] For Western governments, the policy implication of the Trust was clear—the dissident forces within the Soviet state were to be aided by diplomatic recognition, the expansion of trade, and a curb on destabilizing anti-Soviet activism. Everything should be done that might ensure the success of the NEP. As Dziak has summarized this strategy: "the disinformation fostered through the Trust reinforced the initiatives of the NEP, which was also overseen by Dzerzhinsky in his dual capacity as chief of state security and chief of the Supreme Council of National Economy. From this perspective, the NEP itself served a deception purpose in that it helped to refinance Soviet industry at Western political and economic expense.[48]

From the standpoint of the Soviet leadership, the NEP and its associated disinformation exercises were indeed successes. Some ten percent or more of the Russian émigré community returned to the Soviet Union, including several of its leaders such as Savinkov and Kutepov. The émigré movement was never again a significant threat to the Soviet regime. Western powers assisted in the reconstruction of the Soviet economy—above all, Germany, which also built up the Soviet war machine. The NEP period was also a period of political consolidation for the Soviet regime. Vestiges of the old political parties in the Soviet Union were eliminated. Religious activity was brought firmly under political control in the pro-regime "living churches." Powerful nationalist movements in Georgia, the Ukraine, Armenia, and the Asian republics were suppressed, and these nations subjected to full annexation. Mongolia became the first Soviet satellite state. Twelve new Communist parties joined the Comintern. By the time Stalin closed down the NEP and wound up the Trust, it had substantially achieved its goals "to prevent internal revolt, expand foreign trade, attract foreign capital and expertise, gain diplomatic recognition from non-communist countries, prevent major conflict with the Western powers, help to exploit the contradictions in and between the capitalist countries, neutralize the emigre movement, and help to promote world revolution through the communist movement."[49]

There are ominous parallels between the disinformation exercises of the NEP period and current policies of *glasnost*. The objective of financing the reconstruction of the ruined Soviet economy with Western capital and technology is the same. Now, as then, Germany is likely to play a crucial role in supplying capital. An activist diplomacy is gaining major concessions from the Western powers, as a result of which the USSR can proceed with its program of modernizing its military forces while appearing to reduce its offensive capability. Side by side with a diplomacy which divides NATO, diminishing almost to a vanishing point the Western perception of Soviet enmity and so promoting the psychological disarmament of the West, the USSR has increased the activities of its intelligence services, particularly in Germany and Britain, with the objectives of expediting technology transfer and manipulating opinion. (The reorganization in 1987 of key departments within the KGB and GRU is likely to prove one of the more enduring achievements of perestroika.) Such are the clear parallels between current developments and the NEP period. They suggest that perestroika is best interpreted as a reversion to a Leninist strategy of disinformation and activist diplomacy (the latter encompassing exercises in tactical retreat, as in Afghanistan) and the abandonment of the clumsy, costly neo-Stalinist strategies of the Brezhnev period. They suggest that we are now witnessing the "sixth glasnost," the boldest yet, designed to destroy the Western perception of Soviet enmity and permit the Western refinancing of the Soviet system. As Epstein has put it: "By 1989, at virtually no cost to Soviet power, the sixth glasnost had provided the Soviet leadership with not only the tens of billions of dollars in credits it required to further expand its industrial (and military) capacity, but . . . was perceived as less of a threat to Western Europe than the United States."[50]

Granted these parallels, how are present developments to be understood as responses to the contemporary situation in the Soviet Union? I have specified the chief defects of the conventional methodology of Soviet studies as its reliance on standard techniques of analysis in political science and, in particular, its deployment of inchoate notions of political culture. This methodology neglects the structural affinities displayed by all communist regimes. In the present sections, I have argued that the conventional methodology neglects the potential for strategic disinformation possessed and exercised by the Soviet regime (not only in the Trust episode, but in later episodes such as the WIN operation in 1947–51).[51] The alternative line of analysis and theorizing developed here is that of the Soviet Union as a system constituted, from its inception, by Leninist ideology and a terroristic security service. We may even go as far as to concur with Dziak, and refer to the Soviet Union as "a counter-intelligence state."[52] On this view, the Soviet Union is a totalitarian order whose character as such is guaranteed by the KGB and whose role in representing the Soviet Union to the external world ought never to be underestimated. Current policies of *perestroika* and *glasnost,* on this alternative analysis, are authentically Leninist exercises in strategic deception.

The parallels between the present period and that of the NEP, suggested by the alternative methodology I have advanced, are real enough. Nevertheless, they do not of themselves account for the crucial differences in the historical contexts of the two episodes. By comparison with the NEP period, the USSR now confronts far graver problems of ethnic conflict, nationalist and separatist tendencies, religious and fundamentalist movements, and environmental degradation. For reasons I shall try to specify in a later section of this paper, it is far from clear that the economic renaissance of the NEP period, brief and partial as it was, can be repeated. Nor is it obvious or even plausible that infusions of Western credit can facilitate the resurrection of the USSR's senile industries. The financial burdens of the Soviet state, including an estimated 14 billion dollar per annum commitment of non-military support of the Eastern European communist regimes and an analogous commitment to Cuba, are incomparably greater than those of the fledgling Soviet state. Even if it was conceived as a ground deception, the policy of *glasnost* is extraordinarily risky for the Soviet leadership. Indeed, however it was conceived—and a Leninist interpretation of its inception seems by far the most plausible—the current Soviet policy confronts difficulties and hazards far greater than any that the Soviet regime has ever faced in peacetime. To theorize these phenomena, we need to abandon the blinkered perspective of Kremlinology, which has dominated Soviet studies for lack of any disciplined theoretical alternative. We need to ask: what are the real-world constraints that govern and constrain the Leninist strategy and tactics of the Soviet rulers? In order to answer this question, we must attempt, more directly and systematically, to theorize the constitutive features of Soviet totalitarianism.

VIII. Soviet Totalitarianism: Calculational Chaos in a Political State of Nature

Central to the Soviet totalitarian order are the failure of central planning and the political consequences of that failure. The War Communism episode shows that the Bolsheviks took seriously the Marxian commitment to the abolition of the institutions of market exchange. As Roberts and Stephenson have said: "Public ownership of property is not the defining characteristic of Marxian socialism; central planning is. In Marxian socialism, there is no exchange; therefore, there is no private property (rights to exchange)."[53] The suppression of private property follows from the abolition of commodity production, not vice versa. The project of replacing the institutions of market pricing with institutions of central planning confronts massive and insuperable difficulties, best theorized in the work of the Austrian economists Mises and Hayek.[54] The argument of Mises is that economic calculation presupposes market pricing: the information required for national resource-allocation—information about relative scarcities and consumer preferences, for example—is so complex that no central planning authority could possibly collect it. The number of transactions in a modern economy is so enormous that the planner will face an insuperable problem of calculation if he attempts to simulate market processes in a mathematical model. Hayek's argument focusses on the epistemological impossibilities of central planning rather than its practical difficulties: it is a problem of knowledge, not merely a problem of calculation, which is fatal to the socialist project of supplanting market institutions. The knowledge which the planner requires is dispersed knowledge, scattered about society, and it is often local knowledge of circumstances that are in their nature ephemeral. Most importantly, the knowledge possessed by economic agents is often practical knowledge, embodied in skills or dispositions, and only slightly theorized by the agent. Indeed, the tacit knowledge on which we all rely in our economic dealing may be only partly theorizable: it may contain elements, such as entrepreneurial perceptions or traditional practices, which cannot be given any full theoretical statement. Because much of it has this tacit or practical character, economic knowledge cannot be retrieved and collected by the planner. This last argument was developed independently by Michael Polanyi,[55] who saw that it imposed an insuperable limit on the planning both of science and the economy. In economic life, as in science, the planner is defeated by the fact that we always are making use of knowledge containing elements of which we are bound to remain ignorant, and we always know more than we can ever say.

In this Hayekian and Polanyian account, the role of market institutions is that of discovery procedures which allow for the disclosure and utilization of dispersed knowledge. This is a very different model from that of classical economic theory, in which the market is a device for relating scarce resources with competing ends. In the Hayekian-Polanyian model, no one has knowledge of the available resources: if the market exists to economize on anything, it is on knowledge, the most irremediably scarce resource of all.

The implications for economic policy and institutions of the Austrian calculation argument are radical. There is, first, the implication that in the absence of market pricing of most factors of production, there will be calculational chaos. This is a result which puts to rest not only the discredited Lange-Lerner model[56] of competitive socialism through the medium of market-simulating devices, but also the anachronistically fashionable idea of a market socialism of competing worker-cooperatives.[57] It demolishes the latter since, if the calculation argument applies at all, it has its clearest application to capital: it suggests that only market institutions can deploy the dispersed knowledge required for capital to be subject to an efficient allocation. This carries with it a second result for policy—that most factors of production, including most capital, be held in decentralized private ownership; or, in other words, that there is no viable middle way between the institutions of market capitalism and those of central planning.

The radical implication for current policy is that no program of *perestroika,* or economic reform, can hope to succeed which does not encompass dismantling the socialist system of ownership and dispersing its productive assets as private property. Such a policy of privatization is feasible, however, only on condition that the dispersed assets may be securely held and exchanged. This is in turn possible only under a rule of law in which private property is protected from arbitrary seizure by government. (It is the absence of the rule of law, and all that entails, that accounts for the lack of economic progress in non-totalitarian states such as the dictatorships of Latin America and Africa.) It is obvious that the institution of a rule of law would amount to the suppression of one of the key structural features of Soviet-style totalitarianism, since it would impose important constraints on the hitherto unlimited discretionary power of the state. We must ask ourselves: why might the ruling elites of a totalitarian state accept such a constraint on government? Answering this question requires examining the political environment of the Soviet economic chaos and the constraints imposed on feasible reform that it imposes.

IV. The Incentive Structures of Soviet Central Planning: A Public Choice Approach

The argument so far has been entirely epistemic. It has been the argument that central planning, whatever its goals or the motives of the ruling elites that control it, cannot achieve a rational allocation of resources. This is not to say that it cannot succeed in achieving specific and limited goals: the examples of the Soviet space program and the build-up of the Soviet war machine show that it can so succeed. Plausibly, however, it has done so only with the aid of Western technology, and only at the cost of displacing scarce resources from civilian uses and thereby further impoverishing Soviet society, including elements of its privileged *nomenklatura.* The epistemic argument—the argument that central economic planning is an epistemological impossibility—is important precisely because it is insensitive to the incentive structures that govern the planners. Its result is that the planners will fail in most of their objectives, whatever they are—whether or not they, for example, recognize consumer preferences, aim primarily to reward the *nomenklatura,* or simply want to modernize the war machine. As James Sherr has put it in his authoritative study, *Soviet Power: The Continuing Challenge:*

> Whatever its ostensible purpose, the elimination of the market and the creation of a command economy has one clear consequence: the who, what, and how of economic relations is determined by planners, not by those who produce and consume. It is the structure of the system that demands this, not the unimaginativeness or selfishness of those involved. An enterprise director cannot do what he considers best for society since, without the market's signals, he cannot know what this is. He may know the difference between a tractor that works and one which does not, but he cannot know how many tractors are required, what sort of tractors to build, and where they are most needed.[58]

One large part of the rationale of *perestroika* is indeed to achieve the three objectives specified above more effectively than is possible under central planning. The result of the calculation argument, however, is that economic reform is bound to fail—and that these objectives will be unachievable—without the reconstruction of a regime of private property under the rule of law. Failing that, the objectives of *perestroika* can be achieved, if at all, only by a massive Western refinancing of the Soviet system.

The predictive content of the calculation argument is that a centrally planned economy cannot exist. What exists under central planning institutions is a complex structure of parallel markets, relying on historic, capitalist, or black market prices, subject to recurrent episodes of authoritarian intervention. This theoretical result, worked out in Polanyian terms in Paul Craig Robert's *Alienation in the Soviet Economy,*[59] is amply corroborated by such excellent empirical studies as Peter Rutland's *The Myth of the Plan.* Rutland concludes: "it turns out that the structure of the command economy is not what one might naively expect to find—it is messy, overlapping and subject to endless and obscure organizational mutation."[60] At the present time, what exists in the Soviet Union is exactly that which is predicted in the calculation argument—a chaos which reproduces itself by covert reliance on parallel markets and by continuous mutations in the planning structures themselves.

We must consider the environment of incentives within which the planners operate independently of both the problems of knowledge which they confront and the larger structure of incentives which surrounds those who inhabit the Soviet state. For the planners, it is clear, all the incentives of the Soviet system point to conservatism and risk-avoidance rather than initiative or constructive investment. As Sherr has said, "Virtually extinct in the Soviet Union after sixty years of socialism is the linchpin of capitalism, the entrepreneur. (To the extent that he survives, he is apt to make the illegal second economy his habitat.)"[61] Planners are bound to be risk-averse in their investment polices, and, since no error-elimination mechanism for inefficient investments exists under central planning institutions, they have an incentive to conceal malinvestments by diverting further resources into them. Even aside from the insuperable epistemic problems, the command economy contains an incentive structure that is biased against efficiency. The very existence of the massive planning bureaucracies creates powerful interests against the liberalization of economic life. As Sherr puts it, "Replacement of plan by market is in itself a surrender of power, since it means the elimination of planners. At present, Soviet agriculture, and therefore the day-to-day lives of Soviet peasants, are regulated by hundreds of thousands of officials and 33 ministries. If production and exchange were henceforth to be determined by those who produce and consume, what functions would their former controllers then perform? What powers would the state still posses over those thus emancipated?" The economic interests of the planning bureaucracies only reinforce one of the defining features of Soviet totalitarianism, which is the obliteration of the economy as an element of an autonomous civil society. As Sherr concludes: "It is not the KGB, 'indomitable' as it is, which makes the Soviet Union a totalitarian society, nor even the CPSU's monopoly of political power, but the fusion of political and economic power. Monopoly of power—Stalin's first justification of the planning system—will probably be its last defence."[62] The same incentive structure that guarantees the economic inefficiency of the command economy also confers on it a powerful political stability.

The analysis we have developed so far has followed the Public Choice

School in attributing to planners the same motives we attribute to actors in the marketplace—it theorizes the bureaucrat as *homo economicus*. Another tool of the Public Choice School, game theory, may help to illuminate the structure of Soviet totalitarianism as a generalized Prisoner's Dilemma and therefore to explain its phenomenal stability.

X. Soviet Totalitarianism as a Political State of Nature and the New Hobbesian Dilemma of its Subjects

Soviet totalitarianism, like that in Communist China, differs from any kind of traditional despotism in virtue of its near-obliteration of civil life. This has a momentous consequence—that for all of its subjects, daily life must be conducted within the institutions of the Soviet state. It is the state, or one of its arms, that determines the job a person holds, the apartment he lives in, the education available to his children, and all of the other crucial dimensions of his life-chances. In the Soviet Union, to a far greater extent than in any Western country, housing, education, and employment are positional goods in that access to them is achieved primarily through position or influence in the Party or its subordinate hierarchies. It is of vital importance to understand that this is true not only of the exploitative *nomenklatura* but to virtually everybody in the Soviet system; it gives everyday life there an aspect of mutual predation lacking in societies where most goods are allocated by markets. It means that, in the Soviet Union, exchange is often a zero-sum transaction—what one gains, another loses. It means that, however estranged they may be from it, subjects of the Soviet state must daily renew its institutions, and thereby perpetuate it in existence. This is so even when they turn to the ubiquitous parallel economy for sustenance, since the illegal economic networks which enable it to reproduce itself exist only on its sufferance. For this reason, no subject of the Soviet system can escape contamination by its practices.

The characteristics of the Soviet totalitarian order as a political state of nature encompass a paradox, since in Hobbes and other contractarian thinkers the state of nature is (by definition) pre-political. Like all true paradoxes, however, this one contains an important truth. Soviet totalitarianism has in common with the Hobbesian state of nature, first and last, *lawlessness*. Without legal order, there are no protected domains of independence within which individuals may frame and enact their plans. Worse, since there is no law, anything may be judged to be illegal: every Soviet subject must live in a permanent legal twilight in which any act of his may be arbitrarily criminalized. Given that the necessities of daily life demand constant breaches of rules and regulations, every Soviet subject is permanently vulnerable for his infractions—but he would be so, even if by a miracle he had not breached any known rule, since the security organs still retain extrajudicial powers. Further, some laws—such as that against anti-Soviet activity—are susceptible to any interpretation. This condition of lawlessness brings into being an environment of *uncertainty* which also resembles that of the Hobbesian state of nature. For in it no one can be bound to keep agreements with others, save by extralegal means, and there is an incentive for everyone to use all available resources to protect his interests against possible attack by others. Power is vested in the Party and its organs. Thereby arises that process of constant *mutual predation,* so characteristic of Soviet life, in which Soviet subjects use the power of the Party to prey upon one another. Finally, even though it is far from being pre-political (indeed, everything in it is politicized), the Soviet totalitarian order is akin to the state of nature in that it lacks the institutions of civil society. To say that it is a political state of nature, then, is to say that it is a lawless polity, in which the war of all against all is conducted through the medium of the Party and its auxiliary institutions.

It is the genius of the system that it constrains its victims to renew it. The great majority of its subjects, including most of the *nomenklatura,* would undoubtedly be better off without it, but they are compelled to recreate it daily. Their exchanges are often not zero-sum so much as negative sum—they leave each worse off. In this the captives of the Soviet state resemble the denizens of Hobbes's state of nature, condemned by their insecurity to a war of all against all that none may escape. This is the Prisoner's Dilemma in a classic form: rational prudence as engaged in by each produces insecurity and impoverishment for all. The Soviet state is a phenomenon which even Hobbes's dark vision could not have foreseen—a Leviathan in which lawless power and a predatory state of nature are inextricably intertwined.

The darkest side of Communist totalitarianism—its ability to implicate its victims in its worst atrocities—has been well expressed by Simon Leys: "If totalitarianism were merely the persecution of an innocent nation by a small group of tyrants, overthrowing it would still be a relatively easy matter. Actually, the extraordinary resilience of the system resides precisely in its ability to associate the victims themselves with the all-pervasive organization and management of terror; to turn them into active collaborators and accomplices. In this way the victims acquire a personal stake in the defense and preservation of the very regime that is torturing and crushing them."[63] As he acknowledges, Ley's observation parallels many made by Alexander Zinoviev. We need not take literally Zinoviev's assertion that Stalin's power was the ultimate expression of the power of the people[64] to accept the insight it contains—that one of the chief sources of the stability of totalitarianism is its ability to implicate its victims in the terror and repression to which they and their fellows are subject.

One explanation of the stability of totalitarian orders, then, is in the morally compromised condition of their subjects. The endemic scarcity of the necessities of life, and their control by the Party and its subordinate organizations, condemns the Soviet subject to compete with his fellows in collaborating with the system that oppresses him. The impact of this daily necessity to lie, cheat, and distrust one's fellows, and thereby to renew the system by which all are held captive, is not illuminated by standard Arendtian notions of the atomization of social life in totalitarian orders.[65] Such atomization is real, but (as such observers as Havel have noted[66]) the impact of totalitarianism on personality is even more destructive. It tends toward the very fragmentation of personality—to a pervasive demoralization, anomie, and disintegration of the person that perhaps only Orwell foresaw. This is not to accept Alexander Zinoviev's extreme thesis that totalitarianism has indeed created a new man, *Homo sovieticus*,[67] whose personality has been entirely collectivized. The evidence is that, though he exists, *Homo sovieticus* is rare—most Soviet subjects retain their pre-Soviet ethnic, religious, and moral identities. Though they have thus survived intact, for the most part, the indentities of the subjects of totalitarian orders have been injured in ways that further compound the difficulties of moving toward a stable post-totalitarianism—a post-totalitarianism that is not anarchy or chaos.

XI. The Prospects for *Perestroika*

How might the Soviet political state of nature be transcended? Only, it seems, by the emergence of an Hobbesian sovereign. On the most benign interpretation to which it is subject, *perestroika* may be seen as the project of just such a sovereign—on the model, perhaps, of Peter the Great—aiming to construct a framework of law in the Soviet Union within which enterprise and civil society might shelter. In support of this interpretation might be cited Gorbachev's anti-corruption campaign and his frequent invocations of socialist legality.

In fact, the available evidence supports the opposite interpretation—that *perestroika* is in substance the project of suppressing the nascent forms of civil society that had begun to emerge during the Brezhnevite era of stagnation. During those two decades, there had occurred the large-scale growth of illegal businesses throughout the Soviet Union (but especially in Soviet Asia), controlled—and, indeed, owned—by Party bosses enjoying considerable autonomy. The forms of civil life represented and expressed in this "mafia" were thoroughly distorted by the totalitarian environment which they inhabited and on the basis of which their initial power rested. Nevertheless, the extensive network of parallel institutions which this "mafia" operated sustained the manifest prosperity of the provinces in which it operated, most particularly Uzbekistan and Kazakhstan, and it enabled a section of Soviet society to create a space within which quasi-autonomous institutions could exist and in which resources could be diverted from the control of the state to private ends.

In many parts of the Soviet Union, the so-called "era of stagnation" was in fact a period of illegal boom. It is precisely this prosperity which is being threatened or destroyed by *perestroika,* with its campaigns against corruption. Here we reach an insoluble contradiction in the policy: its objective of reasserting central Party control over local and regional satrapies is in irreconcilable conflict with the objective of economic renewal. Free markets and contractural exchange barely existed during the era of stagnation, but simulacra of them flourished on a grand scale in the parallel institutions of the illegal economy. Like black markets everywhere, those of the Soviet era of stagnation were inefficient, inequitable, and unworkable in enterprises requiring large injections of long-term capital. However, they mitigated the catastrophes of the central planning institutions, putting resources that would otherwise have been wasted to productive work and thereby generating a standard of living higher than any achievable by planning.

From the standpoint of the totalitarian Party, however, a flourishing parallel economy means a diversion of resources into a sphere that is not controlled by the state: a key objective of *perestroika* is therefore to reclaim these "privatized" resources for the state sector. In economic terms, the results of this policy have been, and can only be, disastrous. It entails disrupting and often destroying the principal efficient institutions of production and exchange in the Soviet economy. In political terms, *perestroika* expresses the project of renewing totalitarianism, of reincorporating within the totalitarian order the quasi-autonomous social forms that characterized the Brezhnev period. As Francois Thom has succinctly observed: "The Law against Unearned Income has signalled the start of an offensive against civil society in the purest Communist tradition."[68]

The economic aspect of *perestroika* will almost certainly fail. This is so not just because it tends to destroy the parallel institutions that have hitherto partly supplanted the planning institutions, but also because it deprives the planning institutions of signals from the parallel economy by which they have long been guided. A real shift to a market economy—the only way in which economic renewal can be achieved[69]—is excluded because it would entail the reconstitution of a civil society and the end of the totalitarian fusion of the economy with the polity. It is in any case doubtful whether the motives and dispositions needed to run a Western-style economy persist in the Soviet Union—particularly when everyone knows that the profits of enterprises established under *perestroika* are liable to NEP-style confiscation whenever the policy is reversed. After two generations of civil war against civil society, a market economy, along with other elements of civil life, can probably only exist in the interstices of the totalitarian state. The economic objectives of *perestroika* can be achieved, if at all, only in enclaves of the Soviet economy where Western capital is under Western management, and does not disappear into the abyss of the central planning institutions.

X. The Future of the Soviet Union: Ottomanization

If the Soviet case is treated as a paradigm, it has a clear implication: post-totalitarianism, the dissolution of totalitarian institutions and the reconstitution of civil society, is achievable by a process of internal evolution only in states where some civil institutions have remained intact. This result is corroborated by the Polish example, where the Church was never substantially incorporated into totalitarian administration, and by the Baltic states, where a flourishing parallel economy, together with a strong sense of nationhood, combined to limit the effectiveness of the postwar reconstruction on the Soviet totalitarian model. In these states, a reversion to totalitarianism could probably not be accomplished even by recourse to military repression, which (as in Poland in the early eighties) would instead achieve merely an authoritarian despotism. In the Soviet Union, a reversal of the policy of *glasnost* in the wake of economic collapse is, by contrast, likely to shatter the present precarious neo-totalitarian equilibrium and precipitate a return to totalitarianism. It is profitless to speculate on the forms that Soviet totalitarianism will assume in the period after the likely termination of the present policies. A recurrence to Brezhnevite "stagnation" and the "Ottomanization"[70] of the Soviet Union, with the provinces and the republics regaining a measure of *de facto* independence, seems the most benign outcome at present imaginable, but even that does not look very likely. The economic situation in the Soviet Union probably prohibits any such reoccurrence, with a catastrophic collapse and consequent widespread famine being predicted by Soviet economists in mid-1989 as real possibilities in the USSR two or three years hence.[71] A policy of military repression on the model of that applied in China in mid-1989, inaugurated in response to nationalist and religious disturbances themselves manipulated by local Party bosses, is well within the bounds of possibility. In the medium to longer term, a policy of exploiting Russian nativist sentiment—already evident in the leeway permitted to the Pamyat organization—may develop as a means of buttressing the totalitarian regime with populist support. Whatever the specific form it might take, a reversion to classical totalitarianism in the aftermath of economic collapse need not mean that the present policy has altogether failed. If it yields diplomatic victories and an influx of capital—with the current German-Soviet negotiations producing something akin to a second Treaty of Rapallo—the policy of *perestroika* might be assessed as having succeeded despite its economic failure, since it will have secured yet another lease on life for Soviet totalitarianism.

There is, however, another side to this scenario. Even if totalitarianism were to be reimposed in the Baltic states, say, and the neo-totalitarian project of *perestroika* reversed (along with *glasnost*) in the Soviet Union in the wake of economic collapse, the prospects for classical totalitarianism in the USSR over the longer term of a decade or more are poor. For even if the Soviet Union were to emulate the Chinese model, it would not return to wholesale Stalinist terror, which the majority within the Party would resist. It would instead rely solely on military force, together with selective police repression. In such circumstances, the maintenance of ideological conformity—the reproduction of the *Weltanschauung*-state—is likely to be an increasingly low priority. In other words, if there is a reversion to classical totalitarianism in the USSR, it is likely to be relatively brief, being followed by worsening economic crisis and a slow shift to an "Ottomanized" authoritarianism, held together (as in the era of stagnation) by military force, but against a background of worsening economic decline and increasing popular discontent. *Retotalitarianization,* if it occurs in the Soviet Union, will not last long—almost certainly, less than a generation. As Walicki has argued in his contribution to this volume,[72] the days of totalitarianism are numbered once the *nomenklatura* come to be concerned solely with self-reproduction and are no longer animated by a project of expansion. This is a result of our analysis which, when combined with the dire economic consequences of the project of retotalitarianization, bodes ill for the repressive policies of the current neo-Stalinist leadership in China.

It may even be the case that the Soviet Union is itself on the verge of launching into a transitional period of post-totalitarianism. The dramatic collapse of the Communist monopoly of power in the GDR, following on the dismantling of the Berlin Wall and the no less sudden blossoming of popular opposition in Czechoslovakia, may be interpreted (if the analysis developed earlier has any plausibility) as tactical moves in a Soviet strategy of "reverse Findlandization," modeled on the authentically Leninist paradigm of the Treaty of Brest-Litovsk (which in 1918 ceded large parts of Russia, including the whole of the Ukraine, to Germany). The aim of this strategy is to secure the rapid decoupling of the United States and Western Europe (which American economic weakness in any case renders inevitable in the medium term) and the neutralization of most of Western Europe at the cost of Soviet withdrawal from Eastern Europe. Even if, as is likely, this strategy is successful, it is an extraordinarily dangerous one for the Soviet Union to adopt. It risks strengthening secessionist movements within the Soviet Union and triggering new movements for independence in areas (such as Soviet Central Asia) which have, until now, been quiescent. If such a scenario of internal disintegration were to begin to unfold in the USSR, the most likely outcome would not be a project of retotalitarianization, but instead recourse to classical authoritarian measures of martial law and police repression. In that eventuality, however, the Soviet Union would have become irreversibly post-totalitarian.

The prospects of the experiments in controlled democracy in Hungary and Poland will depend mainly on the degree of success each achieves in its policy of economic reform. Even in these comparatively favorable cases, the shift to a market economy will involve dislocations and costs that may destabilize the fragile political settlements achieved there. In Poland, the economic program of Solidarity is not wholly coherent, but even a consistent policy of full marketization carries with it the risk of dividing Solidarity in the country from Solidarity in the city (and for that reason finds little favor outside the Party). In Hungary, which has passed from a non-terroristic totalitarianism sustained chiefly (as was long the case in Czechoslovakia) by economic sanctions to a controlled democracy without any significant intervening phase of post-totalitarianism, the political settlement may appear even more precarious. Recourse to repression in Hungary may, however, be rendered less likely by the role that Hungary may play in Gorbachev's European diplomacy. Here Hungary and Poland are very different: though they have in common an economic crisis, including an unsustainable foreign debt, they are to be distinguished in that developments in Poland have arisen endogenously, whereas in Hungary they occur at least in part in response to exogenous pressures from within the Party and, perhaps, the Soviet Union. For this reason, repression could be achieved more easily in Hungary than in Poland should policy undergo a major reversal in the Soviet Union and its European diplomacy be dislocated, or the domestic Hungarian political process be destabilized by economic collapse.

In both Poland and Hungary, the danger exists of a recourse to a post-Communist dictatorship as the necessary political mechanism for the transition to a market economy. Such a "Pinochet solution" to the transition problems of dismantling the centralized economy is unlikely to occur in Czechoslovakia or Eastern Germany, with the former returning to the strong social-democratic traditions of the postwar years and the latter eventually being integrated into West German democratic institutions as part and parcel of the inexorable process of reunification. In the rest of Eastern Europe, classical Communist totalitarianism is already showing signs of weakness (as in Bulgaria), and even Romania may not prove immune to change or collapse. In these parts of Eastern Europe, however, the project is of *re-Balkanization* rather than of transition to civil society. The model for such a prospect, in these parts of Eastern Europe (and, indeed, in the Soviet Union), may be contemporary Yugoslavia, with its intractable ethnic conflicts, profound economic problems, weak populist governments, and chronic tendencies toward disintegration. In all these areas, post-totalitarianism may mean political authoritarianism superimposed on social and economic chaos.

The answer to the question with which we began—what must be true for post-totalitarianism to be a possibility?—has proved to be that important elements of civil society must remain intact if the transition to a full civil society is to be achieved. Where, as in the Soviet Union, these are lacking, totalitarianism can be succeeded only by authoritarianism or chaos—or, most likely, a mixture of the two. Even in Poland, where civil society was never fully suppressed, the conflicts of interest generated by a policy of marketization could produce considerable political instability and endanger the otherwise well-conceived policy of buying off the *apparatchik* class. The possibility suggests itself, in light of these considerations, that the task of reforming a Communist economy confronts problems that are in most cases insoluble. Like the Soviet Union itself, many of the states of the Soviet bloc (even where a return to classical totalitarianism is not a realistic prospect) cannot be expected to fulfill the first condition of a stable post-totalitarianism, which is a stable market economy. They must expect, not the reconstitution of civil society, but Ottomanization—the process of decline, corruption, and the waxing of the institutions of the parallel economy that characterized the era of stagnation in the Soviet Union, but in a context of worsening economic conditions for the entire bloc.

Except perhaps in Poland, Hungary, Czechoslovakia, and East Germany, the waning of totalitarianism, as it seems likely to occur over the medium term—primarily for economic reasons but accelerated by ethnic and nationalist conflicts—is unlikely to be accompanied by the waxing of civil society. For the foreseeable future, chaos and instability, contained only by the recurrent threat and exercise of military force, seem the most likely outcome for the USSR. The reform policy of *perestroika,* in the end, founders on the overwhelming likelihood that the transition from totalitarianism cannot, save in exceptional circumstances, be conducted in an orderly fashion. Instead, it is to be seen as the prelude to a process of repression, decline, and instability that resembles the beginnings of revolution more than it does any kind of reform.

XIII. The Cultural Origins of Soviet Totalitarianism

On the account I have tried to develop, the Soviet totalitarian regime primarily owes its stability to internal factors—to the public choice problems generated by any move to a civil society and to the new Hobbesian dilemma that constrains its subjects. I have also argued that Western aid has been decisive in enabling the regime to recover from crisis and to expand. The upshot of my account has been to confirm the soundness of Lenin's insight into the dynamics of Western capitalist states—which, Lenin prophetically observed, were bound to compete with each other in forming the Soviet state. This competition, like the Prisoner's Dilemma that sustains the Soviet totalitarian order internally, is doubtless statable in game-theoretic terms. It goes far in explaining the lack of effective Western strategy in regard to the Soviets as well as the strategic advantage the Soviets have in formulating long-range policy in regard to the West.

The question arises as to why Western opinion has systematically misunderstood the nature of the Soviet regime, and in particular why Western opinion lacks any perception of the enmity of the Soviet Union to Western civil societies. I submit that a major part of the explanation for this blindness is in the fact that Soviet Communism has its roots in elements of the most ancient, central, and fundamental Western traditions—and not, as the conventional wisdom supposes, in Russian political or religious culture.

What are the cultural origins of Soviet communism? In order to answer this question we must ask another: what are the intellectual antecedents of Marxism? Kolakowski has located one source of Marxism in the Greek, and especially the Neo-Platonic, preoccupation with the contingency of human existence, which was transmitted to Marx via Hegel.[73] In this account, Marxism is a secularized version of the mystical soteriology of Greek Platonism in which a return to the unalienated human essence replaces reabsorption in the Absolute as the form of salvation and release from contingency. Kolakowski's analysis neglects or underestimates the contribution of Judeo-Christian traditions to the intellectual and moral formation of Marxism. For it was Christianity, with its conception of human history as a moral drama, which allowed the Platonistic soteriology to be transformed into an historical theodicy. This is the insight captured by Voegelin in his interpretation of modern political religions as gnostic immanentizations of Christian eschatology. As Voegelin puts the point: "The characterization of modern political mass movements as neopagan, which has a certain vogue, is misleading because it sacrifices the historically unique nature of modern movements to a superficial resemblance. Modern redivinization has its origins rather in Christianity itself, deriving from components that were suppressed as heretical by the universal church."[74] Voegelin's analysis parallels that of de Jouvenel, who observes, "It is a curious thing, moreover, but true, that political applications of the Christian idea of man grew and multiplied at the very time Christian theology was rejected."[75] The same point is made by Michael Polanyi: "Had the whole of Europe been at the time of the same mind as Italy, Renaissance Humanism might have established freedom of thought everywhere, simply by default of opposition. Europe might have returned to—or if you like relapsed into—a liberalism resembling that of pre-Christian antiquity. Whatever may have followed after that, our present disasters would not have occurred."[76]

On this interpretation, Marxism is a Christian-historicist gloss on a Greek doctrine of salvation. It should be noted here, however, that contrary to the conventional academic wisdom, Western Christianity is far more implicated in the generation of Marxism than Eastern Christianity. For Western Christianity imbibed the elements of Aristotelian rationalism as transmitted via Aquinas into the medieval world, together with the humanist values of the Renaissance and the secularizing impact of the Reformation, which had little impact on Russian Orthodoxy. For Orthodoxy, with the exception of a few iconoclastic thinkers (such as the early Berdyaev[77]), Marxism represented the incursion of a Western ideology into Russian Christianity—and one which, furthermore, had emerged in the West partly because of the decadence of Western Christianity. This is not to deny that, as Besancon has shown,[78] Soviet communism has some sources in an alienated Russian intelligentsia—a point emphasized by Solzhenitzyn[79] and prophetically made by Dostoyevsky.[80] It is to question the common Western belief that Soviet communism was ever sustained by elements in Russian religious life—against which it has waged a perpetual war.

It is from its expression of the central tenets of the European Enlightenment, however, that Marxism—and its embodiment in Soviet Communism—derives its essential appeal to Western intellectual opinion. It is here that the Jacobin lineage of Leninism and the character of the French Revolution as the first precursor of twentieth-century experiments in social engineering via the mass liquidation of entire social groups need to be noted. The recent revisionist historiography[81] of the French Revolution has noted its terrorist nature; in particular the fact that, whereas at the time the Bastille was stormed, it contained fewer than ten inmates, by the time the Terror had run its course around half a million Frenchmen were incarcerated for political reasons, many of whom would perish in jail. We know that Lenin was himself much influenced by the Jacobin precedent as an early experiment in what Talmon has well called "totalitarian democracy."[82] There seems to be good reason, then, to see a clear historical linkage between the two revolutions, both as to their goals, their strategies, and the types of institutions they produced.

It is in the common origins in the secular faith of the Enlightenment that the affinity of the two revolutions is most plainly seen. The ideas of a self-consciously planned society and of a universal civilization grounded in scientific knowledge are central elements of that religion of humanity that is expressed in both Marxism and liberalism. They express, in a distinctively modernist fashion, values and beliefs—rationalistic and optimistic—derived both from the Greco-Roman classical tradition and the Judeo-Christian tradition that are coeval with Western civilization. It is in this truth that the central paradoxes of totalitarianism are to be found: the paradoxes of its enmity to the civilization that gave it birth and the paradox that, though Marxism-Leninism is a modernist ideology, Soviet totalitarianism is at war with the most fundamental institutions of the modern world as it has thus far developed. We may justly judge that von Laue exaggerates greatly when he avows that "it was the West which, by the model of its superior power, has shaped the Soviet dictatorship. Soviet totalitarianism has basically no more than the caricature echo of Western state and society, the best copy feasible under Russian conditions."[83] Von Laue's extreme overstatement, like the claim that Western societies have totalitarian aspects, nevertheless expresses a grain of truth—the truth is the claim that totalitarian ideology has its roots in Western tradition, and totalitarian regimes are episodes in the global process of Westernization, aberrant and distorted not by the traditional societies which they destroy but by elements within the Western tradition itself.

Western opinion's blind spot in regard to the nature of Soviet Communism is congenital and incorrigible. It expresses an integral part of the Western worldview. One may even say without too much exaggeration that just as totalitarianism is only the shadow of modern civil society, so Soviet Communism is only the shadow cast by the European Enlightenment. A realistic perception of Soviet enmity to Western civil societies presupposes an insight into the defects or limitations of Western traditions of which the animating ideology of the Soviet regime is an authentic development. Nothing supports the hope that Western opinion is capable of the self-criticism such an insight requires. If it comes to pass, the fall of Soviet totalitarianism is most likely to occur as an incident in the decline of the occidental cultures that gave it birth, as they are shaken by the Malthusian, ethnic, and fundamentalist conflicts which—far more than any European ideology—seem set to dominate the coming century.[84]

October 1989

NOTES

1. For the use of the word "totalitarian" by Italian theorists of fascism, see L. Schapiro, *Totalitarianism* (London: Macmillan, 1983), pp. 13–15; E. Nolte, *Marxism, Fascism, Cold War* (Assen, The Netherlands: Van Gorcum 1982), pp. 137–8.
2. A good compilation of the postwar literature may be found in C. J. Friedrich (ed.), *Totalitarianism* (Cambridge: Harvard University Press, 1954).
3. For a good survey of the literature that argues against the concept of totalitarianism in the Soviet and Eastern European contexts, see A. Gleason, "Totalitarianism," *Russian Review,* vol. 45 (1984), pp. 145–59.
4. For an argument that modern capitalist societies are totalitarian, see H. Marcuse, *One Dimensional Man* (London: Sphere Books, 1964), p. 105ff.
5. See M. Heller, *Cogs in the Soviet Wheel: The Formation of Soviet Man* (London: Collins Harvill, 1988).
6. R. Pipes, *Russia under the Old Regime* (London: Weidenfeld and Nicolson, 1974), p. 317.

7. Barrington Moore, Jr., *Social Origins of Dictatorship and Democracy,* (London: Penguin Press, 1967), p. 206.
8. Leonard Schapiro, *Totalitarianism* (London: Macmillan, 1972), p. 23.
9. E. Nolte, *Marxism, Fascism, Cold War* (Assen, the Netherlands: Van Gorcum, 1982), sec. B.
10. The economical exposition of the five-point totalitarian syndrome appears in C. J. Friedrich, "The Unique Character of Totalitarian Society" in Friedrich, *Totalitarianism,* pp. 47–59.
11. Perhaps the best defense of this view may be found in Pipes, *Russia under the Old Regime.*
12. A. Walicki, *Legal Philosophies of Russian Liberalism* (Oxford: Clarendon Press, 1987).
13. Norman Stone, *Europe Transformed, 1878–1918* (London: Fontana, 1983), p. 200; John J. Dziak, *Chekisty: A History of the KGB,* (Lexington: Lexington Books, D. C. Heath and Company, 1988), Appendix, pp. 173–76.
14. I owe this, and other statistics, to M. Heller and A. Nekrich's magnificent *Utopia in Power: The History of the Soviet Union from 1917 to the Present* (New York: Summit Books, 1986), p. 15ff.
15. Stone, *Europe Transformed,* p. 197.
16. *ibid.,* p. 200ff.
17. D. Luver, *Russia's Rulers under the Old Regime* (New Haven and London: Yale University Press, 1989), p. 290.
18. Heller and Nekrich, *Utopia in Power,* p. 15.
19. Dziak, *Chekisty,* p. 173ff. The term NKYU refers to the People's Commariat of Justice.
20. *ibid.,* p. 35.
21. Cited in *ibid.,* p. 33.
22. R. Pipes, *Russia under the Old Regime,* pp. 301–2.
23. A. Besancon, *The Soviet Syndrome* (New York: Harcourt Brace Jovanovich, 1976), p. 56.
24. On the significance of the Shakhty trial of engineers, see Heller and Nekrich, *Utopiain Power,* pp. 211–12.
25. *ibid.,* p. 213.
26. *ibid.,* p. 701.
27. *New York Times,* July 31, 1989.
28. See E. H. Carr, *The Russian Revolution from Lenin to Stalin, 1917–29* (London: Macmillan, 1964); and M. Dobb, *On Economic Theory and Socialism: Collected Papers,* (London; Routledge and Kegan Paul, 1955).
29. P. C. Roberts, *Alienation and the Soviet Economy,* (Alberquerque: University of New Mexico Press, 1971); T. Remington, *Building Socialism in Bolshevik Russia* (Pittsburgh: University of Pittsburgh Press, 1984); S. Malle, *The Organization of War Communism, 1918–21* (Cambridge: Cambridge University Press, 1985).
30. Dziak, *Chekisty,* pp. 32–33.
31. *ibid.,* p. 25.
32. *ibid.,* p. 29.
33. A. Nove, *An Economic History of the USSR* (London: Penguin Press, 1969), p. 198.

34. *ibid.,* p. 266.
35. *ibid.,* p. 180.
36. *ibid.,* p. 379.
37. Heller and Nekrich, *Utopia in Power,* p. 264.
38. *ibid.,* pp. 235–36. It is not intended by Heller and Nekrich, I take it, to equate the communist genocides with the Nazi Holocaust, since the latter clearly has dimensions that are incommensurable with other twentieth century genocides. The intention is simply to note that the Stalinist policy of collectivization was genocidal in character.
39. On this, see Robert Conquest's excellent book, *The Nation-Killers* (London: Macmillan, 1960).
40. Eugene Lyons, *Assignment in Utopia* (New York: Harcourt Brace and Co., 1937), pp. 572–80.
41. On this, see N. Bethell, *The Last Secret* (London: Fontaine, 1974).
42. See the path-breaking study by C. Andreyev, *Vlasov and the Russian Liberation Movement: Soviet Reality and Émigré Theories* (Cambridge, Cambridge University Press, 1987).
43. The nuclear Gulag is that portion of the Soviet system in concentration camps in which prisoners are required to service nuclear installations and devices.
44. Dziak, *Chekisty,* p. 52.
45. See *ibid.,* p. 47.
46. *ibid.,* p. 49. Further data about the "changing landmarks" movement and the Trust operation are to be found in Heller and Nekrich, *Utopia in Power,* pp. 148–49; Andreyev, *Vlasov and the Russian Liberation Movement,* pp. 175–77; Golitsyn, *New Lies for Old,* p. 12; Edward Jay Epstein, *Deception,* (New York: Simon and Schuster), p. 25.
47. Epstein, *Deception,* p. 25.
48. Dziak, *Chekisty,* pp. 49–50.
49. A. Golitsyn, *New Lies for Old* (London: Bodley Head, 1984), p. 12. Golitsyn's predictions for the next stage of Soviet development, made no later than 1983, are perhaps worth quoting in full:

    "Political "liberalization" and "democratization". . . . [in the USSR] would be spectacular and impressive. Formal pronouncements might be made about a reduction in the communist party's role; its monopoly would be apparently curtailed. An ostensible separation of powers between the legislative, the executive, and the judiciary might be introduced. The Supreme Soviet would be given greater apparent power and the president and deputies greater apparent independence. The posts of president of the Soviet Union and first secretary of the party might well be separated. The KGB would be "reformed." Dissidents at home would be amnestied; those in exile abroad would be allowed to return, and some would take up positions of leadership in government. Sakharov might be included in some capacity in the government or allowed to teach abroad. The creative arts and cultural and scientific organizations, such as the writers' unions and Academy of Sciences, would become apparently more independent, as would the trade unions. Political clubs would be opened to nonmembers of the communist party. Leading dissidents might form one or more alternative political parties. Censorship would be relaxed; controversial books, plays, films, and art would be published, performed, and exhibited. Many prominent Soviet performing artists now abroad would return to the Soviet Union and resume their professional careers. Constitutional amendments would be adopted to guarantee fulfillment of the provisions of the Helsinki agreements and a semblance of compliance would be maintained. There would be greater freedom for Soviet citizens to travel. Western and United Nations observers would be invited to the Soviet Union to witness the reforms in action . . . .

"Liberalization" in Eastern Europe would probably involve the return to power in Czechoslovakia of Dubcek and his associates. If it should be extended to East Germany, demolition of the Berlin Wall might even be comtemplated.

Western acceptance of the new "liberalization" as genuine would create favorable conditions for the fulfillment of communist strategy for the United States, Western Europe, and even, perhaps, Japan."

I do not intend to endorse Golitsyn's theories, but simply to note the respects in which his expectations have been corroborated by events.

50. For an explanation of the term "the sixth glasnost," see Epstein, *Deception,* p. 279.
51. See, for data on the WIN operation, Dziak, *Chekisty,* pp. 49–50.
52. *ibid.,* p. 5.
53. P. C. Roberts and M. Stephenson, *Marx's Theory of Exchange, Alienation and Crisis* (Stanford: Hoover Institution Press, 1973), p. 94.
54. For an excellent account of the Austrian calculation debate, see D. Lavoie, *Rivalry and Central Planning: The Socialist Calculation Debate Reconsidered* (Cambridge: Cambridge University Press, 1985).
55. See Michael Polanyi, *The Logic of Liberty* (Chicago: University of Chicago Press, 1951).
56. On the Lange-Lerner model, see Lavoie, *Rivalry and Central Planning,* ch. 5.
57. I have criticized the market socialism of competing worker-cooperatives in my book *Liberalisms: Essays in Political Philosophy,* (Routledge: London and New York, 1989), ch. 10.
58. James Sherr, *Soviet Power: The Continuing Challenge* (London: Macmillan, 1987), p. 27.
59. P. C. Roberts, *Alienation in the Soviet Economy* (Albuquerque: University of New Mexico Press, 1971).
60. Peter Rutland, *The Myth of the Plan* (London: Hutchinson, 1985), p. 183.
61. Sherr, *Soviet Power,* p. 30.
62. *ibid.,* p. 31.
63. Simon Leys, *The Burning Forest* (New York: Henry Holt and Co., 1985), p. 167.
64. Alexander Zinoviev, *The Reality of Communism* (London: Paladin Books, 1985).
65. H. Arendt, *The Origin of Totalitarianism* (London: Macmillan, 1958).
66. See V. Havel *et al., The Power of the Powerless* (New York: M. E. Share, Inc., 1985).
67. A Zinoviev, *Homo Sovieticus* (London: Paladin Books, 1985).
68. Francois Thom, *Gorbachev, Glasnost and Lenin: Behind the New*

Thinking (London: Policy Research Publications, 1988), p. 12.
69. For an analysis that parallels mine, see L. Sirc, *What Must Gorbachev Do?* (London: Centre for Research into Communist Economies, 1989) Occasional Paper Two.
70. As far as I know, the term "Ottomanization" was first used in the context of Soviet affairs by Timothy Garton Ash. See his book, *The Uses of Adversity* (Cambridge: Granta Books, 1989), pp. 188, 227–31. For details of the secessionist movements in Lithuania, see *Radio Free Europe Research,* January 5, 1989; for similar developments in Soviet Moldavia, see *Radio Free Europe Research,* February 9, 1989.
71. As reported in *The New York Review of Books,* August 17, 1989, p. 24.
72. See Walicki's contribution to this volume.
73. L. Kolakowski, *Main Currents of Marxism, Volume One: The Founders,* (Oxford: Clarendon Press, 1978), ch. 1.
74. See Eric Voegelin, *The New Science of Politics* (Chicago: University of Chicago Press, 1952), p. 107ff.
75. B. de Jouvenel, *Sovereignty* (London: Routledge and Kegan Paul, 1950), p. 48.
76. M. Polanyi, *The Logic of Liberty* (Chicago: University of Chicago Press, 1951), p. 62.
77. See N. Berdyaev, *The Origins of Russian Communism* (Ann Arbor: University of Michigan Press, 1960).
78. See Alain Besancon, *The Rise of the Gulag: Intellectual Origins of Leninism* (New York: Continuum, 1981).
79. See A. Solzhenitzyn, *August 1914: The Red Wheel,* London: Bodley Head, 1989.
80. See, especially, Dostoyevsky's great novel, *The Possessed.*
81. For a brilliant demystification of the French Revolution, see Rene Sedillot, *Le Cout de la Revolution* (Paris, 1987).
82. See Besancon, *The Rise of the Gulag,* ch. 12, for Jacobin aspect of Leninism. J. Talmon's *The Origins of Totalitarian Democracy* (London: Macmillan, 1952) is also relevant here.
83. Theodore H. von Laue, *Why Lenin? Why Stalin? A Reappraisal of the Russian Revolution, 1900–1930* (New York, Lippincott Company, 1971), p. 213.
84. For their comments on this paper, I am indebted to Fred D. Miller, Jeffrey Paul, Z. Rau, Roger Scruton, S. Sencerz, and A. Walicki. I am particularly indebted to Ellen Paul for her detailed written comments.

Four Stages of One Path out of Socialism

Zbigniew Rau

A generation ago, roughly between Tito's break with Stalin and the Prague Spring, the crucial issue—not only for Marxist intellectuals but for the Communist leaderships and, indeed, for the societies of the socialist countries—was the question of whether there was one (universal Soviet) or there were many (particular national) paths to socialism. In domestic issues, the notion of many paths to socialism was a modification of the previous Stalinist model. While satisfying some aspirations of particular societies (for example, by giving up the notion of collectivization in Yugoslavia and Poland), it still did not challenge the Communist parties' monopoly of control over the political, economic, and ideological spheres of public life. This was the common feature of the national paths to socialism in Yugoslavia after the reforms of the early fifties, in Poland after the "Polish October" in 1956, and (to some extent) in Czechoslovakia during the Prague Spring reform attempts in 1968.

Today, the concept of many paths to socialism still has committed advocates among some Communist leaders. Yet, ironically enough, it is no longer the hallmark of reformers in the Communist ranks, the heirs of Tito, Gomulka, or Dubcek, but rather that of the upholders of the status quo, such as Ceausescu or Castro. These are leaders who are eager to avoid the impact of the current reforms in the Soviet Union upon their countries. Nevertheless, precisely because of the impact of the Soviet "new thinking" on the situation in Eastern Europe, the concept of many national paths to socialism has generally lost its previous political significance. Indeed, especially in light of the obvious Soviet consent to the recent reforms in Poland and Hungary, these days it would be much more tempting to talk about many national paths *out of* socialism.[1]

However, I will argue here that there are not many national paths but rather one universal path out of socialism, both for the Soviet republics and for the countries of Eastern Europe. This is the case regardless of the national variation of socialism—that is, for example, Soviet, Polish or Yugoslav. Unlike the process of following different national paths to socialism, the process of taking one universal path out of socialism does not depend upon the program or policy of the Communist parties. Rather, it results from the activity of social forces independent of these parties. Yet this process may be accelerated by party initiatives (as in the case of *glasnost* and *perestroika*) or slowed down by them (as in the case of the imposition of martial law in Poland in 1981).

The essence of the process under discussion is the shift from the system in which the Communist party enjoys its monopolistic position in society and the state to a system where pluralistic civil society exercises, through a multi-party system, its sovereign prerogatives in a democratic state. In principle, there are four stages of this process: first, the emergence of dissident groups; second, the establishment of massive revindication movements; third, the launching of independent political parties; and fourth, the taking of power in competitive elections by these parties.

The seizure of power by Communist parties or by the conquest of the Red Army, wherever it has occurred, has meant the destruction of civil society. By civil society, I understand a society in which various segments exercise control over (to different extents) political and economic power and ideological influence. In any given Communist country before the Communist takeover, civil society had been, as a whole, an active subject and not a passive object of the political, economic, and ideological processes in the state. Indeed, using various institutions independent of the state, such as political parties, business associations, trade unions, and the media, civil society was in a position to pursue different political, economic, and ideological goals (See Diagram 1). Of course, there had been important differences between the extent to which various segments of civil society were able to pursue the goals of their members under democratic and non-democratic regimes. For example, in the 1930s the Czechoslovakians were much more powerful in expressing their various goals than the Poles, since the Czechoslovakian constitutional system and political practice during that period were democratic while the Polish ones were authoritarian. For precisely the same reasons, the Russians under the provisional government in 1917 enjoyed many more opportunities for self-expression in public life than the Romanians did under the personal rule of King Charles II in the late 1930s. Nevertheless, in the experience of Russia and the East European countries immediately before the Communist takeover, there was no regime which managed—or, indeed, even tried—to deprive these societies of all influence in the political, economic, and ideological spheres.

After the Communist takeover, these independent structures of civil society were replaced by the Center: that is, the party/state leadership. The Center combined three mutually interacting branches: the political (control of the police and army) the economic (planning and control of economic activity and distribution), and the ideological (imposition of the officially established ideology and control of the channels of mass communication).[2] Therefore, the establishment of the Center resulted in political, economic, and ideological alienation of civil societies in socialist countries. Having destroyed autonomous organizations and replaced them with those of its own making, the Center was in a position

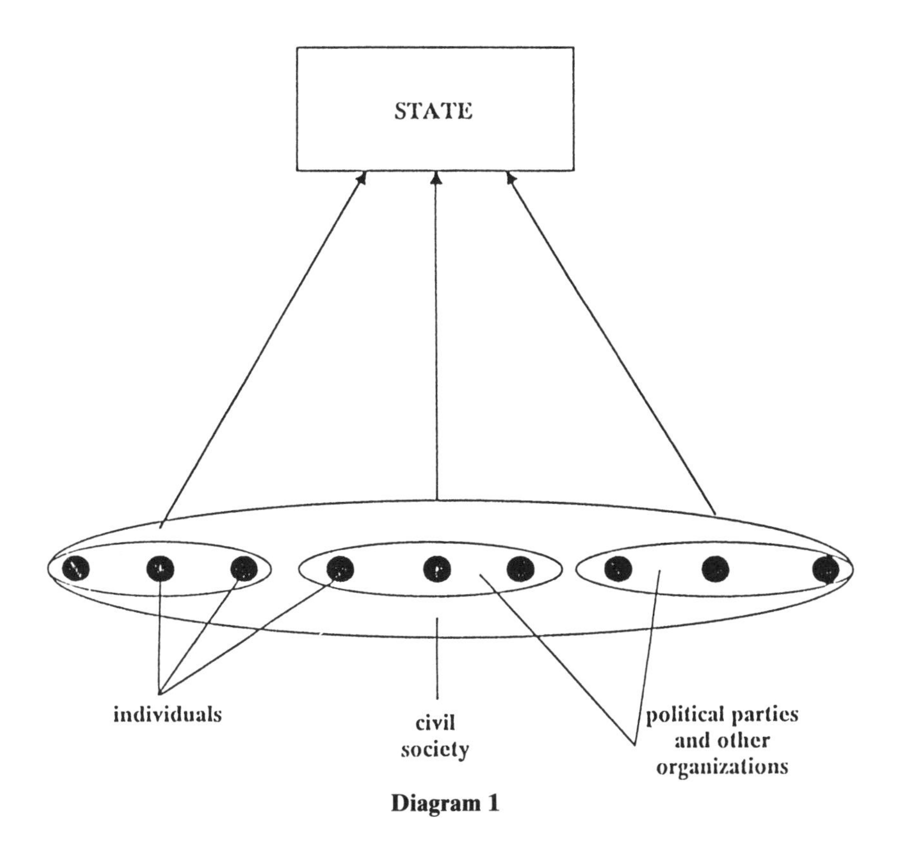

Diagram 1

to implement its policy towards individual members of these societies in almost all aspects of public life (See Diagram 2).

The success of this alienation was based upon the special isolation of the individual. A proper understanding of this isolation is crucial to the argument pursued here. At first glance, the individual seems to live a normal life as a member of the natural community—that is, of the family as well as of other groups such as productive units, professional associations, and so on. Accordingly, this isolation has nothing to do with a physical atomization which would render the business of state impossible. Rather, it is expressed in the ideological, political, and economic sphere of human life. The individual is required to identify himself with and promote the single system of official morality by his membership, participation, and activity in the political institutions and economic structures established and supervised by the Center. The essence of this state of affairs is that the individual makes no attempt to get in touch with others in order to put into effect a concept of ideological, economic, or political arrangements which could serve as an alternative to the official one. Such isolation of the individual and

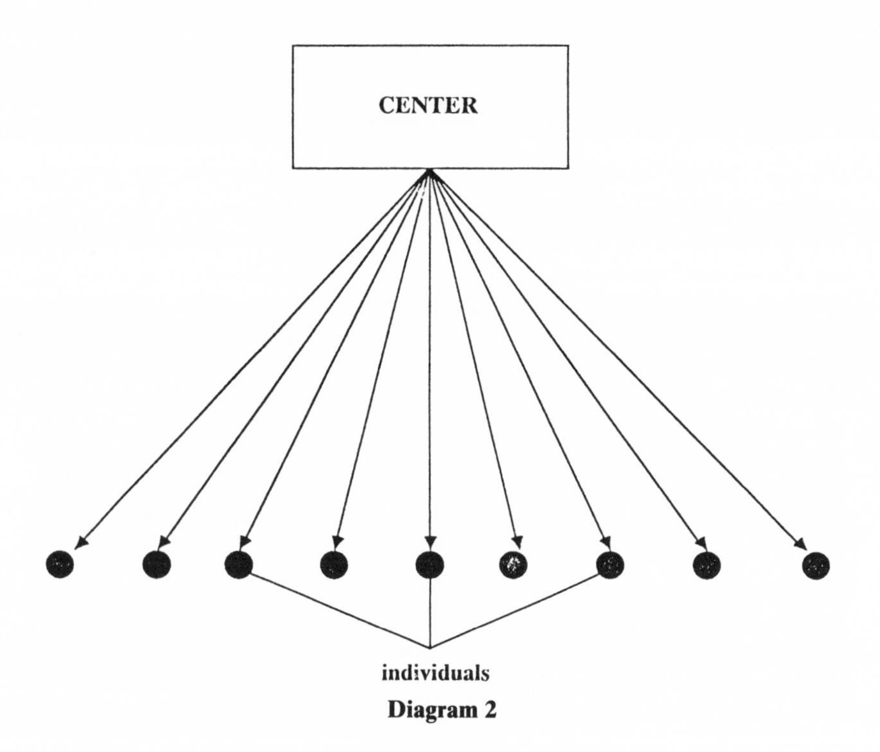

Diagram 2

alienation of civil society was achieved in the political sphere in Soviet Russia and the USSR by the early 1920s when independent political parties disappeared from public life; in the economic sphere, alienation was achieved after the completion of collectivization and industrialization a decade later. In the Eastern European countries, the same isolation and alienation were accomplished in both spheres by the end of the 1940s.

The Emergence of Dissident Groups

The first fundamental challenge to this arrangement, which is characterized by the omnipotence of the Center and the absence of civil society, emerges with the appearance of dissident groups. Indeed, the dissident groups challenge the Center's monopoly over ideological power. First, the dissident groups offer an alternative to the official morality endorsed by the Center by promoting various concepts and interpretations of human rights, religious freedom, social and economic justice, national sovereignty, peace, disarmament, ecology, and the plight of ethnic minorities. Second, the dissidents offer an alternative to the channels of mass communication created and controlled by the Center by establishing their own underground network of unofficial *samizdat* publications.

Promoting independent participation in public life, the activity of the dissident groups overcomes the previous isolation of their members, which in turn leads to the restoration of some elements of civil society (See Diagram 3).[3] The passive form of this participation, which covers the overwhelming majority of these groups' sympathizers, is limited to reading dissident publications and supporting them financially. The active form involves both the formation of such groups and the zealous participation of their members, all of which occurs outside the structures controlled by the system and is therefore independent of it. Both these forms of dissident activity bring about institutional expression and the promotion of independent social goals in public life. In addition, participation in dissident organizations leads to the appearance of the cadre of civil society, individuals with moral authority, leaders, and skillful organizers such as Sakharov in Russia, Chornovil and Horyn in the Ukraine, Havel in Czechoslovakia, and Kuron and Michnik in Poland.

The main weakness of dissident groups—indeed, the fundamental obstacle to their impact upon the system as a whole—is the vulnerability to judicial, administrative, police, and economic persecution[4] of their members. A barrier of fear thus separates the dissidents from the masses of the population. In fact, this barrier hindered the activities of the most powerful organizations in the history of the dissident groups—such as the Committee for the Defense of Workers and the Movement for the Defense of Human and Civic Rights in the late 1970s in Poland—limiting their influence to the main industrial centers and a few rural areas.[5] Therefore, the main achievement of the dissident groups lies not in a profound change of the system but rather in the creation of other concepts and institutions than those promoted and controlled by the system. The dissident groups can deprive the Center of its ideological power over dissident activists and sympathizers, but, at this first stage, the Center's political and economic power remains unchallengeable.

The period characterized by the regular activity of dissident groups began in Russia in the 1960s and in the other Soviet republics, the Ukraine, and Lithuania in the 1970s. In Eastern Europe, the dissidents appeared later. In Poland, Czechoslovakia, and Hungary the first

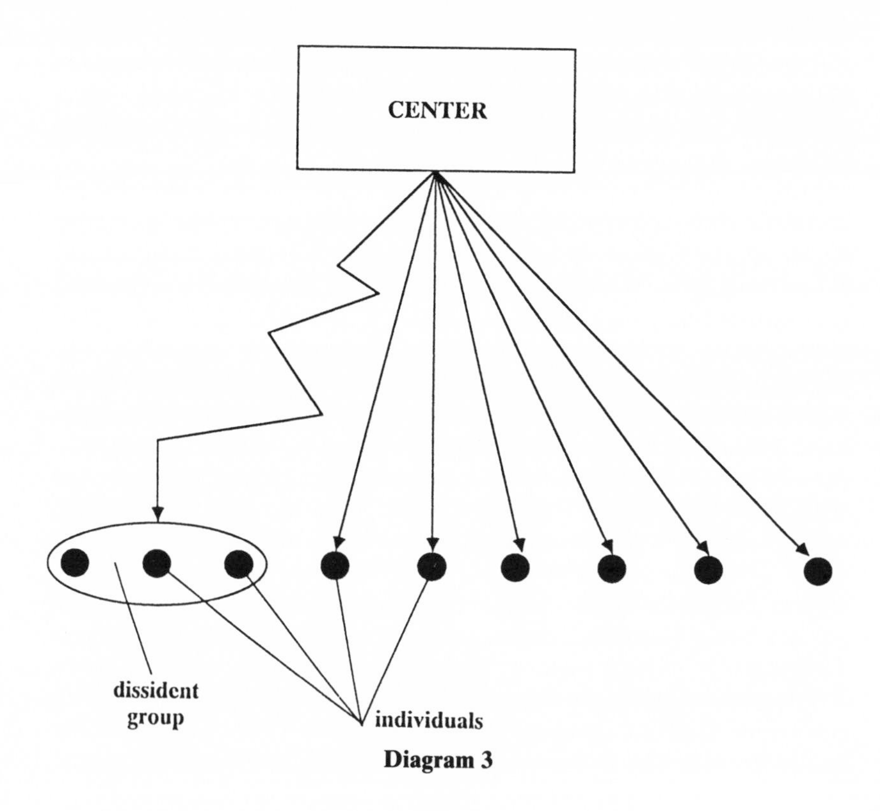

Diagram 3

organizations were launched in the late 1970s, in East Germany in the early 1980s, and in Bulgaria in the late 1980s.

The Establishment of Revindication Movements

The next step in the process of overcoming the system is the emergence and activity of mass revindication movements. This phenomenon is not limited to the appearance of Solidarity in 1980. It is also the case for the organizations which were established in some Soviet republics in the years of 1988–1989: the Popular Front in Estonia; the People's Front in Latvia; the Reconstructing Movement—*Sajudis*—in Lithuania; the Karabach Committee in Armenia; the Popular Movement in Support for Perestroika—*Rukh*—in the Ukraine; the Democratic Movement in Moldavia; the Popular Front in Azerbaijan; The Popular Front—*Adradzhen'ne*—in Byelorussia; and the Popular Front in Georgia. The most recent examples of the launching of a revindication movement are the emergence of the New Forum in East Germany, the Civic Forum in Bohemia, the Public Against Violence in Slovakia, and the Union of Democratic Forces in Bulgaria. There have been some efforts to launch a similar popular movement in Slovenia. The activity of these movements is simultaneously aimed both at society and the Center.

As far as the activity of the movement towards the population is concerned, this undoubtedly leads to a nationwide extension of the ranks of civil society (See Diagram 4). The movement overcomes the barrier of fear—the main obstacle to independent activity which threatened the dissident groups in the past. Indeed, if successful, the movement establishes its branches at almost every workplace or, at least, in any district. In this way, it embraces all the segments of society, including the previous dissident circles. Given the number of the participants in the movement, the Center gives up the previous practice of police repression. In fact, unless it is prepared months ahead and supported by the army (as in the case of Poland when martial law was imposed in 1981), efficient repression is no longer possible at that point. The best indication of the uselessness of the use of force in attempting to control an emerging mass movement is provided by the developments in the Soviet Caucasus republics in the years 1988–1989. Despite the previous deployment of military units to prevent ethnic hostilities in Armenia and Azerbaijan, as well as the decision to use the MVD troops in Georgia in April 1989 (which consequently resulted in the Tblisi massacre), the steady growth and increased influence of the movements in these countries have not been stopped; the presence of the armed forces failed to restore the barrier of fear among the population. Indeed, the most spectacular example of this failure is the activity of the Popular Front of Azerbaijan which managed, in spite of the military presence there, to launch a wave of political strikes in the republic which included the controversial economic blockade of Armenia in September 1989. Given the powerful position of the mass movement, the independent activity outside the structure of the system usually does not imply a personal risk of persecution. Thus, the choice between passive and active participation is no longer determined by fear but rather by the political temperament of its members.

Having overcome the nationwide barrier of fear, the movement is in a position to begin the process of revindicating the old, pre-Communist form of society. Accordingly, for example, the Georgian Popular Front considers itself "a general civic movement that unites Georgia's citizens with the aim of evolving and developing a humane and democratic

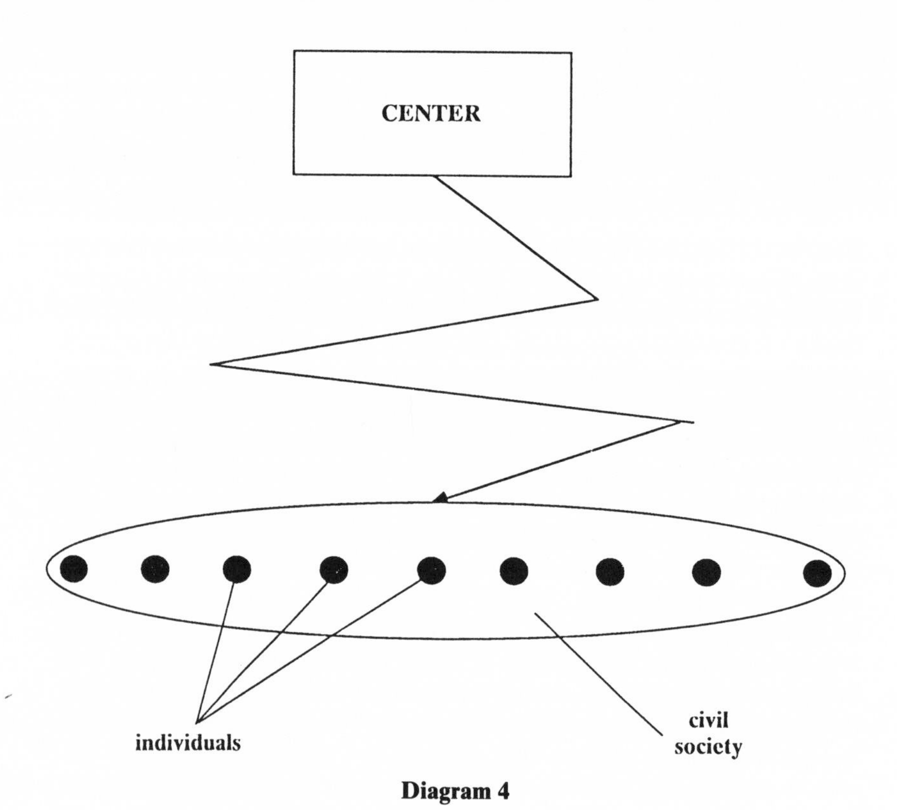

Diagram 4

society in accordance with the wishes of the people".[6] Similarily, its Byelorussian counterpart—*Adradzhen'ne*—states that its aim is the creation of "a sovereign Byelorussia based on the principles of democracy, humanism, and social justice."[7] The revindication under discussion is possible only by freeing society from the implementation of the policy of the Center. This, in turn, comes into being only by countering the traditional instruments of such implementation.

To analyze the process of the countering of these instruments, let us examine the programs of the Democratic Movement in Moldavia and the Popular Front in Azerbaijan.[8] These programs are relatively new—they were both formulated in early 1989—and, as such, they visibly refer to the programs and, indeed, the achievements of their powerful counterparts in the Baltic republics. Moreover, putting aside those of their postulates which are characteristic of the typical conditions of Soviet republics, most of them are striking reminders of many demands put forward by Solidarity, especially during its first period of legal activity: that is, in 1980–1981.[9] There are therefore good grounds for the claim that these two programs may be treated as models for the aims of a typical revindication movement.

The first set of their postulates includes gaining the right to put up the movement's own candidates in elections, achieving local control over election procedures, and establishing principles for the organization of meetings and other mass gatherings. The second set demands the abandonment of the *nomenklatura* system in all spheres of public life. The third set demands that all industry, factories, industrial organizations, and ecological initiatives on the territory of these republics be excluded from the direct control of the central planning system. The fourth deals with the change of property relations and proposes decollectivization of agriculture. The fifth demands that the legislation conform to the provisions laid down in the United Nations Declaration on Human Rights. The sixth calls for society to be cleansed of militarism—for the end of military programs in schools and peacetime drafting of students for military service. The seventh demands the elimination of ideological distortions and "blank spots" from the teaching of history and literature. And the eighth, final set of postulates calls for the reinstatement of the influence of religious organizations, with greater opportunities for the churches to train priests and publish religious literature; free circulation of and public access to domestic and foreign religious publications; access by the churches to the media; and the return to religious communities of churches and monasteries that have been closed or taken over by the authorities.

Although the above demands are typical of almost any revindication movement, they do not embrace the issue that has to be approached by the Popular Fronts of the Ukrainians and the Byelorussians: namely, the problem of national consolidation. Unlike other Soviet republics, the East Slavic movements face—due to a similar language, culture, and history to that of Russia—a relatively low level of national self-awareness, which is especially visible in the cities of the Eastern Ukraine. The phenomenon known as "Little Russian consciousness" (which manifests itself in renouncing one's native language in favor of Russian[10]) is the main obstacle to the Ukrainian and Byelorussian movements' achievement of more widespread participation in their own republics. Therefore, the fundamental demand of these movements is the revindication of their native language, history, and culture as promoted by the republican legislation and political practice of these republics.

On the whole, the demands of the typical revindication movement were previously considered taboo by the Center-run media, and their discussion was usually limited to the dissident community. Given the special sensitivity of the authorities, some of these issues—such as those concerning relations between society and the army, and relationships in the army itself—were not even raised by the dissident groups in order to avoid provoking prosecutions. After the creation of the movement, mass participation in it created the opportunity for independent public discussion of all of these issues.[11] The movement as a whole supports all these proposals as its own program. It has its own nationwide channels of communications—for example, the daily *Gazeta Wyborcza* in the case of Solidarity and the daily *Respublica* in the case of Sajudis—to lobby for these reforms, and its own organizational structures to promote them. Indeed, even without free and regular access to radio and television programs, the movement, if well-established, is in a position to reach an audience as least as numerous as that of the Center-run mass media. It is enough to refer to the spectacular success of Sajudis, which managed to launch a network of about 160 regular magazines and newsletters in a republic with a population of less than 4 million people.[12] When the movement extends its reach to include all of society, therefore, it deprives the Center of its monopoly over ideological power.

The activities of the movement, unlike those of the dissident groups, also have to focus on the Center itself. Regardless of whether the movement is recognized by the authorities *de jure*—as Solidarity was between 1980 and 1982 and has been once again since the agreement reached at the "round table talks" in April 1989—or only *de facto*—as have its counterparts in the Soviet republics and East Germany—its demands constitute a program of reforms which can be implemented only by the Center. Some of the postulates concern the state of affairs created by the arbitrary political practice of the Center; they can therefore only be implemented by a change in political practice. For example, the striking workers in Poland in 1980 who later created Solidarity put pressure on the authorities and eventually forced them to allow the church access to radio programs. Similarily, Sajudis managed in 1988 to enforce the return of the cathedral of Vilnius to the Catholic Church of Lithuania.

However, the implementation of most of the movement's demands requires profound changes in the system of law itself. Again, that can only be carried out by the Center since it still controls the legislature. Note, for instance, the provisions of labor legislation and the law on censorship supported by Solidarity during its first period of legal activity. Fundamental changes in Poland's very constitutional system were achieved by Solidarity as the result of the "round table talks"; they found their expression in the legislation passed in May 1989. These changes embraced the establishment of the Presidency, the second house of Parliament, and the new electoral law which included free and open elections to the Senate and partially to the Sejm (the lower house). Similarly profound constitutional changes were enforced by Sajudis in May 1989. The Lithuanian Supreme Soviet, following the example set up by the Estonian Supreme Soviet in 1988, declared the sovereignty of the Lithuanian state and passed four amendments to Lithuania's basic law. The amendments established separate Lithuanian citizenship and stated that Lithuanian citizens were entitled to all the social, economic, political, and personal rights and freedoms provided in the Lithuanian constitution, the other laws of the republic, and those included in universally accepted international conventions. The amendments embraced the provisions stating that all of Lithuania's natural resources and man-made assets were the republic's national wealth and were under its jurisdiction. Moreover, another amendment stated that Soviet laws would be in force in Lithuania if and only if they were approved or registered by the Lithuanian Supreme Soviet.[13]

The pressure put on the Center by the movement restricts its economic and political powers. As far as economic power is concerned, certain initiatives clearly undermine the omnipotence of the planning system—for example, the revindication of the right to strike achieved by Solidarity at the beginning of its existence, or its insistence on the market-oriented reforms in the April 1989 agreement, or Sajudis's pressure on defying Soviet central economic legislation in Lithuania in the same year.

As for the political power of the Center, it is limited from the very inception of the movement. The movement reestablishes public opinion, which indirectly undermines the political control of the Center. Moreover, in the longer term, when the prospect of free and open elections emerges the impact of public opinion upon policy-making becomes more direct. All in all, the establishment of the movement means that the Center is no longer the only actor on the political scene. As such, it has to react politically to the demands of the movement.

Its political reactions usually take two forms: first, that of confrontation with the movement; second, that of limited cooperation with it. Confrontation is characteristic of the first reactions of the Center to the emergence of the movement. Indeed, in all the countries under discussion, the establishment of each movement was accompanied by hostility on the part of the authorities. This results from the Center's desire to eliminate the movement from public life and to restore the *ex ante* monopoly of political and economic power. The Center has a wide spectrum of means to choose from when confrontation is the preferred option. It may be conducted by launching an anti-movement campaign in the media, like the campaigns still being conducted in the Ukraine and Moldavia. It may take the form of petty administrative annoyances, as in Byelorussia in June 1989. In this instance, the authorities did everything in their power to prevent the founding congress of *Adradzhen'ne* from taking place by putting pressure on factories and enterprises that might otherwise have been willing to lend halls to the Popular Front delegates. The result of this campaign was that the congress of *Adradzhen'ne* was forced to convene "in exile"—namely, in Lithuanian Vilnus under Sajudis's wing.[14] In an extreme situation, confrontation is carried out by using force on a mass scale, as occurred in Poland in December 1981.

The Center usually chooses the option of cooperation because of critical evaluation of its own previous policy of confrontation. Confrontation so antagonizes newly-emerged public opinion that the Center finds itself isolated by society, making the implementation of Center policy virtually impossible. The best example of this state of affairs is the passive resistance launched by the underground Solidarity after the imposition of martial law, which was sometimes described as a "cold civil war." In general, the transition from confrontation with the movement to cooperation with it requires a profound change in the Center's political thinking. Sometimes it is associated with a change of leadership. For example, in Lithuania in the fall of 1988, the previous party boss, Songaila, a hardliner, was replaced by Brazauskas, a more open-minded and conciliatory politician.[15] The essence of cooperation with the movement is the treatment of the movement by the Center as a political partner that constitutes a constant factor in the political constellation.

This results in the Center relinquishing its monopoly on decision-making in favor of negotiations with the movement. This in turn leads to the Center's implementation of the movement's reform program.

The core of the movement's activity is to formulate demands which the Center is pressured to adopt in legislation or to implement in political practice. Therefore, the movement formulates only the demands which it thinks the Center will consider negotiable. In other words, the movement does not formulate strictly political programs which would be unacceptable to the Center and imply its abolition. Regardless of the relationship between the Center and the movement—confrontation or cooperation—the movement avoids a direct political challenge to the Center. This does not mean that the movement rejects such fundamental goals as the restoration of national sovereignty and parliamentary democracy. Nevertheless, these distant goals are not treated as current concessions to be demanded of the Center.

The Launching of Independent Political Parties

The very activity of the revindication movement which restores civil society inevitably creates conditions for the reemergence of independent political parties. Unlike the movement itself, the parties formulate strictly political programs which offer a fundamental structural alternative to the Communist system. They do not seek cooperation with the Center, but competition with it. They do not expect the Center to implement their demands. Rather, they seek its abolition and the implementation of their own programs by a new state structure created after their victory in open elections. The best description of this position is in an interview given by Slavko Susuec, one of the activists of the Socialist Democratic Alliance in Slovenia. Indicating the alternative his party offers to the present Yugoslav system, he declared: "Instead of socialism, we offer parliamentary democracy. Instead of self-management; free private enterprise, and introduction of shares, and co-participation. Instead of one candidate from one party, more candidates from different parties."[16]

However, the appearance of political parties does not immediately deprive the Center of its limited economic and political power. The first task of the newly created parties deals with civil society itself. Establishing their constituencies, the parties launch a politicization of civil society. This leads to the division of civil society along political lines (See Diagram 5).

To understand these divisions, note the difference between those independent political organizations that appeared before the emergence of revindication movements and those that appeared later. The former organizations—the League for a Free Lithuania (1978), the Confederation for an Independent Poland (1979), or the Democratic Union (1988) in the Russian republic—pleaded either for the independence of their countries (Lithuania and Poland) or for the introduction of a multi-party system and parliamentary democracy (USSR). Their programs, even if they were not regarded as realistic by newly-emerging public opinion, were so general that they did not create political divisions in the ranks of the dissidents. In fact, they were commonly considered uncontroversial as final national goals in Lithuania and Poland, and recently became officially adopted as the aims of the mass movements in these countries—Sajudis and Solidarity.[17] Therefore, these long-term political programs did not divide civil society; rather, they united it.

The real political divisions in civil society were brought about by the emergence of parties with more particular objectives that took their

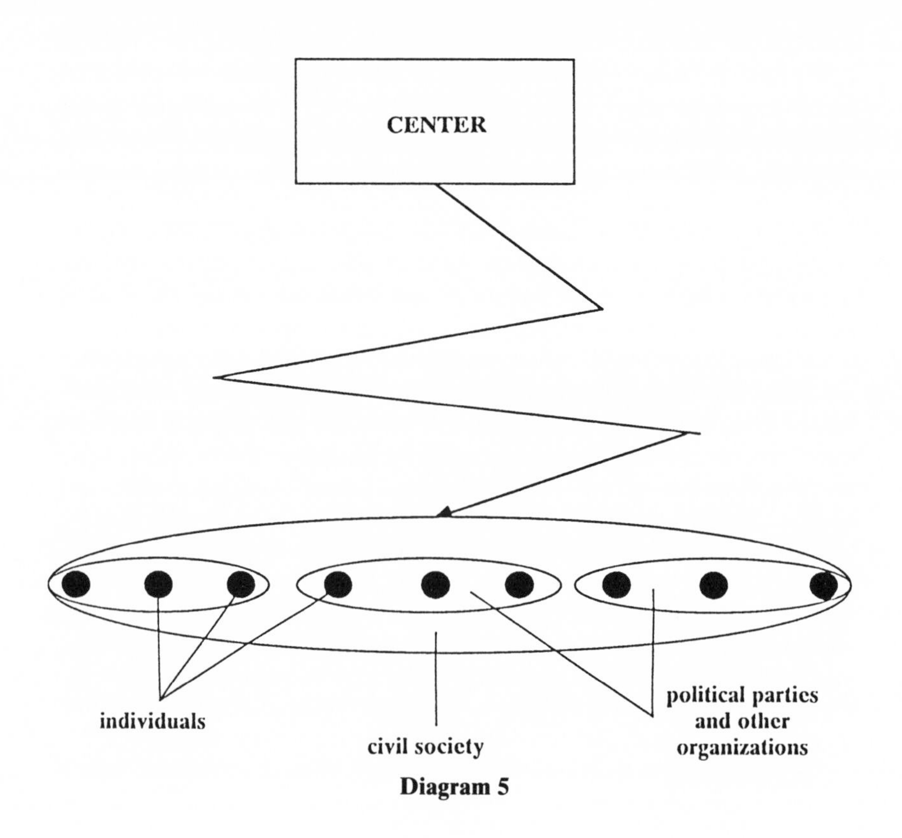

Diagram 5

inspiration from different political traditions and schools of thought. For instance, the group Polish Politics was established in Poland in 1983, basing its program on the tradition of the National Democratic Party, the most influential political party in prewar Poland. In 1984, the Liberal Democratic Party, "Independence," appeared. Although it was influenced by American neoconservatism in its economic program, it also hearkened back to the tradition of the struggle for national independence under Pilsudski after World War I. Moreover, in 1987, the Polish Socialist Party—liquidated after the Communists gained power—reemerged, endorsing policies reminiscent of its prewar predecessor. In Lithuania, the main body of the prewar (that is, pre-Communist) political spectrum of the country was reestablished in 1989. It is enough to mention the reemergence of the Lithuanian Christian Democratic Party, the Lithuanian Democratic Party, the Lithuanian National Association (which had governed the country from 1926 to 1940) and the Lithuanian Social-Democratic Party. Also, in 1988–89 the Ukraine experienced a clear revival of political party activity. The best known and most representative of the main currents of Ukrainian political life include: the Ukrainian Democratic Union/Ukrainian People's Democratic League (previously a regional branch of the Russian Democratic Union), the Ukrainian Christian Democratic Front, and the Social Democratic Federation of Ukraine.[18] In Hungary, among the participants in the Opposition Round Table (that is, those newly emerged political parties which took part in the negotiations with the Communists in the summer of 1989), at least three—the Social Democratic Party, the Independent Smallholders' Party, and the Christian Democratic People's Party—declared their intention to reactivate the traditions of their prewar counterparts.[19]

However, these divisions are not just confined to different political programs. By restoring pre-Communist political concepts and traditions, these parties contribute to differences in the perception of the existing Communist systems and advance diverse ways of overcoming these systems. A case in point is the controversy in Polish civil society during the "round table talks" in April 1989. Moderates and fundamentalists proposed competing approaches to the problem of bringing the ruling Communist party to political competition in fully open elections. The groups which take their inspiration from the social democratic, national democratic, and Christian democratic traditions endorsed a moderate approach and opted for negotiations with the Center, treating them as a political partner with some limited credibility. The representatives of the organizations which continue the tradition of Pilsudski's struggle and that of the more radical social democrats took a fundamentalist position. They denied the credibility of the Center in negotiations and argued that more pressure should be put on the Center by launching strikes and mass demonstrations.[20] A similar controversy was visible in Hungary in the fall of 1989 when two parties refused to sign the agreement which resulted from the negotiations between the Communist party, the Opposition Round Table, and the so-called Third Side that represented the official institutions dependent upon the Communists. The same type of divisions are evident in the recent launching of the Hungarian Independence Party, which is a negative reaction to these negotiations. The Independence Party rejects the negotiations on the grounds that the agreement restricts political competition—which, in turn, favors the Communists.

Taking Power in Competitive Elections by Independent Political Parties

The last stage in the process of overcoming the system is the creation of a non-Communist government as the result of open elections. Such an event would restore the same relationship between civil society and the state that prevailed before the Communist takeover (See Diagram 6). While this stage has not yet been achieved in any Communist country, its general outline can nevertheless be projected from the present developments in some Eastern European countries.

The basic condition which has to be met in order to reach this stage is the abolition of the Center. This, in turn, can be achieved by the separation of the Communist Party from the state. This separation is usually anticipated by processes in the party itself. These processes cause the party to give up its previous leading role in society and the state as well as its Leninist structure and impel it to adopt a new social democratic orientation. It is now possible to indicate at least four ways in which the party can be separated from the state. The case studies offered refer to the situations in the Soviet Union (in the Baltic republics, in particular), Poland, and Hungary.

As far as the Soviet Union is concerned, the new trend began after the somewhat free election for the Congress of People's Deputies in March 1989. A considerable number of established figures in the Communist Party of the Soviet Union failed to get elected, even though most of them had contrived to run unopposed and only needed to obtain 50 percent of the vote. The reaction in the Party to this humiliation did not include formulating a new political program or organizational changes which could have improved its performance in the future. Indeed, at the Party meetings in the following months, a profoundly defeatist atmosphere prevailed. At the session of the Central Committee in April, one of its members said that not a single Party official in his region was prepared to stand in the forthcoming elections to republican and local soviets—defeat seemed certain. No one rose to paint a more optimistic picture of the situation in any other area.[21] In July, when 200 leaders of the Party apparatus from across the country met to discuss the Party's new role and what its course should be, the mood of disorientation and pessimism was still present and no reforms were on the agenda. In fact, Prime Minister Ryzhkow insisted that Gorbachev, as general secretary, should take on the task of reconstructing the Party, but Gorbachev ignored this call in his concluding speech.[22]

The obvious state of torpor among the Party establishment led the radical members of the Congress of People's Deputies and the Supreme Soviet to launch the Interregional Group at the end of July. While the number of Party members in the group is unknown, its officeholders—including Yeltsin—are Party members. Given the fact that their behav-

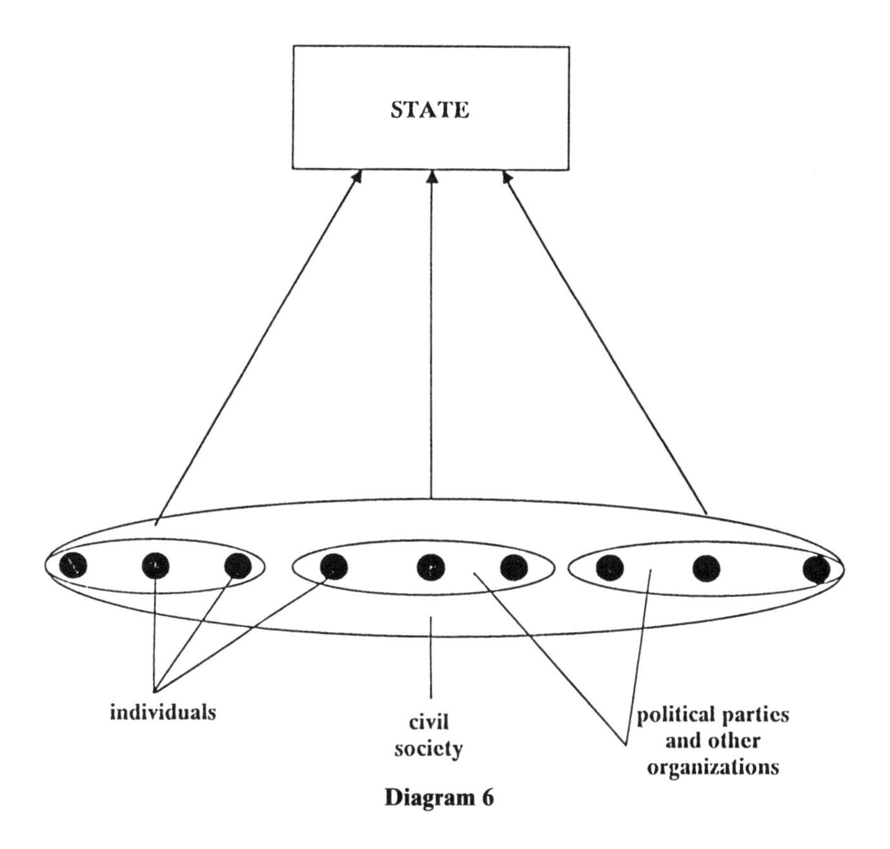

Diagram 6

ior as legislators does not conform to Party discipline, it is justified to treat them as a faction within the Party. The existence of a faction in the Party deprives it of its Leninist character, since it clearly undermines the principle of democratic centralism. Moreover, some statements of the group's leaders indicate that they wish to promote political programs which are alternatives to that of the official Party establishment. For example, Yeltsin, speaking for the group, was reported to have promised "to help the mensheviks defend their ideas against the conservative bolsheviks" in the Supreme Soviet. Another leader of the group, Goncharov, advocated a multi-party system, stating that, with the acceptance of the pluralism of opinion, "the next step is organizational pluralism."[23]

The fact that a faction of the Party makes its own relatively independent policy in the Congress of People's Deputies and in the Supreme Soviet (that is, in the constitutional organs to which considerable political power was recently shifted from the central Party institutions) contributes to a visible separation between the Party and the state. Indeed, given that most members of the Supreme Soviet owe their seats not to the recommendation of the Party apparatus but to the voters, the Supreme Soviet has proved to have a much more flexible and open-minded attitude than the Party on a number of political issues. These issues include economic autonomy for the Baltic republics, the punishability of so-called "anti-state" offenses, transfer of land to the farmers under the land-lease scheme, and the democratization of the procedure for elections to republican and local soviets.

However, the present separation between the Party and the state does not mean the abolition of the Center. Ultimate authority still seems to reside in the Politburo. At least for the time being, the Party—due to Gorbachev's presidency and his personal authority among the members of the Supreme Soviet—is in a position not to allow a permanent division of policymaking. And this present constellation may hold in the near future. Central to the permanent division of policymaking is the existence of a political party which can challenge the CPSU throughout the Soviet Union. Not only is there no such party (since the Democratic Union still cannot perform this task), but elections for the Congress of People's Deputies before the expiration of its five-year term are unlikely. Nevertheless, the present constellation constitutes a spectacular departure from the old system; indeed, it is the first step in the direction of the abolition of the Center. For this reason it is treated by Ligachev, Gorbachev's conservative rival in the Politburo, as *dvoevlastie*—dual power.[24] In the Russian experience, this means instability—which, in turn, leads to a change in the political system.

In the Baltic republics, the separation between the Party and the state is even more advanced, but it takes a very different form. Under pressure from the local popular fronts, the Communist Parties of Lithuania, Latvia, and Estonia have steadily been adopting the main body of these fronts' programs to their political agenda. In such issues as the reevaluation of history (especially the illegality of the Molotov-Ribbentrop Pact) and the concept of autarky of their republics, these parties follow the initiatives of the popular fronts. Moreover, the Communist parties in the Baltic republics favor the change to a new status which would give them organizational independence from the CPSU. Since the Lithuanian Party has declared that it will decide in December 1989 whether or not to cut its ties with Moscow (following the example set up by the Lithuanian Komsomol), it seems to be the party closest to a break with the CPSU.

Despite these changes, the Communist Parties in the Baltic republics do not constitute genuine political forces at home; they therefore have no chance to compete successfully for power. For example, in Lithuania during the March 1989 elections for the Congress of People's Deputies, Brazauskas, the first secretary of the Party, was elected only because Sajudis took his moderate and conciliatory approach into consideration and refrained from fielding a candidate against him, as it did against other party officials—who lost. In Estonia, according to an opinion poll conducted in April 1989, only 7 percent of Estonians and 32 percent of non-Estonian residents said they would vote Communist in a free multi-party contest. Given the relative size of the two ethnic groups, the Communists would receive a total of 16 percent of the vote while the Estonian Popular Front would win 35 percent.[25]

Therefore, provided that: first, these Parties do not have their own original political programs which they could implement through the state structure; second, that they do not implement the program of the CPSU from which they seek to cut their ties; and third, that they implement the programs of the popular fronts with which they are not in a position to compete, the Center no longer exists in any of the Baltic republics. Indeed, in its traditional sense, the Center—a party/state leadership that implements its own political, economic, and ideological program through both the structure of the party and the state—has ceased to exist there. The structure of the state in the Baltic republics, especially the republican supreme soviets, no longer serves the Communist parties. Rather, it serves civil societies represented by the popular fronts. For the time being—that is, before elections for republican and local soviets—the fronts use the Communist Parties (its members still dominate in these soviets) in order to express their national aspirations in their disagreements with Moscow. This could be seen in Lithuania in May 1989 when the Communist-controlled Supreme Soviet passed "A Declaration of Lithuanian State Sovereignty." Therefore, ironically enough, the Communist Parties there perform the role of transmission belts through which the popular fronts control the structure of the state.

In Poland in the spring and summer of 1989, the Polish United Workers' Party experienced a chain of humiliating setbacks which profoundly changed its position in the state. They included the blow at the polls in June, Jaruzelski's one-vote victory in the presidential election in July (which he clearly owed only to the support of some Solidarity members), and—finally—the failure to form a Communist-run cabinet in August, which eventually resulted in the establishment of the Solidarity-led government under Mazowiecki. Nevertheless, these events have not caused much change in the Party itself. First of all, there is no indication that groups of reformists who have formulated a program of adjustment to the new situation are gaining ground.[26] The majority of the Party's intellectuals have defected, and the character of the organization is determined as never before by the apparatus. Given the Party's experience with repeated confrontations with Polish society after World War II—especially in 1956, 1968, 1970, 1976, and 1980–1981—as well as with the firm if unsteady increase of the influence of the opposition since the emergence of the first dissident groups in 1976, there is little prospect for a change of its present bad luck in its future performance at the polls. Moreover, Rakowski, the new first secretary, is commonly treated as a personal enemy of Solidarity and the former instigator of confrontation with it. In sum, the present process of Party decline seems irreversible.

The newly arranged separation between the Party and the state seems no less permanent. The separation is especially visible in the relations between the Party and the Parliament, between the Party and the Presidency, and between the Party and the government. In the summer of 1989, the minor parties—the United Peasant Party and the Democratic Party (who had traditionally been seen as the Communists' protégés)—declared their intention to cooperate with Solidarity, rather than the Party, in the creation of the government. The Communists unexpectedly lost their control over the majority in the Parliament, even though it had seemed assured by their preelection agreement with Solidarity following the "round table talks." The relations between the Party and the Presidency are still relatively strong, since a veteran Party leader was elected President. After Jaruzelski's election, he nevertheless kept a promise made earlier and gave up all his Party posts, including his position as First Secretary of the Central Committee and his membership in the Politburo. After the establishment of the Solidarity-led government, the separation between the Party and the state became even more visible. It is true that the Communists run four powerful ministries, those of interior, defense, foreign trade, and transportation. Nevertheless, their presence in the government is not a result of the sole decision of the Party leadership, as it was before. Rather, it resulted from the geopolitical considerations of the other partners in the coalition. In admitting the Communists to the government, the other partners of the coalition recognized the Communist Party as the guardian of Warsaw Pact interests in Poland but not as a leading political force in society and the state. The strategic character of the ministries led by the Communists confirms this interpretation.

Given the changes that have separated the Party from the state in Poland, it is clear that the Center no longer exists there. Indeed, ultimate authority has shifted from the Politburo to the Parliament and decision-making powers to the government. In this situation, it is highly likely that, if nothing extraordinary happens, independent parties will gain control over the whole structure of the state in the free elections scheduled for 1993.

Hungary's Communist Party was the only party in the countries under discussion which had the ambition of taking an active part in leading the country out of socialism and adopting a social-democratic character for itself. After the end of Kadar's rule in May 1988, the new leaders launched a nationwide discussion about the future of the country and the place of the Party in it. Despite visible controversies between the innovators such as Pozsgay and the less reform-minded such as Grosz, the Party as a whole managed to enter and lead the discussion with the opposition organizations in the summer of 1989. The aim of the talks was to work out the rules of the democratic game in the period of transition to parliamentary democracy and a market economy. In August 1989, the Party—for its own part—issued its "draft manifesto" that was both a party program and an election platform.[27] Both were adopted at the extraordinary Party Congress in October 1989, at which the Party also changed its name to the Hungarian Socialist Party.

It was admitted in the document that the Party "is aware that no historical example exists for the transition from dictatorial socialism to a democratic socialism that is based on a market economy." However, it was stated that "this goal cannot be reached by copying foreign models and the application of abstract ideologies." The Party itself declared its intention to become a "socialist party" ready to compete with other parties for power. It promised to "acknowledge the common will of the nation as it is manifested at the elections, while at the same time striving to obtain a major governmental influence." The manifesto promoted the idea of a welfare state in Hungary; it stressed the need to provide social security for those who could not fend for themselves and to secure freedom of the individual, social justice, and equal opportunity. A great deal of emphasis was placed on "versatile ownership forms," including private, cooperative, and state ownership; ownership by towns, villages, and foundations; and ownership by foreign capital. Enterprising groups and individuals would be encouraged to make profits, and private enterprise would be invited to engage in improving health care and other social services.

The Party's unprecedented decision to play such an active role during the transition period obviously resulted from its relatively strong position in the country and the weakness of its adversaries—that is, the opposition parties. Indeed, since the uprising of 1956—over the period of Kadar's so-called "soft dictatorship"—the Party has managed to avoid serious confrontations with society. On the other hand, the opposition is a new phenomenon. The dissident groups in Hungary in the late 1970s were less active and lacked the ethos of their Polish and Czechoslovakian counterparts. Moreover, all the independent parties were created in the years of 1988–1989 and still have not managed—with perhaps, the one important exception of the Hungarian Democratic Forum—to establish constituencies outside the ranks of urban intelligentsia. In this situation, the Communist Party assumes that after the elections—which are due no later than in June 1990—it could rule in a coalition with some independent parties. However, these calculations seem a little over-optimistic; in the August 1989 runoff elections, only one seat was won by a Communist Party candidate in the elections of four provincial towns. Interestingly, his election posters neglected to mention his party affiliation. The other three seats went to the Hungarian Democratic Forum.

Nevertheless, regardless of the outcome of the elections in 1990, it is already possible to indicate that the abolition of the Center in Hungary has taken the fullest form among the countries under discussion. Indeed, all political forces in Hungary support and implement the separation of the Party and the state. Therefore, it is highly likely that Hungary will be the first country to meet the main condition of the fourth stage: that of independent political parties taking power in competitive elections. This step will complete the country's long march out of socialism.

Conclusion

The reasons for the rebirth of civil society in Communist countries are beyond the scope of this paper. My aim is only to indicate that the four stages outlined above constitute a pattern that may be universally applicable to the Soviet republics and the countries of Eastern Europe. Each state falls fairly neatly into some aspect of this pattern. Given the lack of any appreciable dissident activity in Albania and Romania, they have not yet reached the first stage.[28] The Soviet republics of Estonia, Latvia, Armenia, Azerbaijan, Georgia, Moldavia, and Byelorussia are already at the second stage, precisely because of the activity of such movements. East Germany, Czechoslovakia, and Bulgaria have also just reached that stage, since their revindication movements managed not only to unify the loose dissident groups under their wings but also to attract new constituencies. Due to the politicization of civil society by independent parties, Poland, Hungary, Lithuania, the Ukraine, Slovenia, and, to some extent, the Russian Republic have reached the third stage. It is likely that Hungary, and then Poland, will approach the fourth stage before the others.

Despite the fact that this paper is focused on the Soviet Union and the East European countries, I would argue that the model developed here could be extended beyond Europe. Indeed, it is justifiable to assume that with the significant presence of dissident groups, Cuba has achieved the first stage. As a result of the student demonstrations supported by the workers and intellectuals in China, there was a chance to launch a revindication movement there and to approach the second stage. The massacre in Tiananmen Square restored the previous barrier of fear and pushed the country back to the first stage.

The overcoming of the system is a multidimensional process in which the four conditions have to be met. They are: first, the challenge to the omnipotence of the Center; second, the restoration of civil society; third, the politicization of civil society; and fourth, the abolition of the Center and the restoration of pre-Communist relations between civil society and the state. The essence of this process is that the chronology presented cannot be changed—it has to be maintained. The meeting of any succeeding condition depends upon the meeting of the previous conditions. For example, the abolition of the Center and the restoration of pre-Communist relations between civil society and the state can only take place if there are political parties which will compete for power in open elections. In turn, the existence of such parties may result only from the fact that the civil society has undergone politicization, which is characterized by the emergence of various political attitudes and programs. The restoration of civil society can occur only if the Center's monopoly over the channels of mass communication has been successfully challenged and the isolation of the individual has therefore been overcome.

Nevertheless, this does not mean that all these conditions have to be met in the four specific stages of the path out of socialism. Sometimes, in the experience of some particular country, one of the stages may be missing but all the conditions are met anyway. Take, for instance, the experience of Hungary and of the Russian republic. Given the rebirth of independent parties in Hungary and the spectacular nationwide activity of the Democratic Union in Russia, both these countries have already reached the third stage—despite the fact that a mass revindication movement has not been launched in either country. Therefore, in both countries, the second stage is missing. The consequence of these developments is that the conditions usually met at the second and third stages—that is, the restoration of civil society as well as its politicization—are met simultaneously at the third stage. In other words, civil society is being restored there not by the activity of a revindication movement but directly by the newly-emerged political parties and other informal groups such as those having as their main focus human rights, the environment, and religion.

However, it is necessary to stress that the lack of one stage inevitably weakens the process of overcoming the system in its fullest dimension. In this context, it is enough to compare the extent of the ranks of civil society in the Russian republic to that of Poland. The absence of a mass revindication movement in Russia has kept its civil society from expanding to the majority of the population. Indeed, before the wave of miners' strikes in the summer of 1989, the workers had shown little interest in the political debate going on in their country. Moreover, there is still not much indication of active independent participation in public life on the part of the farmers. In Poland, by contrast, in the year Solidarity became active (1980–1981), the ranks of civil society spanned all social strata. They embraced the workers and intellectuals organized in Solidarity proper, the farmers who launched Farmers' Solidarity, and even some representatives of private business who were the members of what was called Craftsman's Solidarity.[29]

The creation of a mass revindication movement in the Russian republic is important for the successful abandonment of socialism. However, it is crucial that such a movement exists in order to determine what political constellation will replace socialism. The lack of a movement clearly leads to a less promising destabilization of the country, which may lead to chaos. The presence of a movement would offer both a nationwide democratic alternative to the present destabilization and a liberal democratic alternative to replace the past totalitarian system in the country of its birth.

September 1989

NOTES

1. By socialism, I understand the system which has prevailed in the Soviet-bloc countries.
2. I do not think that the non-totalitarian explanations of Soviet-type systems have been very successful in proving the lack of the omnipotence of the Center. See Allen Kassof, "The Administered Society: Totalitarianism without Terror." *World Politics,* vol. xvi, no. 4, pp. 558–75; John Kautsky, "Comparative Communism versus Comparative Politics," *Studies in Comparative Communism,* vol. vi, nos. 1 and 2 (1973), pp. 135–70; Stephen White, "Communist Systems and the 'Iron Law of Pluralism'," *British Journal of Political Science,* vol. viii, no. 1 (1978), 101–17; Valerie Bunce and John Echols, "Soviet Politics in the Brezhnev Era: 'Pluralism' or 'Corporatism'?" D. Kelly, ed. *Soviet Politics in the Brezhnev Era* (New York: Praeger, 1980), pp. 1–26. For a brilliant discussion of the usefulness of the concept of totalitarianism in the perception of Soviet-type systems by independent Eastern European intellectuals in the last three decades, see Jacques Rupnik, "Totalitarianism Revisited," John Keane ed., *Civil Society and the State* (London: Verso, 1988), pp. 263–89.
3. For different conceptual and ideological approaches to the phenomenon of the reemergence of civil society in Eastern Europe, see Ivan Szelenyi, "Socialist Opposition: Dilemmas and Prospects," Rudolf L. Tokes ed., *Opposition in Eastern Europe* (London: Macmillan, 1979), pp. 187–208; Andrew Arato, "Civil Society against the State: Poland 1980–81," *Telos,* vol. 50 (1981), pp. 23–47; Zbigniew Rau, "Some Thoughts on Civil Society in Eastern Europe and the Lockean Contractarian Approach," *Political Studies* XXXV (1987), pp. 573–592; and Zbigniew A. Pelczynski, "Solidarity and 'The Rebirth on Civil Society' in Poland 1976–81," John Keane ed., *Civil Society and the State* (London: Verso, 1988), pp. 361–80. For an attempt at an analysis of civil society in the USSR, see Gail W. Lapidus, "State and Society: Toward Emergence of Civil Society in Russia" in *Politics, Society and Nationality inside Gorbachev's Russia,* Seweryn Bialer ed., (Westview Press: Boulder & London: 1989), pp. 121–47. See also Richard Sakwa. *The State and Civil Society in the USSR* (Cambridge: University Press, forthcoming).
4. By economic persecution, I understand the loss of a job: a common way

in which authorities try to discourage independent activity. For an illuminating discussion of this issue, see Milan Simecka, *The Restoration of Order: The Normalization of Czechoslovakia 1969–1976,* (London: Verso, 1984) and Wlodzimierz Brus, " 'Normalization' " Processes in Soviet-dominated Central Europe," Zdenek Mlynar ed., *Relative Stabilisation of the Soviet Systems in the 1970s, Research Project Crises in Soviet-type Systems,* Study No. 2 (1983).

5. See Jan Jozef Lipski, *KOR: A History of the Workers' Defense Committee in Poland 1976–1981* (Berkeley: University of California Press, 1985).
6. Quotation from Elizabeth Fuller, "Towards Georgian Independence: Georgian Formal and Informal Groups and their Programs," *Report on the USSR,* Vol. 1, no. 25 (June 25, 1989).
7. Quotation from Kathleen Mihalisko, "Belorussian Popular Front Holds Founding Congress in Vilnus," *Report on the USSR,* vol. 1, no. 28 (July 14, 1989).
8. See Vladimir Socor, "Popular Front Founded in Moldavia," *Report on the USSR,* vol. 1, no. 23 (June 9, 1989) and Mirza Michaeli & William Reese, "The Popular Front in Azerbaijan and Its Program," *Report on the USSR,* vol. 1, no. 34 (August 15, 1989).
9. Compare Jerzy Holzer, *"Solidaritat": Die Geschichte einer freien Gewerkschaft in Polen.* (Munchen: Verlag C. B. Beck, 1986).
10. On the question of Little Russian consciousness, see the article of the Ukrainian writer Mykola Raybchuk. "Ukrainskaya literatura i malorosisky 'imidzh' ", *Drushba Narodov,* no. 5 (1988).
11. For the Sajudis demands for Lithuanian territorial divisions in the Soviet armed forces, see Kestutis Girnius, "No Love Lost Between the Military and the Lithuanian Reconstructing Movement," *Radio Free Europe Research,* January 5, 1989.
12. See, Saulius Girnius, "Sajudis Plans a Daily Newspaper," *Report on the USSR,* vol. 1. no. 30 (July 28, 1989).
13. See Saulius Girnius, "Lithuania Declares Its Sovereignty," *Report on the USSR,* vol. 1, no. 22 (June 2, 1989).
14. On the hostile treatment of *Adradzhen'ne* by the Byelorussian authorities, see *Pravda,* July 1, 1989. On its congress in exile see Kathleen Mihalisko, "Belorussian Popular Front Holds Founding Congress in Vilnus," *Report on the USSR,* vol. 1, no. 28 (July 14, 1989).
15. See Kestutis Girnius, "Six Months of the Lithuanian Reconstructing Movement," *Radio Free Europe Research,* vol. 14, no. 8 (January 5, 1989).
16. See Milan Andrejevich, "The Social-Democratic Alliance of Slovenia Holds Its Founding Convention," *Radio Free Europe Research.* February 24, 1989.
17. On February 16, 1989, the Sajudis National Assembly deputies took an oath that stated: "We, the deputies of the Sajudis National Assembly, having come to the Monument of Freedom on Lithuanian Independence Day, say: 'Lithuania should be as its people desire. Our goal: A free Lithuania! Our fate: Litusania! May God and all people of good will throughout the world help us'," quoted in Kestutis Girnius, "Lithuania: Independence Day Celebration," *Radio Free Europe Research* (March 16, 1989), p. 20. Similarly, after the completion of the "round table

talks," Walesa—in a statement which was broadcast nationally by Radio Warsaw on April 5, 1989—stressed that the new agreement with the government was "a starting point on the road to democracy and a free Poland."

18. For the latest developments in unofficial political life in the Ukraine, see Taras Kuzio, *Dissent in the Ukraine under Gorbachev* (Ukrainian Press Agency: London, 1989).
19. The other independent political parties which were involved in these negotiations are the Federation of Young Democrats, the Democratic League of Independent Trade Unions, the Hungarian Democratic Forum, the Alliance of Free Democrats, and the Endre Bajcsy-Zsillnszky Friendship Society.
20. For this controversy in the ranks of Polish opposition, see Jan Dziandl, "Opozycja w opozycji," *Polityka* (Warsaw), March 4, 1989, as well as the declarations of the Liberal-Democratic Party, "Independence" and "Fighting Solidarity" in *Kultura* (Paris), March, 1989.
21. *Pravda,* April 27, 1989.
22. *Pravda,* July 21, 1989.
23. Scott Shane, *The Baltimore Sun,* July 31, 1989.
24. *Pravda,* July 21, 1989.
25. The poll was commissioned by the Finnish daily *Ilta Sanomat* and published in the newspaper on May 3, 1989. See also Baltic Area Situation Report/5, *Radio Free Europe Research,* May 31, 1989.
26. Some attempts to launch a faction which advocates the dissolution of the Polish United Workers Party and the establishment of a social democratic one is to be found in the activity of the "Initiative of July 8th." Nevertheless, the influence of this group does not seem to reach beyond some academic circles. See Jan Dziadul, "Sztandary i Proporce," *Polityka,* September 30, 1989.
27. The manifesto appeared in *Nepszatadsag,* August 19, 1989. Quotations in this essay are from *Radio Free Europe Research,* vol. 14, no. 35 (September 1, 1989).
28. No dissident activity has been reported in Albania. As far as Romania is concerned, the most important independent group, Free Romania (*Romania Libera*), was launched by ethnic Romanian refugees in Hungary in 1987. Nevertheless, the supporters of this group in Romania have not managed to give considerable public dimension to their activity.
29. Following this line of argument, it is possible to make an even stronger point and to speculate that, for example, in Albania or Romania, a violent uprising or foreign intervention (as in Grenada) would overthrow the Center. In this case, all four stages would be missing. The reemergence of civil society would take place in a different, less organized (or even chaotic) way. Changes that do not develop along the lines of the four stages cannot easily establish stable structures of civil society. Those societies which do abolish socialism along the four-stage path have a better chance of creating a smooth transition to stable structures, since there is a steadier increase in the involvement of broader segments of the population. Therefore, the model offered here does not apply to foreign intervention or violent uprising.

Totalitarianism and the Rule of Law

*Roger Scruton**

It is widely conjectured that totalitarianism is incompatible with the rule of law. However, the reasons for this incompatibility remain obscure, and nobody knows whether totalitarian systems can evolve in a legal direction. In this paper I shall define both totalitarianism and the rule of law; I shall try to show why they are incompatible, and what this incompatibility amounts to; and I shall conclude with some reflections on the possibilities of change.

I. Totalitarianism

Hegel distinguished 'state' and 'civil society'—the first being the system of unified sovereignty, typically expressed through law, and the second being the sum of autonomous associations, formed through peaceful commerce, and lying within the jurisdiction of a sovereign power.[1] It is sometimes said that totalitarian systems are those in which civil society is controlled by the state. Such a definition fails to describe modern totalitarianism, in which neither civil society nor the state exist except in mutilated versions. Hegel's distinction applies to political organisms in their natural development, and totalitarian systems are not natural. They involve an attempt to constrain all associations towards an over-mastering purpose. And this can be done, I suggest, only by destroying free association (which is the natural condition of society)

*Previous versions of this paper were read by Professor Ellen Frankel Paul, Professor Joseph Raz, Professor Paul Q. Hirst, Mr. Justice (Sir Edward) Cazalet, and Dr. Milowit Kuninski; I am extremely grateful to them for many helpful criticisms and suggestions. I am also grateful to the participants in the Liberty Fund conference who saved me from many errors, to the Liberty Fund itself for making the conference possible, and to Pavel Bratinka for inspiration and advice.

and legal order (which is the natural condition of a state). In calling these things 'natural' I mean roughly what Hegel meant and what Aristotle meant before him—namely, that these are the ways in which societies and states "flourish according to their nature." Society is fulfilled in free association, just as the state is fulfilled in law.

A totalitarian system contains a power which recognizes no part of society as outside its concern, and against which there is no veto. A veto is a power to forbid: it creates a threshold which cannot be crossed. If I possess a veto over some action, then it can occur only with my consent; the existence of individual vetoes is therefore a sign (perhaps an indispensable sign) of consensual government. In Western systems, vetoes take the form of legal rights. If there are genuine rights, a society is not totalitarian.

Vetoes may also lie with groups and institutions. The rights of associations are vital to civil society and are anathema to totalitarian powers—whose first purpose is to control the ways in which people come together. Associations exist under totalitarianism only to the extent that they are tolerated; they can always be subverted or abolished at the behest of the controlling power. (Consider the churches, universities, orchestras, etc., which have survived under Communist rule.)

Totalitarian power does not reside in the state. Usually the controlling power is a party—i.e., a conspiratorial body, hierarchically organized, which controls the state while remaining independent of it. The party structure, which offers renewable privileges to the party membership, is more effective in achieving social equilibrium than is personal dictatorship. Indeed, under a properly organized party, totalitarian government perpetuates itself by an "invisible hand," without anybody explicitly intending it, merely because the rational pursuit of self-interest guarantees the ruling monopoly.[2]

The attempt to define totalitarianism has an interesting history. Some (notably Hannah Arendt[3]) have scarcely noticed the Leninist variety, seeing the roots of totalitarian order in nineteenth-century nationalism. Others—C. J. Friedrich, for example[4]—have recognized the centrality of the Soviet case, while emphasizing personal dictatorship of the kind exercised by Stalin. Others have drawn attention to the 'ideocratic' nature of totalitarian regimes,[5] or to the need—especially in the early years—for a gnostic pseudo-religion, a promise of salvation-through-knowledge, which mobilizes the party and justifies its crimes.[6] All those definitions and explanations point to important features of a complex historical process. Nevertheless, they have little application in the contemporary world, in which totalitarian regimes continue to spring up (Ethiopia, Syria, Iraq, Vietnam), which lack many of the characteristics that have seemed so important in the history of modern Europe. The definition I offer is more general and possesses greater explanatory power, since it captures a 'kind' of political organism, with its distinctive dynamic and innate powers of survival. A totalitarian state, I suggest, is one in which a monopoly power (usually a party, whether or not subject to a dictator) attempts to exert control over every aspect of society by controlling the individuals who compose it.

That definition has certain useful consequences. First, the concept of totalitarianism is distinct from that of authoritarianism—i.e., from the concept of a system in which commands are legitimized by authority. In an hereditary monarchy, for instance, descent confers authority (in the sociologist's sense[7]) on the Crown and therefore on the officers appointed by the Crown. The resulting authoritarian regime is compatible with limited government; indeed, it is favorable to it. It is in republics that the seeds of totalitarianism are most fruitfully sown. Those who see the origins of Soviet totalitarianism in Tsarist Russia are, for reasons summarized in this volume by John Gray,[8] profoundly mistaken—not only in their reading of history but also in the concepts which they use to understand it. (This is not to deny that there can be authoritarian regimes which are *also* totalitarian in my sense.)

Second, totalitarian control can persist in the absence of terror, and even with a considerable area of 'permission' over which it is not overtly exerted. Some commentators have argued that the USSR, for example, has ceased to be totalitarian, since the party has permitted areas of social and economic autonomy which it could not eradicate without damaging its own economic interests. What matters, however, is whether groups and enterprises can exclude the party and disobey its commands. To exist by the party's permission is not to possess a veto against the party's power: on the contrary. The point here is a logical one: the party may possess *control*, even though it no longer rules by *force*. Control rests in the one who must be obeyed, should he choose to command. And in this sense the Communist Party of the Soviet Union probably still aims to control the whole of society.

Finally, totalitarianism as I have described it is a project which may be realized to a greater or lesser degree. The project is to control society by abolishing every rival will. There is also a goal which is held to justify this project: the goal of controlling the *outcome* of social processes in the interest of some favored group (the proletariat, the Aryan race, the "people"). Confusion between the project and the goal is another source of the view that societies like the Soviet Union today are not really totalitarian.

No matter how much men may wish to control events, they cannot do so. Indeed, by attempting to control them, they may lose the little influence that they might otherwise have had. If we had no other proof, the experience of totalitarianism itself is sufficient to establish that the attempt to direct society to a comprehensive goal is irrational: as Hayek and others have persuasively argued, men can neither possess nor imagine the information that is needed for success in such an enterprise.[9] In referring to 'control', therefore, I do not mean the control of social outcomes, which emerge in unforeseeable ways and create their own intrinsic obstacles to the central plan. I mean the control of *people*: the ability to overcome their will, so that they do what one wants them to do. (Hitler's name for this—*Gleichschaltung*—is still appropriate.) The control of rational beings can be reliably achieved, provided one has complete information about their activities, unlimited power to harm them, and the preparedness to exercise that power.

It is often said that in modern Communist states, the bureaucracy, the black-market economy, the system of privileges and favors—all of which emerge inevitably as if by an invisible hand from the totalitarian project—place limits on that project, producing a social residue which obeys laws of its own. The outcome of any measure undertaken by the party will depend upon this structure of unintended interests, and cannot be seriously predicted by the party itself. "Five year plans," "accelerated development," and "*perestroika*" make interesting slogans, but they are shouted in increasing awareness that nothing can be done to realize what they propose. In this sense, indeed, the party may have less influence over social *outcomes* than any elected legislature. Every new attempt to *control* the social process leads to a new form of disaster—whether industrial, spiritual, economic, or ecological.

Nevertheless—to repeat—while the totalitarian *goal* is to control events, the totalitarian *project* is to control *people*, in the absurd and dwindling *hope* of controlling events. In full totalitarianism all activities, no matter who performs them, can, once known to the party, be stopped by it. If they persist, therefore, they persist either secretly or with the party's permission. That is what it means to say that there is no veto in the citizen's hand. As Lenin saw, the Communists can maintain the totalitarian project only so long as their will is undivided—hence the hierarchical structure of military command within the party, which he ironically called 'democratic centralism'. If there is a true threat to the totalitarian project in the Soviet Union, it comes as much from within the party—and from the possibility that its will may be unpredictably and irresolubly divided against itself—as from the subordinate social structures.

What I have said by no means provides a full analysis of totalitarianism in its current manifestations. But it enables me to say something about the decline of totalitarian systems—a subject which is of considerable importance to my later argument. This decline, I suggest, passes through two stages. The first consists in what Weberians would call the 'routinization' of the totalitarian order. The party still controls society, but its instructions are contained in rules and habits rather than in individuals. Of course, individuals may use the party machinery to assert their will and to establish local dictatorships. But it is the party *machinery* that provides their power—a power which therefore depends upon a general habit of obedience, itself the legacy of terror. This routinized condition is a totalitarianism of the "invisible hand," in which force and terror have been minimized, and people cooperate in their own enslavement. It has been called 'post-totalitarianism' by Václav Havel,[10] and certain writers, impressed by its rule-guided aspect, have supposed it to involve a kind of rule of law.[11] In order to show that this is not so, I discuss the case of Czechoslovakia below, until recently the purest remaining instance of a routinized totalitarian state.

The second stage of decline occurs as a result of routinization. The habit of terror dwindles, and neither the party *apparatchiks* nor their victims can really believe in the durability, and certainly not in the legitimacy, of their "mind-forg'd manacles." It becomes impossible to starve, hang, and shoot people in the proportions which the totalitarian project requires, and bit by bit the life of society begins to escape the party's vigilance. Eventually, the police force suffers from a vast insufficiency of information and a paralysis of the will.

When conformity is no longer guaranteed by regimentation, but merely encouraged by habit, the party cannot know how to exert the right degree of force towards the right target on the right occasion. People like Wałęsa, who should have been "liquidated" years before, suddenly appear at the head of a mass movement of opposition; people go secretly to Mass and have their children baptized; "anti-social" activities begin to occur in the crevices between monolithic blocks of interdiction—private charities for the relief of the poor; the circulation of poetry and philosophy; the growth of love and friendship with no socialist purpose. In time, even the party membership begins to feel the gravitational pull of these forbidden things, and in any case it no longer has the information that would enable it to suppress them. The system begins to fragment, as in Eastern Europe today. Can this decline be arrested, and can a rule of law emerge during the course of it? If a rule of law *can* emerge, then this is one way, I contend, in which the decline of totalitarianism will become irreversible (or reversible only by massive use of force).

What do we mean by the rule of law? This is the question to which I now turn. I shall be as brief as possible, and shall endeavor to remain neutral in the longstanding controversies of jurisprudence.

II. The Rule of Law

A law is a prescriptive rule, applying uniformly and determinately to those within its jurisdiction.

The terms of the definition need clarification:

(a) "*Prescriptive.*" A law is a command or permission. There are laws which appear to be descriptive: for example, laws specifying "jural interests" (rights, privileges, duties, etc.).[12] But interests are jural only if they are defined by commands: I have a right in law only if the law obliges you to respect it. Some laws are (to use the language of Kant) not categorical but hypothetical imperatives—for instance, laws establishing the *validity* of certain transactions: "if you want to make a will, then obtain two witnesses"; "if you want to make a contract for the sale of a house, then do so in writing." In other ways, too, the law can depart from the central paradigm. The law specifying the liabilities of an occupier of land, for instance, is not phrased in the language of command, but simply states the legal consequences of certain hypothetical acts and ommissions. Nevertheless, these consequences are legal only if they can be described in prescriptive terms: as legal duties which the subject is commanded to perform (the duty, for instance, to remedy any dangerous defect or, failing that, to pay compensation to the one who is injured as a result of it). Where there is no prescriptive statement which conveys the content of a putative law, then the law is no law at all but a sociological observation.

I have used the expression "prescriptive rule" rather than the more common "norm," since a norm can be either a rule that is obeyed or a habit that is followed. Commands and permissions belong to the same logical class: the command to walk is the negation of the permission not to walk, and vice versa. It is a logical truth that those things which are not forbidden are permitted. This is the prescriptive equivalent of a fundamental axiom of modal thinking.[13] Often the complaint is made against totalitarian criminal systems that the inference from '*x* is not forbidden' to '*x* is permitted' cannot be safely made. If that is so (and the evidence points strongly in this direction), then those systems are not systems of *law*. In what follows, however, I shall assume that this defect has been either cured or circumscribed: it is the other, and more interesting, defects that I wish to consider.

(b) "*Rule*." A rule has universal application: it applies to all members of a class.[14] As already indicated, we should distinguish rules (which are instructions to be obeyed) from regularities or habits, in which people *happen* to conform to a rule while not in any sense obeying it.

(c) "*Uniformly*." A law applies when and only when the agent and his action fall under the description given by the law. Exceptions may be provided for, but these also must be defined by law.

(d) "*Determinately*." It must be possible for a rational being, endowed with normal faculties, to know whether an action is forbidden or permitted by the law.

(e) "*Jurisdiction*." It must be possible to determine whether or not some given person is subject to the law. Jurisdiction is characteristically defined in terms of territory, citizenship, or religious confession.

All laws are prescriptive rules, but not all prescriptive rules are laws. What, then, are the distinguishing marks of law? This is the principal question over which naturalists and positivists contend. I therefore offer only a provisional answer. The positivists, I suggest, are right in thinking that the existence of a law is a social fact, which may or may not coincide with any precept of 'natural' justice. A rule is a law if and only if it forms part of a legal *system*. And while writers in the positivist tradition dispute over what this involves (conformity to a "basic norm," to a "rule of recognition," to a judicial procedure, etc.),[15] their various theories are variants of a single idea. A legal system is seen as a device for governing a community of rational beings. And so it is.

The truth in positivism is therefore summarized in a dictum of Lon Fuller's: "Law is the enterprise of subjecting human conduct to the government of rules."[16] But the dictum also hints at the truth in naturalism. For if we ask ourselves what is meant by "subjecting" and "government," we come quickly to the conclusion that not just any body of rules could count as a system of law. There are rules that emerge naturally in human society, by which rational beings are guided even when not constrained by some sovereign power. The rules that agreements are to be upheld (*pacta sunt servanda*), that disputes are to be referred to an impartial judge, that the life, limb, and property of the innocent are sacrosanct—such rules emerge spontaneously, as rational responses to the ordeals of social life, and no government which defied them would have the spontaneous consent of its subjects.[17] Left to itself, law would develop so as to incorporate these 'natural' rules, and impartial courts would spontaneously tend to affirm them.

Such naturalist thoughts are true and profound, though the defense of them lies beyond the scope of this paper. As we shall see, however, they place a question mark over the very idea of a "socialist" legality.

Not all laws are enforced. Some—for example, international laws—are maintained by a system of voluntary compliance. Others—moral laws, the 'natural laws' just referred to—are enforced only here and there. A *rule* of law, however, requires the enforcement of law against transgressors.

A law is enforced if a sovereign power commands general obedience to it, and retains the right to punish all proven transgressions.

The principal terms again need clarification:

(a) "*If*"—but perhaps not "only if." Perhaps there can be a habit of obedience, even when there is no sovereign power. (See Section IV below.)

(b) "*Sovereign.*" A sovereign power is supreme over (i.e., able to impose its will upon) all other powers within the jurisdiction, and subject to none outside it. A sovereign typically claims authority (in addition to power), and ought to *possess* the authority that it claims. Frequently, as in the UK and the US, this claim to authority is based on the very law that the sovereign is appointed to uphold. Thus the Queen holds office by virtue of the law, while the law is binding because the Queen commands it. (The air of paradox can be dispelled, but not in the space available to me here.)

(c) "*Command.*" A command is an order addressed to all within the jurisdiction.

(d) "*General obedience.*" All agents, individual or corporate, are commanded to obey.

(e) "*Punish.*" A punishment is a penalty arising when and because the law is broken. The right to punish may not be exercised: thus the enforcement of law is compatible with the practice of clemency, and also with the practice of issuing "cautions" and rebukes to certain categories of offenders. Civil laws are enforced through the criminal offense of "contempt of court." In such cases the court settles a dispute by making an order, and the sovereign then enforces that *order* in the usual way.

Law, and its enforcement, are essential ingredients in the rule of law. In addition: *there is a rule of law only if: (i) every power within the jurisdiction, including the sovereign power and its agents, is subject to the law; (ii) law is enforced against all proven transgressors and only against proven transgressors; and (iii) the law is comprehensive.*

To explain:

(a) "*Power*:" a decision-making body. Powers include corporations, political parties, and conspiracies.

(b) "*Agent*:" one who acts under orders from, and on behalf of, another.

(c) "*All transgressors*:" enforcement may prove difficult in a particular case, but the difficulty should not be the sign of an exemption.

(d) "*Only against proven transgressors*:" punishments should be administered only after a trial establishing the guilt of the victim. In the language of classical jurisprudence, *nulla poena sine crimine*.

(e) "*Comprehensive*." There is a rule of law only where the majority of judiciable matters are covered by law.[18] A state in which the law is scrupulously enforced, but in which most conflicts lie outside of it, is a lawless state. For example, if there is no law of tort, private justice will become the norm. (It has been one of the major defects of Communist legal systems that the disputes that would, in natural societies, be settled before a court of law often could not even be discussed there.)

The definition admits of many refinements. It also raises philosophical questions which are beyond the scope of this paper. For instance: what is it to follow a rule? What is a command? How are laws justified? Are all laws of equal status? The conception of law recently advanced by Ronald Dworkin,[19] according to which law involves a chain of interpretations, linking legislature to judge and the judge to his successors, may be thought to cast doubt upon the idea of law as a system of prescriptive rules. In fact (although Dworkin's extravagant language conceals this) the "interpretive" theory is compatible with the view that I have advanced. As we know from Wittgenstein's discussion of the foundations of language, it is no easy matter to say what 'rule-following' involves.[20] But for all Dworkin's attempt to redescribe the law as a form of meditation, its subject-matter is a system of rules, and the 'interpretation' to which he refers is something that is always required when a reasonable being either lays down a rule for others or follows a rule himself.

III. How is a Rule of Law Established?

It is best to approach this question by considering the ways in which a society might *fail* to enjoy a rule of law. Failure comes in five common varieties:

(i) The laws are not really laws.
(ii) The laws are not enforced.
(iii) The laws are not enforced against some transgressors.
(iv) The laws are enforced against non-transgressors.
(v) The law is not comprehensive.

Let us consider each of these in turn.

(i) *Not really laws*. Laws usually fail to be laws for one of three reasons: either they are not prescriptive rules, they are not impartially applied, or their application is indeterminate.

A law must conform to the principles of 'legality' (as Hart has called them[21]). It should be (a) general, with no arbitrarily defined exceptions, (b) free from ambiguities and obscurities, (c) publicly promulgated, and (d) not retroactive. Each of these conditions raises difficulties.[22] Nevertheless, they follow directly from the fact that prescriptive rules are addressed to rational beings. A rule that falls short in one of the four respects is a rule that we could not easily incorporate into our day-to-day plans. Therefore, although all legal systems are forced to admit the need for retroactive legislation, it is an established principle of Western jurisprudence that the effect of such legislation must be clearly foreseeable (as in the budget laws), and necessary to the purpose for which the law is made.[23]

A law is impartially applied only if judges are independent and truth is respected. A judge is independent to the extent that he has no personal interest in the outcome of the case. His sole interests should be legal: i.e., (narrowly) in upholding and applying the law, and (widely) in doing justice. The judge must take instructions from no one, and stand neither to gain nor to lose from his verdict.

When one of the parties is the State, the judge can be independent only if there is a "separation of powers." The failure of judicial independence in totalitarian systems, however, comes not through the judge's dependence on the *state*, but through his obedience to the *party*.

Truth and impartiality are inseparable. Legal rules can be impartially applied only by a judge who truly believes that the case before him is covered by them. He must therefore follow rules of evidence which are calculated to deliver the truth. (Trials by ordeal or by forced confession are therefore incompatible with a rule of law.)

The application of a law must be determinate: it must be clear which facts are operative and why. This condition is implied by the rule forbidding obscurities and by the demand for evidence. In practice, however, determinacy means the clear apprehension, in the mind of all concerned, as to why and how the law has been transgressed. To secure this is no easy matter, as we shall see. Indeed, absolute determinacy is an asymptotic condition—one which can be approached but never exactly attained.

(ii) *Really enforced*. The law is really enforced if (but, again, perhaps not only if) there is adequate policing, a sufficiency of courts, and determined investigation. Punishments must be adequate, and in civil cases the remedies must rectify, so far as possible, the mischiefs complained of. Civil law must therefore offer the remedy of injunction.

(iii) *Against every transgressor*. All those powers which can commit the acts which constitute crimes or civil wrongs must be subject to the law. This means that the law should accord legal personality or the equivalent to all moral agents. The state must also be subject to the law, and agents of the state who exceed their instructions should not be immune from legal action. Hence, there must be procedures of judicial examination—including trials of those who act *ultra vires*—in order to force the agents of the state to comply with the law.

It is arguable that there are no examples, in modern conditions, of a *full* rule of law, on my definition. The existence of diplomatic and other immunities ensures that, in all legal systems, some classes of wrongdoer lie outside the law. In a sense, however, this is because they are outside the *jurisdiction*: the law does not apply to them, because they are not *subject* to it. Alternatively, we might say that the law applies to them,but is not enforced against them.

(iv) *Only against transgressors*. Penalties should be imposed only after "due process of law," where due process involves the conditions elaborated under (i) above.

(v) *The law must be comprehensive*. Law must extend into all areas where obedience is the only guarantee of order. The law must provide penalties wherever the normal conscience demands them (although it may not provide exactly the *kind* of penalties that the normal conscience would prefer); it must also exact compensation for all generally acknowledged wrongs. The alternative is the "black market" in justice—in other words, anarchy.

Comprehensiveness normally requires a system of appeals, whereby problems demanding legal solution are signaled at their first occurrence. There must also be a process of legislation and discussion—either through the courts, as in common law systems, or through some legislative body, endowed with legal expertise.

Appeals are also important as a corrective device: that is, a way of compelling the legal system to police itself. It is possible for justice to be done without appeal, but to deny appeal is to jeopardize the distinction between a valid and a bogus verdict.

IV. Legal Reasoning

Law is addressed to rational beings, and whoever lays down laws commits himself to a system of thought with its own principles and procedures. Legal reasoning exists at many levels, and it is one of the miracles of our rational nature that we can spontaneously comprehend its lower levels, just as we spontaneously comprehend morality, language, and elementary mathematics.

The lower levels of legal reasoning involve two operations: interpretation and subsumption. By interpretation I mean the discovery of the law from statute, precedent, rules of equity, and abstract principles of adjudication. By subsumption I mean the description of the individual case so as to bring it under a law. The judge both discovers the rules and applies them. As with mathematics, the ease with which we grasp these operations contrasts with the difficulty we find in giving a philosophical account of them.[24] That should not prevent us, however, from making two distinctions which are essential to understanding the rule of law.

The first is the distinction between rules and their justification. A legislator, who must justify the rules, may rely on several considerations: for example, expediency, utility, or justice. It is an important philosophical question whether each of these is equally authoritative or equally central to the idea of legal order. A judge, too, must sometimes consider how a law is or ought to be justified if he is to interpret it. (Consider the English judge, searching for what Parliament "really intended.") Nevertheless, laws may exist unjustified, and to interpret is not in itself to justify.

The second distinction is that between internal and external reasoning. In interpreting laws, a judge engages in legal reasoning; his reasoning, although it answers some questions, raises others. For example, how is this statute to be reconciled with that, this decision with that? What law applies to this case, and how? To validate a decision is to derive it by valid steps from valid laws and principles. Legal positivists and legal naturalists give different accounts of validity. But they both recognize that, in every legal system, decisions are validated by reasoning which is internal to the law.

Sociologists and politicians look on law from the outside. For the sociologist, law has certain functions—coordinating actions, resolving conflict, maintaining order, and ensuring predictability. For the politician, it has certain purposes—changing society, helping his constituency, or maintaining his party in power. We may reflect on these natural functions and our own (often unnatural) purposes, and ask ourselves how the law should be constructed in order to further them. We then take an external viewpoint. Our reasoning is not legal; it answers no legal questions.

External reasoning tends to be instrumental: law is considered as a means to an end. When the jurist Ernest Weinrib distinguishes the "internal intelligibility of law" from the "external" and "instrumentalist" conceptions which threaten it,[25] one thing he might mean is that the legal validity of a decision is established by internal and not external reasoning. External reasoning may justify a law, but it cannot validate a legal decision. It does not follow from this that the law is an end in itself, or that it is self-justified, without reference to external purposes. The law may be a means to an end, even if it ought not to be considered in that light by the one who applies it. (In this, law resembles morality.)

But ought law to be considered instrumentally by the one who *makes* it (the legislator), even if it cannot be so considered by the judge? It has frequently been assumed—and not only by socialists—that the law may be used to shape society in accordance with a plan. It may even be thought that this is the primary function of law. Thus "the science of law," according to Roscoe Pound, "is a science of social engineering, having to do with that part of the whole field which may be achieved by the ordering of human relations through the action of politically organized society."[26] And those who accept what Robert Nozick has called an "end-state" conception of justice would be likewise disposed to think that, if law is an instrument of justice, it must be directed towards producing a certain kind of society, with a certain distribution of goods and opportunities.[27] Even the mildest and most constitutionally-minded socialist may be tempted by this conception, and the widespread use of legislation as an instrument of social reform can only encourage the belief that law is, at bottom, an instrument of our social purposes and a subject of our political will.

Against that, however, there is a tradition of thought—exemplified in our century by Hayek and Oakeshott[28]—which regards legislation in general, and reformist legislation in particular, as a deviation from law and a threat to its autonomy. Such thinkers will argue (though not always with the clarity that the subject demands) that law limits the purposes to which it can be put. For law has an *internal* purpose, which may be incompatible with the external purpose of the social reformer. This internal purpose is the administering of justice. Just as you cannot use an orchestra as a private army and expect it to retain its nature as a musical gathering, so you cannot use the law as an instrument of reform and expect its primary function—the dispensation of justice—to remain unimpaired.

Philosophers influenced by this appealing picture have tended to consider the common law (the law which has emerged from judicial decisions) as their paradigm. For common law arises spontaneously, from the attempt to do justice in the matter of conflict and crime. It is the common law which Hayek expressly contrasts with "legislation,"[29] and it is to the common law that Dworkin turns, in contrasting "principle" (which is internal to legal reasoning) with "policy" (which is not).[30]

An instance of the potential conflict between the "natural justice" administered by common law and the "social justice" which is the goal of socialist legislation is to be found in the United Kingdom 1968 Rent Act and its successors. By this law, many tenants acquired security of tenure, regardless of any contractual relation with their landlord. They also acquired the right to undo the terms of the contract which they had signed, and to ask the court to fix the terms (including rent) by which the landlord would henceforth be bound. In common law, however, a judge is bound to uphold the terms of a lawful contract, unless it should prove void or voidable (through deception, incompetence, or some similar defect). If all legislation were to have the character of the 1968 Rent Act, the court would become a device for the redistribution of property and the reform of human relations. It would then be doubtful that the court could also do justice, or be perceived to do justice, among the parties to a particular dispute.

Of course, it is a philosophical contention that "doing justice" is to be characterized in the Aristotelian way that I have assumed—as a matter of holding people to their bargains and giving to each man his due. Some might say that to do justice is to bring about the "just distribution," and that this involves precisely the kind of social engineering that Pound endorses and Hayek deplores. At the same time, however, the idea that justice is primarily a procedural matter ("adverbial," as Oakeshott puts it), resolving disputes according to the principles of natural law, is deeply ingrained in human nature. Even if there *is* no "natural law," there is a vivid disposition to believe in it. Decisions which defy the principle that *pacta sunt servanda* will never be regarded as *just* by those upon whom they are imposed, even if one party accepts them as advantageous. Hence the first result of the 1968 Rent Act was that arrangements between landlord and tenant became private, and were concluded only on the understanding that no party would ever go to law. Where no such understanding could be obtained, no rental agreements were made. (Hence the Rent Act was eventually repealed—an interesting instance of the way in which the short-term social benefits which may ensue from discounting natural justice are rapidly overtaken by the long-term social costs.)

Similarly, some activities could never be regarded as crimes (i.e., as acts deserving punishment) by those commanded to avoid them. Here, too, our instincts for 'natural' justice always seek to prevail. The attempt to criminalize activities which the normal conscience regards as innocent will inevitably bring the law into disrepute, and lead to its being neither perceived as law by its subjects nor applied as law by those charged with enforcing it.

Here I touch on a deep and difficult issue, but it is pertinent to my theme, since nothing illustrates the arguments of the preceding paragraphs more vividly than the practice of economic law in the "socialist" countries. In order to bring about "socialist relations of production," a system of law was devised which, far from facilitating those economic transactions which are natural to man, systematically obstructed them in the (absurd) hope of introducing a "socialist" economy. Normal buying and selling were both criminalized and covertly permitted (though selectively). (The permission was necessary, since no rational substitute for the market has ever been found.) The chaotic legal consequences of this in the Czechoslovak case have been patiently described by John Walter.[31] Apart from leading to the arrest and imprisonment of all the most productive elements in society, the operation of economic law has been fraught with such uncertainties and such arbitrariness that nobody can use it as a guide to economic conduct. Few citizens are disposed to regard the breach of it either as a crime or as a civil wrong, even when they themselves are victims. As Walter rightly says, the "pre-war (legal) system, based upon an abstract conception of justice and some balance between individual and state rights, has given way to a strictly instrumental approach to the law."[32] As a result, law has all but disappeared from the regulation of economic life, to be replaced by extra-legal devices and *ad hoc* decrees. Far from resolving social conflict, socialist economic law actively fosters it by punishing those who are most useful to the community and most disposed to live peacefully and decently within its bounds.

Even in those branches of the law which are not directly concerned with securing the socialist goal, totalitarian systems of law are made permeable to instrumental reasoning, so that the reasoning which justifies a law can also be used to set it aside. The real reason for many "socialist" laws is that they protect the party's monopoly of power. But if a law is treated as a genuine legal rule, circumstances may arise in which it supports the individual *against* the party, and so corrodes that monopoly. (The party's aims and interests are not always predictable.) In such cases, the law must be instantly reinterpreted in the light of the instrumental reasoning which led to its adoption. The decision is not validated legally, but instrumentally; expediency acts behind a facade of law. I give several instances of this below, as well as of other ways in which the idea of law as a system of thought, with its own internal principles, is eroded under totalitarian rule.

V. Common Law, Civil Law, and the Code Napoléon

The argument of the preceding section raises a question. To what extent does my discussion apply beyond the Anglo-American legal system? It is therefore worth making a few observations concerning the forms of legal order in the modern world.

"Common-law" systems include those of England (though not Scotland), the United States, and the former British colonies. These systems recognize the pronouncements of a legislature (statutes) as authoritative sources of law. But their procedures remain those of the common law, according to which previous decisions are binding until overruled by a higher court. Whole areas of English and American law are therefore creations of judicial reasoning. In addition, common-law courts remain bound by principles of "equity" that are derived from medieval ideas of natural justice. Where there is a conflict between equity and law, equity prevails. Hence the courts are far more independent of the legislature than in rival legal systems, and their decisions (especially in civil cases) retain much of their traditional character as attempts to "do justice" in the particular circumstances of the particular case.

"Civil law" or "civilian" systems are derived from the Civil Law of Rome. Roman law originated as a system of common law. However, following its codification by Justinian and his advisors, it assumed its novel character as an exclusively written system. This character is retained by its modern European derivatives, which claim to regard statute as the sole source of law. Nevertheless, even if that claim were true (which it is not), written law must still be interpreted, particular cases must still be brought *under* the law, and gaps in the law must still be filled. All those facts give a place to judicial reasoning, which may be as responsive in civil-law systems as it is in those based in common law, to the ideas of justice that I discussed in the foregoing section. Moreover, as Lon Fuller has persuasively argued,[33] no system can be applied without a background of "implicit law," governing the interpretation of statutes, the procedure of the courts, and the regulation of judicial conflicts. Particular cases therefore come to have almost as great a significance in civil-law systems as they have in the common law of England.

The Code Napoléon, which forms the basis of several European systems, was derived from the Roman Law, the common law of regal France, and the theories of Enlightenment jurists. Like the civil law, it is entirely written, and its leading cases are decided by a *Cour de Cassation*—a purely jurisprudential court, concerned with the interpretation of statutes. The clarity and subtlety of this court have caused its influence to extend far beyond the states which are governed by the Napoleonic system.

Most Communist legal systems were introduced into countries with a civil-law tradition. In some of these (Czechoslovakia and Hungary, for example), the civil law theoretically remained in force wherever it had not been explicitly or implicitly repudiated by "socialist" enactments. However, the absence of authoritative recent cases made it impossible to say what the remnants of civil law meant, and no judge could be certain how to apply them. In theory, the structure and procedure of the courts remained civilian, and statutes were the sole source of law. Matters of interpretation, however, were not settled by a jurisprudential court, but by an annual "commentary," which was usually more vague than the laws that it purported to clarify.

It is clear that cases cannot have the same significance in civilian and Napoleonic jurisdictions as they have under the common law. Nevertheless, their significance is almost as great, since it is only through individual cases that the meaning and application of statutes can be securely ascertained. Moreover, in all three systems, the background of implicit law gives to the judges a real, if limited, freedom to obey those procedures of reasoning which are internal to the law. The defects which I discern in socialist law are therefore not to be attributed to the civilian tradition. Wherever "socialist legality" has triumphed, that tradition is dead. And socialist legality is not a form of law.

In what follows I shall use the expression "civil law" in two ways: sometimes to denote systems derived from Roman law, and sometimes to denote the civil (as opposed to the criminal) branch of some particular system. The context will make the meaning clear.

VI. Sovereignty

Traditional legal positivists argued that law becomes a reality only when it is enforced. They also supposed that enforcement requires a sovereign, who is the source of law. Law is therefore the command of a sovereign who enforces it.[34]

Legal positivism was criticised by Sir Henry Maine for ignoring the existence of societies governed by customary law.[35] In such societies the habit of obedience may be sustained by no punishment beside the community's distaste, and by no sovereign higher than the conscience of the criminal. Alternatively, enforcement may be at the initiative of the injured party, as in Bedouin law, or in the highly sophisticated civil law of 18th century Poland and Lithuania, the "enforcement" of which is vividly described in Mickiewicz's *Pan Tadeusz*.

Perhaps Maine is right. Perhaps there can be law without sovereignty. And even when there is sovereignty, the law may be so stamped with the character of customary adjudication as to be irreducible to a set of sovereign commands. (Consider again the common law systems.[36]) However, these possibilities do not undermine our definition of the rule of law. We might respond to the fact of customary law in two ways: first, by arguing that enforcement does not require a sovereign, since the habit of obedience is enough; alternatively, by arguing that in such cases sovereignty vests in the community itself, and is exercised through its moral sanctions. Law may be enforced in unorthodox ways, but it must *be* enforced if there is to be a rule of law.

We should recognize, too, that even customary law has a prescriptive force. Only commands, or directives backed by commands, can be laws. This is equally true of those principles of legal reasoning which we might liken to rules of inference, as opposed to the substantive axioms of the law.

Our concern is not with "traditional" societies, but with modern forms of political order in which a sovereign power is recognized as the sole effective means of law enforcement. We may not agree with Bodin that such a power is necessary,[37] or with Hobbes that it is justified by contract.[38] But we must acknowledge it as a fact. In realistic discussions of the rule of law, the question will therefore focus on the sovereign power: how and to what extent is it legally disciplined?

VII. The Problem

The major difficulty is contained in a paradox: how can the sovereign power which enforces the law also be subject to it? Bodin and Hobbes wrote as though there were some kind of logical impossibility in this. The law is the sovereign's will, and the sovereign can therefore release himself from its provisions merely by changing his mind. If he cannot do so, then he is not truly free and not truly sovereign. The law places limits only on the action of subjects, not on the action of the one who commands them by means of it. This view is reflected in the English doctrine that the sovereign cannot be tried in person for any crime—

although the "crown" (i.e., the corporation whose sole member is the sovereign) can be liable for civil wrongs. On the other hand, English Common Law has recognized from the earliest times that the sovereign is subject to his own laws. The Year Book of Henry VI, following Bracton,[39] holds that "the law is the highest inheritance that the King has, because he himself, and all his subjects, are ruled by it."[40] Notwithstanding Crown immunities, such a view was accepted by jurists until Sir Edward Coke and James I crossed swords over it, and was effectively reaffirmed in 1688.

A simple response to this paradox takes its inspiration from Rousseau and Kant.[41] There is no contradiction, their argument holds, in the idea of a self-imposed law. Freedom means autonomy: i.e., making laws for oneself. Hence the will of a free being must be subject to the laws which it chooses and bound by those laws when the choice is made.

Sovereign powers are, as a rule, not individual human beings, and their laws are not moral laws (even if they sometimes coincide with moral laws). It is arguable, nevertheless, that the state *is* (in its normal and natural form) a moral person, and that the law of such a state expresses its will as a settled policy. A conciliar legislature, bound by constitutional rules, cannot change a law without debate: in the meantime everyone, including the state and its agents, remains bound by it. If laws change rapidly and continually, then the rule of law will break down, since the state and its agents will acquire the habit of avoiding legal penalties.[42] But the state then ceases to be a moral person, and the law ceases to be an expression of its will.

It is for this reason that the judicial examination of administrative decisions is a cornerstone of the rule of law. Judicial examination is one of those self-limiting habits which make the conscience of a state. For the judiciary can apply the power of the state against the state itself. However, administrative trials are effective only in certain conditions. The judiciary must be independent, and not replaceable by administrative edict. The procedure for initiating the trial must also be available to every citizen. (Trial of administrative decisions are sometimes called "judicial review"; but I shall avoid that phrase, which, in American law, means the judicial examination of the *constitutionality* of a law. There is no such procedure in English law.)

VIII. The Role of Constitutions

It should be evident that a written document is neither necessary nor sufficient for a constitution. A constitution is the sum of those procedures through which the will and personality of the state find expression. It is not identical with law, since it is that whereby law is made. Nevertheless, it has much in common with law, and one purpose of legislation is to protect and interpret the constitution. A constitution confers rights on the citizen only if the citizen can claim those rights by due process of law.

Written constitutions are of two kinds: prescriptive, like that of the United States, or descriptive, like that of the Soviet Union. A prescriptive constitution is a command addressed to all persons, including the sovereign, against whom it can be enforced by anyone entitled to its protection. A descriptive constitution merely states how things are, while making no provisions for its own enforcement. Only prescriptive constitutions are reasonably regarded as the generator of a country's law; even so, it is not the document that matters, but the human disposition to obey it. A descriptive constitution is not, properly speaking, a constitution at all, but an exercise in legal anthropology. Most descriptive constitutions are wildly inaccurate (like that of the Soviet Union), and contain contradictions and conflicts which remain forever unresolved, since they lay down no legal process for their resolution. The United States' constitution is a *program,* and its meaning is inseparable from the judicial reasoning that has governed its application.

Wherever there is a rule of law, there is a prescriptive constitution—whether or not embodied in a document. But it would be very foolish to infer from the existence of a constitutional document to the existence of a constitution. It would be even more foolish to argue from the existence of a *descriptive* constitution to the existence of a rule of law.

IX. Totalitarianism and the Rule of Law

Neither Nazi Germany nor the Soviet Union should be described as totalitarian *states*. In both cases the ruling power resides in the party and its agents, including the army and the secret police (which Lenin described as "the sword and shield of the party"[43]). Indeed, there may be something wrong in describing the Soviet Union as a state at all. It has only defective personality, and can be held accountable in law to no one, not even to itself. The sovereignty which it claims is a fiction, since all its decisions can be overridden by the party. Its law does not express its will, and is indeed (as I shall suggest) probably wrongly described as law. Of course, we must consider Mr. Gorbachev's reforms—but what, so far, have they amounted to? Laws are passed uniquely by the Supreme Soviet, which claims to be a legislative chamber, analogous to the British Parliament. But the operation of these laws can be canceled at once by decrees (*postanovleniia*) issued by the party high command (the Council of Ministers). These decrees may become law, should the Supreme Soviet so decide at its next meeting (which may be months away), or they may be withdrawn. In either case, the effect is one of retroactive legislation; moreover, the decrees can at once be renewed. The result is a kind of legal twilight in which nothing is clearly defined and the law's function of introducing certainty into areas of potential conflict is cancelled. Even if there *were* certainty between citizen and state, it would be of no significance. For the state is a phantom, without personality, and its sovereignty has been usurped by the Communist Party. Between the party and the citizen there is no certainty whatsoever, even if the citizen is a member of it—even if he is its chief secretary. (Witness recent events in China.) Yet it is only in his dealings with the party that the citizen *needs* the certainty which law could provide, since only the party has unlimited power over him.

In the conditions that prevail in the modern world, a rule of law requires full sovereignty in the state, as well as the limitation of the state by law and by the procedures necessary to change the law. Neither of these is compatible with full totalitarian power. For law confers vetoes on all legal persons, both individual and corporate, and these vetoes create the space in which a civil society can grow outside the reach of the ruling power. In saying this, I do not refer to written guarantees of rights, still less to "natural" or "human rights." Rights are of no effect without the method which may claim them. This method exists only where there is a rule of law. But where there *is* a rule of law, rights need not be explicit, since their existence is at once guaranteed by the legal procedure. As Dicey put it: "The *Habeas Corpus* Acts declare no principle and define no rights, but they are for practical purposes worth a hundred constitutional articles guaranteeing individual liberty."[44]

X. Some Facts

The goal of totalitarian power is the total control of society. (By "total control," I do not mean the constant use of overriding force, but rather the *capacity* to use overriding force should the need arise.) A rule of law involves the attempt to bring all powers *under* the law. Are these goals compatible? If not, can the rule of law be gradually extended to the point where the totalitarian imperative must be renounced? Let us look at the facts.

Modern revolutionaries are by nature hostile to legal restraint. Fouché put the matter succinctly: "he who acts in the spirit of revolution is allowed everything." From the beginning of the Revolution, we observe a rapid destruction of the law in France to the point where it can hardly be said to exist.[45] On the other hand, the French emerged from their revolutionary period with law restored and improved: the Napoleonic code now forms the basis for many rules of law in Europe and elsewhere. However, we should not draw too many conclusions from this, since it is doubtful that the French Revolution succeeded in establishing a totalitarian order despite sustained attempts. I propose, therefore, to study the Eastern European states—specifically Czechoslovakia—where totalitarian rule was imposed on countries hitherto governed by a genuine, if imperfect, rule of law, and where totalitarianism, until very recently, persisted in its 'routinized' derivation.

According to Marx, law is part of the 'superstructure', whose function is to maintain and reinforce the 'production relations' which are the 'material base' of society. "Bourgeois Law" is an instrument of class rule, with no ability either to change the law in a socialist direction or to survive the revolution which puts the proletariat in power. After that revolution, the disappearance of "antagonistic production relations" brings an end to class domination and to the state which is its instrument. The "withering away of the state" entails the withering away of law. Not only does the law therefore offer no legitimate impediment to the revolutionary purpose, it is strictly powerless to prevent it, and its survival after the demise of 'bourgeois' power is at best an anachronism.

Outside American universities, nobody now believes any of that.[46] This is hardly surprising, since it is in almost every respect the opposite of the truth. It is not capitalism which made the legal systems of Europe and America, but those legal systems—developing under their own inherent momentum—which created the free economy, and which also deflected it, in due course, in a 'welfarist' direction.

Nevertheless, Lenin believed the Marxian theory, as did his entourage. It was, after all, a useful thing to believe under the circumstances. Thus the Council of Peoples' Commissars, composed wholly of Bolsheviks, issued a 'Decree on Courts' on December 5, 1917, which abolished the entire legal system of the country with the exception of the local courts which dealt with minor crimes. A body of statute law remained, but the Decree instructed local judges "to be guided in making their decisions and rendering sentences by the laws of the overthrown governments only to the extent that these have not been annulled by the revolution and do not contradict the revolutionary conscience and the revolutionary sense of legality." By November 1918, all statutes of the pre-Revolutionary governments had been abolished, and a vast legal vacuum ensued in which the new "revolutionary conscience" could work as it willed—or, rather, as the party dictated. The bolshevik "jurist" N. V. Krylenko—later to become Stalin's procurator, active in several of the show trials—justified these moves in 1918 in a vulgar version of the Marxist philosophy of law:

> It is one of the most widespread sophistries of bourgeois science to maintain that the court . . . is an institution whose task is to realize some sort of special 'justice' that stands above classes, that is independent in its essence of society's class structure, the class interests of the struggling groups and the class ideology of the ruling classes . . . Bourgeois 'law', bourgeois 'justice', the interests of the 'harmonious development' of bourgeois 'personality' . . . Translated into the simple language of living reality, this meant, above all, the preservation of private property . . .[47]

Later, participating in Stalin's creation of a 'socialist legality', Krylenko argued that expediency ('*tselesoobraznost*'), not justice, is the ruling principle of the new Soviet legal system—expediency being defined not by the courts but by the party.[48]

The result, therefore, was the total abolition of legality, and its replacement by a Potemkin legality in which the party retained complete control over the outcome of every trial. Moreover, whole areas of law—in particular, the civil law of tort, contract, and administration—were simply wiped out, leaving a society rife with conflicts that could never be adjudicated, but which must be settled, if at all, by force—i.e., by the party, as the monopoly provider of force. This deficiency has never been fully remedied, and was passed on to the conquered countries of Eastern Europe. One vital condition for the rule of law—the comprehensiveness of adjudication—has, therefore been removed; it could be recovered only by a sustained effort of independent judicial thought and practice.

There are other interesting and transmissible consequences of the new socialist legality. One, notorious to students of the Soviet system (with the exception, once again, of those in American universities), is the new style of 'descriptive' constitution. Certain peculiarities of this device deserve mention. First, there is the habit of specifying rights and then at once taking them away. For example, Article 59 of the Soviet Constitution of 1977 tells us that the rights seemingly granted in the foregoing paragraphs (inviolability of the person and of the home, privacy of correspondence, etc.) are "inseparable from" certain duties and obligations, including the duty to "comply with standards of socialist conduct." Only the party is qualified to discern who does or doesn't comply with that duty, so that there are in fact *no* rights against the party (i.e., against the sovereign power). The list of duties accumulates thereafter, and no effort is made to show how they are to be reconciled with the rights that are plainly contradicted by them. (This peculiarity seems to be displayed by all Communist constitutions. See, for instance, Articles 174 and 203 of the Yugoslav constitution, which similarly give the party full power to cancel any right at any time.)

Secondly, there is the failure to specify or provide the means whereby an individual citizen may enforce those rights which the constitution describes.[49] It is worth reminding ourselves here of an observation made a century ago by Dicey:

> The proclamation in a constitution or charter of the right to personal freedom, or indeed of any other right gives of itself but slight security that the right has more than a nominal existence, and students who wish to know how far the right to freedom of person is in reality part of the law of the constitution must consider both what is the meaning of the right and, a matter of even more consequence, what are the legal methods by which its exercise is secured.[50]

Indeed, from the beginning there has been an explicit attack on those institutions such as judicial review ("bourgeois judicial review" as Stalin's notorious Minister of Justice Andrei Vyshinsky described it in 1938[51]) which would place the constitution at the citizen's disposal. As one Polish communist jurist expressed the point in 1946:

> The constitutional control of statutes by extra-parliamentary bodies, particularly judicial and quasi-judicial, is a reactionary institution and because of that, there is no room for it either in a socialist State, or in a State of people's democracy, which trusts the people's justice and the will of the people.[52]

Demands for judicial review and judicial examination of administrative acts are now frequently made by reformers in the Communist countries—particularly in Poland, Yugoslavia, and Hungary. The matter is also debated in the Soviet press, and in certain areas a measure of judicial scrutiny is now available. Nevertheless, it seems fairly clear that nothing like judicial examination in our sense has yet been established.[53] Hence the Soviet Constitution can contain the bare-faced assertion (Article 56) that "the privacy of citizens, and of their corresponding telephone conversations and telegraphic communications is protected by law," even though the KGB needs no permission to tap telephones, interfere with correspondence, or cancel telegrams. No citizen can do anything to prevent this, nor has the "law" ever been tested before a court. Article 56 is not only purely descriptive; it is also blatantly false.

Pressure for reform led the Czechoslovak Communist Party in 1969 to sanction the setting up of a Constitutional Court, which would have the express role of supervising the application of the constitution and providing a means whereby the citizen could appeal from the decisions of other courts, so that he could have his constitutional rights and privileges exerted against them. It is interesting to note, therefore, that this Constitutional Court has (at the time of this writing) never met, exists only in theory, and can be cited as authority for no decision. Recent appeals to it by the Jazz Section of the Musicians' Union (an organization which had become too popular for the party's comfort, and which was therefore 'criminalized') went unanswered, and it seems that no judge has ever been appointed to serve on its bench. Such fictions are entirely normal in socialist legal systems, and it would be foolish to conclude, from the apparent moves elsewhere, that a real structural change is just over the horizon.

In fact, it is difficult to know what judicial examination would really amount to in the absence of judicial independence. Although Soviet-style constitutions generally contain a clause stating (on no evidence) that judges are independent, President Novotný was more honest when, addressing the Czechoslovak Communist Party on April 5, 1960, he pledged that the new socialist constitution would eradicate "all remnants of the liberalistic, pseudo-democratic principle of the separation of powers." (Novotný was responding to directives issued at the time in Moscow.)

The destruction of judicial independence was a deliberate policy pursued by Communist governments following the takeover of Eastern Europe. After 1948 Czechoslovakia's Communist Party trained a whole new generation of judges in the following way: politically reliable factory workers were sent to '*dělnická přípravka*' ("workers' training"—in effect, indoctrination classes) for three months and then to law school for two to three years, where they were placed in special classes designed to guarantee their political orientation. They were then given the most important posts in the legal structure, which they were to operate as a system of "class justice." All untrustworthy elements were removed from the Courts and the procuracy, under a law advocating the 'democratization' of the Judiciary (Act no. 319, 1948); a two-year plan was then instituted, to introduce a completely new criminal law. Meanwhile, the party would directly intervene wherever required. The horrendous results of this have been described by one judge who escaped into exile—Otto Ulč.[54] Crimes by party officials went unpunished, no civil action could succeed against a party member, and all 'unreliable' elements could be sent down for long years in prison on the instructions of the local party machine. Similar abuses, surviving unchanged into our times, have been reported by other émigrés—notably by the Soviet jurist Olimpiad Ioffé.[55] An interview with a practicing judge in 1986, carried by the Polish *samizdat* bi-weekly KOS, made it quite clear that the secret police could still, at the time, determine the outcome of many serious trials.[56]

It is important to realize that this absence of judicial independence takes effect as much in civil or ordinary criminal cases as in political trials. Ulč gives many examples of Party "protection"; since *glasnost*, the Soviet press testifies to their regularity while stopping short of proposing a serious remedy. The difficulty in finding such a remedy is well illustrated by the following case, which was reported by a former defense lawyer in 1985: Leningrad bus drivers had sought compensation for monoxide poisoning due to faulty maintenance of vehicles. The first few cases were decided in favor of the plaintiffs; however, as soon as it was realized that hundreds more would follow, the party issued a secret directive forbidding any further decisions against the management.[57] The evidence is that such practice is entirely normal.[58]

Although the system of legal education introduced into Czechoslovakia in 1948 was abolished during the reforms of the sixties, it is nevertheless true that the party has endeavored to ensure that new lawyers are automatically obedient to its commands. Those seeking entry into the law school of the Purkyně University [now Masaryk] in Brno must currently fill in an application form which demands the following information: first, details of the part played by parents in "political and social organizations" (the intention being to favor the children of Party members, and to check on their record); second, of attendance and studies at school; third, of the applicant's social and political activism (*angažovánost*), for which a whole page is reserved; fourth, of the candidate's "character traits, personal values, and moral-political qualities" (*moralně politické kvality*—a peculiar phrase of Newspeak); and finally, among a group of ancillary questions, the actual examination results (which need be considered only *after* the political information has been positively assessed). The candidate must then name those "expert and political supporters" who could influence his application.

No doubt there have now been radical changes. But the courses announced for 1989 involved compulsory Marxism-Leninism "as the basis of higher study in general, and of legal studies in particular"; final examinations require, in addition to a knowledge of Czechoslovak law, an understanding of the "principle of the leading role of the Communist Party," of "democratic centralism," and of the part played by the "workers" in judicial practice. Teaching of Roman Law—the intellectural basis of legal education under the First Republic (1918–1939)—has dwindled to a fragment, while comparative law and jurisprudence were absent from the first degree.[59] The student therefore had no point of comparison against which to measure the rectitude of Czechoslovak law, and no training in judicial—as opposed to ideological—thinking. The textbooks reinforce the content of the courses, being for the most part ideological tracts written in Communist slogans, with a paucity of reference and argument that renders them useless as instruments of study.[60] The net effect is entirely to cancel the idea of law as a system of internal reasoning with its own principles and results, and to present it instead as a collection of political decrees, justified by purely instrumental considerations.

Occasionally, notwithstanding those precautions, people emerged from a legal "education" who had not been entirely purged of their sense of legality. In order to safeguard its position against the mistakes that such people might make, the party instituted in the early seventies an unpublicized "Police University"—the *Vyšoká Škola SNB*. This taught no Roman Law; it concentrated entirely on the political and ideological content of decision-making. Officially, it provided the basic training for interrogators and policemen. However, it also issued doctorates and was empowered to provide the qualifications needed by procurators and judges. Its graduates could always be relied upon, even in the most delicate cases, to put the will of the party before considerations of "bourgeois" justice.

Lest there should be any doubt about the judge's role in reaching a verdict, the matter was explicitly provided for by statute: Act 36 of February 26, 1964, "Concerning the Organization and Election of the Judiciary"—as amended by subsequent provisions. Section 24 of this, laying down the "basic duties" of the judiciary, includes the provision that judges shall interpret statutes and other legal regulations "in the interests of the working people." Since no legal process can determine what is meant from day to day by "the interests of the working people," the interpretation of statutes must therefore be determined by the party, as the working people's sole representative. The point has been expressed in Newspeak by the jurist Stefan Daniš:

> Judicial independence does not mean that a judge may arbitrarily assert his own, subjective, opinion. It is an independence which at the same

> time involves the judge's dependence on the socialist legal system which expresses the will of the ruling working class.[61]

In other words, the law is not determined by judicial reasoning at all, but by an extralegal, metaphysical entity—"the will of the ruling working class"—whose concrete embodiment in the world of mortals is all too familiar under another name.

Of particular significance is the position of the defense lawyer. Even in the Polish courts, the defense lawyer would gain access to the case files only after the investigation has been completed, usually with insufficient notice to prepare a full defense.[62] In Czechoslovakia, the defense, like the prosecution, was primarily a servant of the party. If, in a political trial (or any other trial in which the party has instructed the judge to deliver a verdict of 'guilty'), the defense lawyer made the mistake of defending his client, he ran a serious risk of being discharged, or even of being tried for "obstructing the course of justice." This has been the fate of several advocates in recent political trials—Josef Daniš, for example (no relation of the Stefan Daniš referred to above), and Ján Čarnogurský, both of whom were disbarred for defending signatories and spokesmen of Charter 77, and the first of whom was also tried on a variety of charges leading to a long spell in prison. (At the time of writing Čarnogurský has just been acquitted of "subversion," a truly historic event.) In the VONS trial (see below), the defense therefore made the point of publicly disavowing his clients, dismissing his own arguments as wholly insufficient, and congratulating the judge on a verdict which was richly deserved. In the circumstances, such behaviour is entirely rational: the alternative would be to follow his clients to prison. This, the advocate was likely to reason, is of no help to anyone. As for the circumstance of judges with a conscience—these were increasingly rare.[63]

More important than the conduct of the courts is the structure of the law that they apply. This is worth studying in some detail, since it shows the extent to which the "leading role" (i.e., the totalitarian ambition) of the party has acted as a solvent of the *law itself*, and not merely of the virtues of those charged with applying it. As Ioffé and others have made clear,[64] a great amount of Soviet law remains secret. This is because the judges are subject to secret party directives—also known as "instructive law"—which tell them how a given paragraph of the law is currently to be interpreted. This persistence of secret law is made possible by the wide and vague definitions given in the law itself.

The habit of vagueness dates from the earliest days of Bolshevik power. Article 6 of Lenin's Criminal Code of 1922 defines crime as "every socially dangerous action or inaction that threatens the foundations of the Soviet system." The purpose of this article (followed in subsequent codes) is to judge criminal behavior not by reference to the law, but in terms of its perceived political consequences—in other words, to replace internal with external reasoning as the true ground of a verdict[65]. Over the years, the development of "socialist legality" has introduced a variety of articles—worded in the most abstract language—designed to transmit this "higher" purpose throughout the legal system.

Consider Article 203 of the Czechoslovak Criminal Code as of 1989. This tells us that those who "consistently shirk honest employment and allow themselves to be kept by somebody, or acquire the means of existence in some other wicked manner, are liable to punishment." (All systems of "socialist law" include such a provision, sometimes known as the "anti-parasite" law.) Nowhere does the Czechoslovak law define what "honest" employment is, what "consistently" means, or the nature of a "wicked" manner. In normal systems of law, such vagueness is removed either by judicial reasoning and precedent or by jurisprudential argument (as in the Napoleonic *Cour de Cassation*). In either case, an authoritative record is required of the facts and arguments of each important case. (In true systems of law, the law itself is tried in the court.) It is through the record that law translates itself from merely formal principles to concrete rules that can be obeyed or disobeyed. Some philosophers—including Hegel[66]—have therefore argued that the record is always and necessarily part of the law. In Czechoslovakia, there is no authoritative record. Indeed, those (notably VONS—see below) who have tried to provide one have themselves been condemned to prison, on the grounds that such an attempt is criminal. Partial summaries have been published of certain cases, and a police record was also kept. But neither was available to public, and only lawyers issued with a special pass could obtain access to judicial records in the National Library.

It is true that Czechoslovak laws were provided with a commentary, which was supposed to be a summary of judicial practice and a guide to interpretation. But not only did the commentary provide no such thing, it often served to introduce vagueness where none previously existed. Consider, for example, Article 112 of the Code, which punishes those who "damage the interests of the republic by . . . dissemination of untrue reports in foreign countries about conditions in the republic." Paragraph 7 of the commentary tells us that an untrue report is not only

> a report which is wholly fabricated, but also a report which was originally wholly or partly true, but which has been modified by means

> of half-truths, tearing details out of context or other distortion, so that it assumes a tendentious sense directed against the republic and becomes as capable of inducing analogous unfavorable opinions about the republic as a wholly fabricated report.

Any Czechoslovak would see at once, through the verbal flummery, a single operative phrase: "capable of inducing unfavorable opinions." The term "untrue" has in effect been entirely subverted by the commentary, and replaced by a phrase of Newspeak whose standard meaning is "counter to the interests (whatever they might chance at the particular moment to be) of the party."

Equally significant is the practice of amending the commentary, so as to change retrospectively the application of the law. Article 29 of the Constitution holds that "citizens and organizations have a right to apply to the bodies of the elected deputies and other state organs with proposals, suggestions and complaints." In 1977, taking advantage of this article, a group of citizens signed Charter 77, which they presented to deputies and to the Ministry of Justice. The Charter accused the agents of the state of acting in breach of Czechoslovak law and in contempt of international pacts which had been incorporated into the law. The authorities responded with accusations of "subversion" against "persons unknown": this was to serve as a warning to the Charter signatories and as an instruction to those who employed them, who promptly sacked them from their jobs. There was no clear way in which the existing (1975) commentary could be reconciled with this charge of "subversion." The next edition (1980) therefore added two new clauses:

> A subversive character may also be attributed to so-called open letters containing distorted data and slanders about conditions in the republic, which, though addressed to the party, state or other central organs in the ČSSR, are handed over to the correspondents or other organs of imperialist powers to be used against the ČSSR in international forums. . . . the provisions [of this article] are not at variance with Article 19 of the International Pact on Civil and Political Rights . . . which was signed by the ČSSR.

Those clauses reinterpret the law so that it applies to an act committed three years *before* the interpretation was promulgated. Such adjustments to the commentary show how important it is for the law to be vague, so that its interpretation remains infinitely flexible and all prosecutions and persecutions can be retrospectively legalized. Judicial practice is therefore never a clear guide to the law, which can be used to criminalize any activity at any time.

Such laws fail the criteria of legality proposed above. It could be said that they enabled the party to imprison whomever it liked. It would be more accurate to say, however, that the party's ability to imprison whomever it liked explained the existence of such laws.

The ability to persecute at will goes hand in hand with the ability to exonerate. Discussions in the ruling party are bound to involve the communication of negative assessments intended to influence people against existing policies. Under Article 100 of the criminal code, this constitutes incitement. An implied exoneration of the party and its members, therefore, is already built into the article. This fact is not intended to go unnoticed. Indeed, to interpret the code as it is meant to be understood by the ordinary citizen, we must generalize the exoneration. The citizen must recognize that the party is released from the law, and also that the party *could*, should it so choose, ensure the prosecution of any of its members at any time for breaches of law which it commands him to commit. This is one of the ways in which membership of the party involves enslavement by the party.

Even if the law seems explicitly to permit an activity, the fact of engaging in it may be cited as proof of a criminal intention. Consider the case of Drahomíra Fajtlová, sentenced for incitement in Hradec Králové on July 18, 1984. The prosecution proposed (and the court accepted) the following proof of hostile intent towards the socialist system:

> The accused negatively influenced some of her fellow workers in front of whom she read letters from the family of Jiří Lederer [a dissident writer who was forced to emigrate]. She praised the western way of life and positively evaluated persons who had taken part in Charter 77. She often spoke about the Pope, and displayed his picture. Her opinions about various occurrences were in direct contradiction with generally accepted opinions in our society. Neither she nor her family voted in the last elections—by that abstention she expressed her attitude to our republic in a clear manner.

"Negatively influenced" is added in order to establish the crime of incitement under Article 100. But the acts complained of were all explicitly permitted by Czechoslovak law—including the abstention from elections. (Not even Czechoslovak law has criminalized "opinion.") The obvious conclusion to draw from this and similar cases is that laws like Article 100 are not rules describing acts which are to be avoided, but ritual formulae which must be pronounced whenever someone is being punished.

Particularly interesting in this respect is the fate of VONS (the Committee for the Defense of the Unjustly Persecuted), whose main purpose was to report and publicize miscarriages of justice, and as a means to that end to keep a record of cases which would indicate the meaning of the laws. In the first and most important trial of the VONS committee, in 1979, its members were accused of subversion because they expressed disagreement with verdicts of subversion. The party wished to show that it had ways of making clear what "subversion" meant. This notwithstanding, both the Czechoslovak Constitution and the International Pacts which Czechoslovakia incorporated into its law in 1976 permit the activities for which the VONS members were condemned. All that the citizen could understand from the verdict—and all that he was supposed to understand—was that he is not permitted even to *discuss* the meaning of the laws which bind him. It is a punishable offense to try to discover how punishment is avoided.

The vagueness of the law means that canons of evidence are also unclear—or, when clear, not respected. In one case a man wrote a letter to his friend in England, expressing the view that the outcome of the VONS trial was unjust. He received a three-year sentence for damaging the interests of the republic abroad through knowingly disseminating "untrue" statements. The only evidence offered for this was his opinion about the justice of the verdict. It is also implied that he lied in giving this *as* his opinion: how else could he be said to "knowingly say something untrue"? No rules of evidence known to English or American courts could possibly establish such a verdict on such facts.

As we have seen, the defects of the law mean that retroactive legislation is normal. The retroactive force of the law is felt in both civil and criminal cases. Consider the law relating to emigration. Under Article 109 (now repealed), emigration without permission was a crime. In order to punish those who successfully escape, the party devised indirect punishments—both legal (the confiscation of goods) and extra-legal (the systematic persecution of relatives). People who intended to emigrate, therefore, sold what they could before leaving. One day, the police confiscated a car that had been bought from an emigrant six months before his departure. The court upheld the confiscation, on the grounds that anything sold by the emigrant for up to one year before his departure had been sold in preparation for the criminal act, and was "therefore" already forfeit to the state. The owner, in other words, had no claim against the police.

The purpose of such retroactive law is to instill the practices of buying and selling with immovable anxiety, forcing the citizens themselves to maintain the pressure against emigration through the principle of *caveat emptor*. A like purpose can be discerned in all socialist law: to create a self-policing society which does not need law, but only punishment, in order to maintain its precarious equilibrium.

XI. Civil Law

There is not space here to do justice to the civil law and its problems—though some of these problems can be inferred from what I have written. The civil law in socialist states is radically incomplete—especially in tort (including vital areas such as product liability and nuisance), administration, and contract—and seems to lack important remedies, particularly the remedy of injunction. (The best a citizen can hope for is a "declaration of illegality"—strictly useless against any activity which has the support of the party.)

Consider the law of nuisance. In Czechoslovakia there are currently upwards of 300 laws designed to protect people and the environment from polluters. But the Ministry of Industry has had complete discretion to exempt any enterprise from these laws on the grounds of its economic importance. (The local party officials could also issue discretionary edicts, creating similar exemptions.) The effect is that *no* major polluter in Czechoslovakia has been subject to control, and the law has been applied only to those small and relatively harmless activities which were of no interest to the party.

This is but one instance of a general principle. Since the party has a monopoly of economic power (as well as every other kind of power), it is necessarily the greatest tortfeasor. But no action could be successfully brought against any enterprise through which the party's power was exerted. Hence the law of tort played no real part in regulating human conflict. This can be vividly seen from the case of Chernobyl: no victim of this disaster has brought an action for compensation, nor has such a course even been suggested by the party, which confines its response to a criminal prosecution of those "responsible."

Indeed, the existing sources of Soviet civil law[67] show virtually nothing corresponding to the "law of obligations" as it has arisen in the civilian tradition. Instead, activities liable to cause damage to others are governed by extensions of the criminal law. The primary form of negligence is therefore criminal negligence, a vast and expanding field of socialist "legality." As John Walter remarks, "the concept of imposing criminal responsibility and even prison sentences for negligent damage to property is unique to the socialist bloc, having no parallel in Anglo-Saxon law. Even Western civil-law countries such as Sweden and

West Germany penalize negligence only in the case of arson."[68] A vivid illustration is provided by Soviet maritime law, which endeavours to regulate shipping and guard against accidents and hazards entirely by imposing criminal penalties on the personnel involved.[69] Not only is criminal law an extremely clumsy device for the regulation of such delicate conduct, but the absence of a civil action leaves the resulting conflicts unresolved. The victim of tort has no guarantee of damages, while the perpetrator will not suffer for his fault if he can call on those party immunities which cancel the effect of petty crimes. Once again, the paucity of written reports—and the unauthoritative nature of the few available—makes it difficult for a citizen to know whether he *does* have a civil action. Even in the case of injuries received during the course of employment (for which compensation is guaranteed by statute), the courts—as the case of the Leningrad bus drivers shows—will obey party directives rather than the written law whenever the two are in conflict.

Those defects in the civil law of socialist countries do not stem from the Roman-law background. Although branches of law such as tort, contract, and property have a very different *appearance* in common-law and civil-law jurisdictions, they are founded on identical principles. Both the common law and the civil law acknowledge the principle of restoration—the principle that 'the person who is bound to make compensation must restore the situation which would exist if the circumstances making him liable to compensate had not occurred.' (This principle is explicitly incorporated into the German Civil Code at section 249.)[70] The principle applies whenever one legal person is tortiously injured by another. Two consequences follow: first, that there is neither cause nor need for the criminal law in punishing negligence; second, that there is a general and predictable cost attached to negligent behavior, so that all business tends to be conducted according to a "duty of care." The effect of this in such matters as product liability (for instance, in the leading case of *Donoghue v. Stevenson*[71]) is well known. In socialist systems, people can be poisoned with impunity and will have no redress: hence the rapidly declining life expectancy and rising infant mortality in Eastern Europe.

Nor should the paucity of reported cases be regarded as a trivial defect. As I have already argued, reports of leading cases are as important in Napoleonic and civil-law systems as in common-law systems; without them, the law remains indeterminate. If you wish to know how liability is assigned under the Napoleonic system, then you must look at the cases. For instance, the law says that "*l'on est responsable des choses dont on a la garde*" ("one is responsible for the things of which one has charge"). But what is a '*chose*', what is meant by '*garde*', and how is this responsibility assigned? The answer is not given by statute, but by the *Cour de Cassation* in a lengthy judgment.[72]

No such answers have been available to lawyers living under socialist systems. As the editor of a collection of Soviet civil law cases has put it: "a peculiarity of the Soviet legal system which separates it from its continental cousins is the manner in which court cases are published, which is, in a word, selective at best, woefully incomplete at worst."[73] Once again, the party interest is at work in concealing information. For the party must ensure that the law is maintained in a state of vagueness, lest liability for wrongs should fall on those who (principally) cause them—namely, the party and its agents.

There are other problems, too, some of them legacies of the Marxist jurisprudence upon which Stalin drew for his first "socialist" codes. Engels said that in the communist society of the future, the government of men would be replaced by the administration of things. The Soviet jurist E. B. Pashukanis took this to provide a clue to the "socialist" law that would prepare the way for the law-free paradise that had been promised in the sacred texts. Legal regulation, he argued, is required only where interests conflict. Where there is true unity of purpose, only "technical regulation" is needed.[74] Hence, socialist enterprises and cooperatives—which have already transcended the "antagonistic" production relations of capitalist society—have no need of law. If disputes arise between them, these are of transitory significance, due to this or that recalcitrant element and not to any real conflict of interest. Such disputes can therefore be resolved by socialist means—through discussion and arbitration, rather than through law.

From such pie-eyed reasoning there developed, in time, an extraordinary branch of quasi-law called "state arbitration" (*státní arbitráž*, in Czech). Socialist enterprises can never claim realistic damages against each other for either negligence or breach of contract, and their relations exist in a legal twilight in which corruption spawns, stock perpetually vanishes, and accounts are only spasmodically presented. The loser in every conflict is the state, which must compensate for the follies of its favored progeny. And by doing so, the state advances the spiral of inflation.

The absence of true commercial law goes hand in hand with the fact that corporate personality is defective almost everywhere. The real decisions have rested, in the last analysis, with the party, not with the firms, cooperatives, schools, universities, etc., which are the subject of legal action. And all such bodies can avoid liability by invoking party immunities. For example, bankruptcy has been a real possibility only in Hungary: elsewhere, all 'socialist enterprises' have been protected indefinitely from the legal and economic consequences of their actions. In fact, corporate personality in such a system seldom amounts to anything more than "Potemkin personality," in which arbitrary decision-making exists behind a facade of accountability.[75]

And what of the party itself? Is it a legal person? Officially, yes. But can it be sued in civil law? Can it be held guilty of crimes? There are no known instances where this has occurred, and no advisable procedures for initiating a trial: the principal agent of the party—the secret police—has had its own way with those who challenge it before the law. In effect, therefore, the greatest wrongdoer lies outside the reach of the law—which, as an instrument of rectification and compensation, can hardly be said to exist.

XII. An Interpretation

My brief review of facts should be set against others, more notorious though perhaps less revealing: the fact that in political trials in the Soviet Union no verdict of guilty has ever been overthrown on appeal;[76] the fact that figures for prison populations in Communist countries are official secrets; the fact that prison sentences, which account for only 2½% of sentences in British courts, comprise 30% of the punishments administered in Polish courts;[77] and the most revealing facts of all—the low number of acquittals in criminal cases (15% in Czechoslovakia, a mere 1% in the Soviet Union[78]), and the truly incredible number of convictions. In Czechoslovakia in 1970, 1 person per 120 members of the population was sentenced for a criminal offense: i.e., 1 adult in 50. This figure has varied over the years, but not so much as to defeat the startling implication: until the recent changes in Czechoslovakia, *one criminal sentence was passed for each adult life-span.*[79]

All those are signs that the law has a different function in socialist states from the function that we know. In fact, if we go back and look over my brief survey of the facts, we can quickly see that none of my conditions for a rule of law obtain. The laws themselves are defective: they admit arbitrary exceptions, they are maintained in a state of ambiguity and obscurity, and they may apply (as interpreted) retroactively. It is doubtful that they can be called prescriptive rules, and they are certainly not intended to draw a clear line between what is permitted and what is not. The laws are indeterminate and unsupported by any judicial record.

There is neither judicial independence nor a clear rule of evidence. Indeed, the guarantees against judicial independence are so deeply entrenched in the system of legal education as to suggest that the law is a kind of conspiracy against its own application.

Laws are not enforced against all transgressors, nor only against transgressors. Legislation is not (and cannot be) comprehensive, and the most important power within the jurisdiction lies outside the reach of law. Its members may suffer penalties, but *it* cannot. Corporate personality is either defective or (as in the party's case) merely fictional: in neither case does it permit certainty in civil action. And the standard limiting devices—such as constitutional rights, judicial review, and citizen's access to the courts—exist only in Potemkin form.

The facts speak for themselves: since law is subjected to the aims of the party, the totalitarian project is incompatible with the rule of law. In order to establish a rule of law, the following would be necessary: the party must become a legal person; its agents must become fully liable for the consequences of their acts in both civil and criminal law; the law must become precise and comprehensive; the judiciary must be independent; and it must be possible for any citizen to obtain adequate redress against the party itself—including injunction.

The reforms currently proposed in the Soviet Union include a few moves in this direction. Thus the CPSU Central Committee presented certain 'theses' to the 19th All-Union Party Conference, on May 23, 1988, in which—wedged within sturdy walls of Newspeak calling for the "completion" of the "socialist legal state" and the "further enrichment" of "social rights"—we find, here and there, phrases reminiscent of genuine legal thinking: a call for "adversarial competition," for instance, as well as one for "the presumption of innocence." (Officially, those things already exist, which perhaps shows the likely effect of any new attempt to introduce them.) The "theses" even argue that "judges, procurators and investigators should be protected from any pressure or interference in their activity," and that "they must be subject to the law and the law alone."[80] No mention is made, however, of the procedures required to achieve those goals, and the phrases are no sooner uttered than negated by the flow of Newspeak, which calls for a "resolute enhancement of the militia's responsibility for combating crime," "the broadening of the potential of state arbitration" . . . etc.[81] We can guess how difficult it will be for the few real aspirations expressed in this document to translate themselves into policies.

The fact is that things will remain in the present unsatisfactory state so long as reform is conducted from "above," i.e., in such a way as to confirm the "leading role" of the party and maintain its monopoly of power. Even moves towards judicial review are worthless, so long as the judges remain—as, in the USSR, they are now—servants of the party.[82]

'Socialist law' should be seen as an instrument of social control in the hands of the party. Such law is not the will of a sovereign state, since the state, like the law, is a mere instrument of the controlling power. Neither the state nor the party nor any other corporate agent is a responsible person before the law. Indeed, personality has been effectively chased from the law, which instead operates as a mask of unanswerable power. The government of men has indeed been replaced by the administration of things: things, not persons, exercise power in this system—and although persons are subject to the power, it treats them, too, as things.

XIII. The Future

What are the prospects for a true reform—a reform from below that will subject the party to the law? Recent events in Eastern Europe must give us hope. Calls for judicial independence are now standard in the Polish and Hungarian press, and will no doubt become so in East Germany and Czechoslovakia as well. They have also been made by unofficial groups in Yugoslavia.[83]

The Solidarity-led government recently installed in Poland aims, indeed, to establish a genuinely post-totalitarian order, and the first moves towards judicial independence have already occurred. A National Judiciary Council (*Krajowa Rada Sądownictwa*) has been promised. This will be an independently elected body, which will propose candidates for judicial office to be nominated by the President. And it is certain that no member of the Communist Party will be on its list of nominees. A National Council of Defense Lawyers (*Narodna Rada Adwokacką*) now exists, and it is already impossible for the party to issue instructions to those who appear on behalf of its victims. These reforms issue from bodies other than the Communist Party. Hence they will both limit the party's power and, at the same time, establish the virus which could destroy the totalitarian system.

Nevertheless, further reform requires a clearer perception of the goal than has hitherto been expressed by opposition writers. Judicial independence is not enough; and the call for "human rights"—i.e., for rights defined universally and without reference to the legal procedures needed to secure them—must inevitably overshoot the target. The most important demand must be for the legal incorporation of the Communist Party and its agents. It must become possible for a civil action to succeed against the party itself, and for penalties to be imposed on it that are adequate compensation for its wrongdoing. Genuine laws of contract, tort, and administration must come into place, and in commercial dealings "state arbitration" must cease to take precedence over judicial trial. Finally, a record of cases must be kept, along with a full account of the reasoning used to settle them.

If such reforms are instituted, however, the impersonal, unanswerable law of Communist government will give way to genuine law, expressing the personality of a sovereign state, which will govern and restore the personal relations between citizens. Such a law would treat the citizen as an end in himself, and not as a means to his own replacement by the more pliable "socialist man." And then, at last, the administration of things will give way to the government of men.

NOTES

1. G. W. F. Hegel, *The Philosophy of Right*, trans. T. M. Knox, (Oxford: Oxford University Press, 1942).
2. On the "invisible hand" of totalitarian order, see V. Havel, "The Power of the Powerless", in V. Havel et al., *The Power of the Powerless*, ed. John Keane (London: Verso, 1985). Also, R. Scruton, "The New Right in Central Europe I: Czechoslovakia", *Political Studies* XXXVI (1988), 449–62.
3. Hannah Arendt, *The Origins of Totalitarianism*, (Harmondsworth: Penguin Books, 1982).
4. C. J. Friedrich, "The Unique Nature of Totalitarian Society", in C. J. Friedrich (ed.), *Totalitarianism*, Encyclopedia of the Social Sciences vol. 15, New York 1968, pp. 106–12.
5. The term 'ideocracy' was coined by N. Berdyaev. See the discussion by A. Walicki in his contribution to this volume.
6. A. Walicki, in this volume; W. Gurian, "Totalitarianism as Political Religion", in C. J. Friedrich (ed.), *Totalitarianism* (Cambridge: Harvard University Press, 1954), pp. 119–29. The "gnostic" elements in Leninist thinking have been well documented by Alain Besançon, *The Intellectual Origins of Leninism*, trans. Sarah Matthews (Oxford: Basil Blackwell, 1981).
7. In this sense, a person has authority if others are disposed to treat him as though he had a right to be obeyed.
8. See John Gray's essay in this volume.
9. This argument has many forms. See, for example, F. A. Hayek, "Cosmos and Taxis" in *Law, Legislation and Liberty, vol. I; Rules and Order* (London: Routledge, 1973).
10. See V. Havel, "The Power of the Powerless."
11. See, for example, Paul Q. Hirst, *Law, Socialism and Democracy* (London: Allen and Unwin, 1986), ch. 3.
12. See W. N. Hohfeld, *Fundamental Legal Conceptions* (New Haven: Yale University Press, 1923), ch. 1, for the classic account of "jural interests."

13. See Joseph Raz, "Legal Gaps," in *The Authority of Law* (Oxford: Clarendon Press, 1979), pp. 75–77.
14. The idea of the universal nature of prescriptive rules has been greatly clarified by R. M. Hare in his moral philosophy, notably in *The Language of Morals* (Oxford: Clarendon Press, 1951). The point is not that such rules apply generally, but that they apply to particulars only as instances of a universal. See also Karl Olivecrena, *Law and Fact* (2nd ed.; London: Stevens and Sons, 1971).
15. The "basic norm" theory is that of Hans Kelsen, *The General Theory of Law and State*, New York, 1945; the "rule of recognition" theory is that of H. L. A. Hart, *The Concept of Law* (Oxford: Clarendon Press, 1961); while the emphasis on judicial procedure and institutions is characteristic of Joseph Raz, *The Concept of a Legal System* (Oxford, Clarendon Press, 1982).
16. Lon L. Fuller, *The Morality of Law* (rev. ed.; New Haven: Yale University Press, 1969), p. 106.
17. Hence such rules will be incorporated into the terms of a social contract, if there could be such a thing. (Which is why social contract theorists pay such attention to "natural law.")
18. My use of the term "comprehensive" should be distinguished from that of Joseph Raz, who uses it to indicate that legal systems claim the authority to regulate any type of behaviour. (See *The Authority of Law*, pp. 116–17.)
19. Ronald Dworkin, *Law's Empire* (Cambridge: Harvard University Press, 1986).
20. See L. Wittgenstein, *Philosophical Investigations* (Oxford: Basil Blackwell, 1952), pt. I, and S. Kripke, *Wittgenstein on Rule-Following and Private Language* (Oxford: Blackwell, 1985).
21. H. L. A. Hart, "Problems of the Philosophy of Law," in *Essays in Jurisprudence and Philosophy* (Oxford: Clarendon Press, 1983), p. 114.
22. See my discussion in "*Rechtsgefühl* and the Rule of Law", ed. J. C. Nyíri and Barry Smith, *Practical Knowledge: Outlines of a Theory of Traditions and Skill* (London: Croom-Helm, 1987), and the discussion of these and four similar principles by Lon Fuller, in *The Morality of Law.*
23. There are problems, however, concerning the common law, and the correct description of what happens when a previously binding authority is overturned by a higher court. See R. Dworkin, "Hard Cases," *Taking Rights Seriously* (London: Duckworth, 1976).
24. See the important considerations raised by Ronald Dworkin in "Hard Cases" and "Taking Rights Seriously," both in *Taking Rights Seriously*.
25. Ernest Weinrib, "Legal Realism," *Yale Law Journal*, May 1988.
26. Roscoe Pound, *Justice According to the Law* (New Haven: Yale University Press, 1951), p. 30.
27. Robert Nozick, *Anarchy, State and Utopia* (New York: Basic Books, 1974), pp. 153–55.
28. F. A. Hayek, *Law, Legislation and Liberty*,; Michael Oakeshott, "The Rule of Law", *On History and Other Essays* (Oxford: Basil Blackwell, 1983).
29. F. A. Hayek, *Law, Legislation and Liberty*.
30. See R. Dworkin, "Taking Rights Seriously."

31. John Walter, "Law as an Instrument of Economic Regulation: Economic Crime in Czechoslovakia, 1947-1987," in *Review of Socialist Law*, vol. 14, no. 3 (1988), pp. 209–39.
32. *ibid.*, p. 238.
33. Lon L. Fuller, *Anatomy of the Law* (Harmondsworth: Penguin Books, 1971), pp. 71–99. Compare Karl Olivecrona, who argues (p. 108) that, under any system, whether or not codified, "rules have always, and on a large scale, been introduced into the legal system through the wish of the courts."
34. This is the view expounded by John Austin in *The Providence of Jurisprudence Determined* and by Jeremy Bentham in *Principles of Law and Legislation.*
35. Sir Henry Maine, *Village Communities, East and West* (London: John Murray, 1881), pp. 67–71. The point has been made in a more sophisticated manner by Hart, in his argument that the rules for punishing deviants "may indeed be indispensable but they are ancillary" to the legal system, and not part of what it is to *be* a legal system. (*The Concept of Law* (Oxford: Clarendon Press, 1961), p. 38).
36. See the criticisms levelled against H. L. A. Hart's updated form of legal positivism by Ronald Dworkin in *Taking Rights Seriously*.
37. Jean Bodin, *Six lives de la république*, 1576.
38. Thomas Hobbes, *Leviathan*, 1651, ch. 17.
39. Henry de Bracton, *De legibus et consuetudinibus Angliae*, quoted in George H. Sabine and Th. L. Thorson, *A History of Political Theory* (4th ed; Hillsdale: Dryden Press, 1973), p. 211.
40. *La ley est le plus haute inheritance, que le roy ad, car par la ley il même et toutes ses sujets sont rulés*, Year Book xix, Henry VI.
41. J. J. Rousseau, *The Social Contract*; I. Kant, *The Foundations of the Metaphysic of Morals*.
42. See Joseph Raz, "The Rule of Law and its Virtues" in *The Authority of Law*, pp. 214–15.
43. John Dziak, *Chekisty* (Lexington: Lexington Books, 1988), pp. 3, 16.
44. A. V. Dicey, *Introduction to the Study of the Law of the Constitution*, 7th Edn., London 1980, p. 195.
45. I have discussed this matter in "Man's Second Disobedience: A Vindication of Burke", ed. Ian Small and R. Crossley, *The French Revolution and British Culture* (Oxford: Basil Blackwell, 1989).
46. One instance of a believer (or near-believer) is Bob Fine, *Democracy and the Rule of Law*, Liberal Ideals and Marxist Critiques (London: Pluto Press, 1984).
47. "Revolutsionnye Tribunaly", in *Vestnik zhizni*, no. 1 (1918), p. 31.
48. "Proekt ugolovnogo kodeksa Soiuza SSR", in *Sovetskoe pravo*, No. 1/2 (1935), p. 99.
49. See D. D. Barry and C. Barnes-Barry, *Contemporary Soviet Politics*, 1931, pp. 82–83.
50. Dicey, *Law of the Constitution*, p. 202.
51. *The Law of the Soviet State, 1938*, English Edn. (Moscow: Foreign Language Publishers, 1948), p. 339.
52. S. Rozmaryn, "Kontrola Sprawiedliwosci Ustaw", *Panstwo i Prawo*, 11–12 (1946), p. 886.

53. See Rett Ludwikowski, "Judicial Review in the Socialist Legal System: Current Developments", *International and Comparative Law Quarterly*, 37 (1988), pp. 89–108. (This deals primarily with Polish, and some Soviet, developments). Also Hiroshi Oda, "Judicial Review of Administration in the USSR", *Public Law*, Spring 1989.
54. See Otto Ulč, *The Judge in a Communist State*, 1972.
55. Olimpiad Ioffé, and Peter B. Maggs, *Soviet Law in Theory and Practice*, New York, 1983; Olimpiad S. Ioffé, *Soviet Law and Soviet Reality,* Dordrecht, 1985; Fridrikh Neznansky, *The Prosecution of Economic Crimes in the USSR*, Falls Church VA, 1985; Louise I. Shelley, *Lawyers in Soviet Work Life*, New Brunswick, 1984.
56. The interview is translated in the report of the Committee in Support of Solidarity, issue no. 46 (November 10th, 1986).
57. See Yuri Luryi, "Soviet Labor Law: New Concepts or Relationships?", *Columbia Journal of Transnational Law*, vol. 23, no.2 (1985), pp. 423–24.
58. Ioffé, *Soviet Law and Soviet Reality*, pp. 42, 191, for example; and Shelley, pp. 63–64, 72.
59. Information from the *Seznam Přednašek na Pravnicke Fakultě*, ed. M. Pekárek, Brno 1986.
60. See, e.g., J. Kroupa, *Socialisticky Konstitucionalismus a Jeho principy* (Brno, University J. E. Purkyně: 1985), and the horrendous study guide *Základy Obecné Teorie Státu a Práva*, ed. E. Kučera, (Prague: Ústav státní spravy, 1986).
61. Stefan Daniš, "The Organisation and Role of the Courts in the Czechoslovak Socialist Republic," *Bulletin of Czechoslovak Law*, (1980).
62. See the excellent survey from the pen of an anonymous Polish lawyer in *Uncensored Poland*, no. 22 (1987), pp. 17–20.
63. See, however, the remarkable novel by Ivan Klíma, *Soudce z milost* (*A Judge by Favor*) (London: Rozmluvy, 1986).
64. See F. Neznansky, *Prosecutions of Economic Crimes in the USSR,* p. 30.
65. See Richard Pipes, *Legalised Lawlessness: Soviet Revolutionary Justice* (London: IEDSS, 1986), pp. 9–11.
66. Hegel, *Philosophy of Right*, par. 224.
67. See *Soviet Civil Law*, ed. O. N. Sadikov, being vol. XXI, no. 1 (1984) of *Soviet Statutes and Decisions*, a journal of translations.
68. John Walter, "Law as an Instrument of Economic Regulation," p. 233.
69. See the volume on maritime laws in *Soviet Statutes and Decisions*.
70. Cited in F. H. Lawson, *Negligence in the Civil Law* (Oxford: Clarendon Pres, 1950), p. 201.
71. [1932] AC 562.
72. *Jand'heur c. Les Galéries belfortaises* D. P. 1930.1.57
73. *Soviet Civil Law, Cases and Case Studies*, ed. William B. Simons, being *Soviet Statutes and Decisions*, vol. XXIII (1985).
74. E. B. Pakushanis, cited in Hans Kelsen, *The Communist Theory of Law* (London: Stevens & Sons, 1955), p. 106.
75. On Potemkin personality, see R. Scruton, "Corporate Personality," *Aristotelian Society*, Supp. Vol LXIII (1989), pp. 260–64.
76. This was certainly true in 1979; see Tufton Beamish and Guy Hadley, *The*

Kremlin Dilemma, London 1979. As far as I can ascertain, the situation has not changed since then, though it likely must soon.

77. See the survey referred to in *Uncensored Poland*, p. 20. On the operation of Polish justice under communism, see Andrzej Rzeplinski, *Sadownictwo w Polsce Ludowej* (Warsaw: Pokolenie, 1989). This is a samizdat publication, which gives a scholarly account of abuses during the last decade.
78. See Z. Karabec, "Prameny statistických údajú o Kriminalitě", *Československá Kriminalistika*, no. 2. (1974), p. 95; and P. H. Solomon, "The Case of the Vanishing Acquittal," *Soviet Interview Project Paper*, no. 28 (1987), (University of Illinois at Urbana-Champaign), p. 35.
79. See the table in John Walter, "Law," p. 214.
80. *Pravda*, May 27, 1988.
81. Those unfamiliar with communist Newspeak (*dubovoj jazyk*) should consult, for the true meaning of these particular phrases, Françoise Thom, *Newspeak*, trans. K. Connelly (London: Caridge Press 1989), ch. 1.
82. See again Ludwikowski, "Judicial Review of the Socialist Legal System."
83. See the petition sent to the Yugoslav Assembly in 1986 by the Committee for the Defense of Freedom of Thought and Expression: reprinted in *South Slav Journal*, vol. 9, no. 3–4 (Autumn–Winter 1986), pp. 52–55. The demand for judicial independence and for a non-communist judiciary is made more explicitly in another petition from the same group, dated November 25, 1987. It has also been made by the recently formed "Movement for Civil Liberty" (*Hnutí za Občanskou Svobodu*) in Czechoslovakia in its manifesto "Democracy for All" (October–November 1988), published by CSDS, Scheinfeld-Schwarzenberg, West Germany.

Contributors

Ellen Frankel Paul is deputy director of the Social Philosophy and Policy Center and professor of political science. She received her doctorate from the Government Department at Harvard University in 1976. She is the author of numerous scholarly articles and is also the author or editor of sixteen books. She has written three books: *Moral Revolution and Economic Science* (1979), *Property Rights and Eminent Domain* (1987), and *Equity and Gender: The Comparable Worth Debate* (1988). She is the editor, with Philip Russo, of *Public Policy: Issues, Analysis, and Ideology* (1981); and editor, with Dan Jacobs, of *Studies of the Third Wave: Recent Migration of Soviet Jews to the United States* (1981). She has also coedited thirteen other books.

Vladimir Bukovsky is one of the most renowned Soviet dissidents living in the West, and is regarded as a prescient observer of the contemporary Soviet Union. Educated at Moscow State University, his efforts on behalf of political prisoners and human rights brought him into conflict with Soviet authorities. For thirteen years, between the ages of twenty-one and thirty-four, Mr. Bukovsky was incarcerated virtually full time in Soviet prisons, labor camps, and psychiatric hospitals. He was ejected from the Soviet Union in 1976.

Since his departure, Mr. Bukovsky has received degrees from Cambridge and Stanford University and carried out research work at the Department of Psychology at Stanford. He has written a number of books, including *Short Stories of Russia's Other Writers* (1970); *Opposition—Eine neue Geisteskrankheit in des USSR* (1972); *A Manual on Psychiatry for Dissenters* (1974); his autobiographical memoir, *To Build a Castle: My Life as a Dissenter* (1978); *Cette lanicinante douleur de la Liberte* (1981) [published in English as *To Choose Freedom* (1987)]; and *The Peace Movement and the Soviet Union* (1982). Mr. Bukovsky is the founder and president of Resistance International.

Adam Ulam is the director of the Russian Research Center and the Gurney Professor of History and Political Science at Harvard University. He is the author of numerous books and articles dealing mostly with Soviet and Russian history and politics. Among his twenty books are *Expansion and Coexistence* (1968), *Dangerous Relations: The Soviet Union in World Politics 1970–1982* (1983), and *Stalin* (1987). His most recent work is a novel, *The Kirov Affair* (1988). Apart from his work in history and political science, he has also written on the role of the university in American society. A member of the American Philosophical Society and the American Academy of Arts and Sciences, he has taught at Harvard since 1945.

Andrzej Walicki is a historian of ideas, specializing in Russian and Polish intellectual history and (more recently) in the history of Marxism. He is the O'Neill Professor of History at the University of Notre Dame. For many years he was a professor and department head in the Institute of Philosophy and Sociology of the Polish Academy of Sciences in Warsaw. From 1981–86 he was a Senior Research Fellow at the Australian National University in Canberra. He has written 14 books and more than 150 scholarly articles. His books in English include *The Slavophile Controversy* (1975), *A History of Russian Thought from the Enlightenment to Marxism* (1979), *Philosophy and Romantic Nationalism: The Case of Poland* (1982), *Legal Philosophies of Russian Liberalism* (1987), and *Stanislaw Brzozowski and the Polish Beginnings of 'Western Marxism'* (1989).

John Gray is an Official Fellow and Tutor of Jesus College, Oxford University and a Lecturer in Politics at Oxford University. He was educated at Exeter College, Oxford, where he received his B.A., M.A., and D.Phil. degrees. Between 1973 and 1976 he was a Lecturer in Government at the University of Essex.

Dr. Gray's principal interests are in political philosophy and political economy. His books include *Mill on Liberty: A Defence* (1983), *Hayek on Liberty* (1984), second edition 1986, *Conceptions of Liberty in Political Philosophy,* edited with Z. A. Pelczynski (1984), *Liberalism* (1986), and *Liberalisms: Essays in Political Philosophy* (1989). His current projects are a book-length manuscript on post-totalitarianism, and a volume of essays on post-liberalism.

Zbigniew Rau teaches at the University of Texas at Austin where he specializes in the politics of the Soviet Union and Eastern Europe. Professor Rau was educated at the University of Lodz and received his Ph.D. from the Polish University in England. From 1985 to 1988, he was a Visiting Fellow Commoner at Trinity College, Cambridge University. Rau is currently completing the first Polish edition of Locke's *Two Treatises of Government* as well as a book entitled *Contractarianism versus Holism: The Argument of Locke's Two Treatises of Government.* He has written several articles for *Political Studies* which present a liberal interpretation of the emergence and growth of civil society in Eastern Europe.

Roger Scruton is a professor of aesthetics in the philosophy department at Birkbeck College, University of London. He was educated at Cambridge University, where he received three degrees, including a Ph.D. He has been a Fellow of Peterhouse College, Cambridge University; a Visiting Fellow at Princeton University; and a Visiting Professor at the University of Waterloo and the University of Guelph. His books include *Art and Imagination* (1974), *The Aesthetics of Architecture* (1979), *The Meaning of Conservatism* (1980), *Fortnight's Anger* (a novel) (1981), *A Dictionary of Political Thought* (1982), *Thinkers of the New Left* (1986), and *Sexual Desire* (1986). A second novel, *Francesca,* is forthcoming, and he is currently working on a book about the meaning of Wagner's *Ring.* He is the editor of *The Salisbury Review.*